MOTHERS, SEX, AND SEXUALITY

Edited by Holly Zwalf, Michelle Walks, and Joani Mortenson

T0294088

DEMETER

Mothers, Sex, and Sexuality
Edited by Holly Zwalf, Michelle Walks, and Joani Mortenson

Copyright © 2020 Demeter Press

Demeter Press
2546 10th Line
Bradford, Ontario
Canada, L3Z 3L3
Tel: 289-383-0134
Email: info@demeterpress.org
Website: www.demeterpress.org

Demeter Press logo based on the sculpture "Demeter" by Maria-Luise Bodirsky www.keramik-atelier.bodirsky.de

Printed and Bound in Canada

Cover image: Francisca Vanderwoude
Cover design and typesetting: Michelle Pirovich

Library and Archives Canada Cataloguing in Publication
Title: Mothers, sex, and sexuality/edited by Holly Zwalf, Michelle Walks, and Joani Mortenson.
Names: Zwalf, Holly, 1981- editor. | Walks, Michelle, 1978- editor. | Mortenson, Joani, 1964- editor.
Description: Includes bibliographical references.
Identifiers: Canadiana 20200160419 | ISBN 9781772582222 (softcover)
Subjects: LCSH: Mothers—Sexual behavior. | LCSH: Sex. | LCSH: Motherhood.
Classification: LCC HQ29.M68 2020 | DDC 306.7085/2—dc23

For my child's day-care centre,
without whom none of this would have been possible.
On those occasional days when my child was well enough
to go in the first place, that is.
Or wasn't sent home with conjunctivitis
or a temperature
or a cough
or a cold.

—Holly Zwalf

Thank you to Jake for supporting my career and
cooking delicious meals!

—Michelle Walks

For my mother, for my sons, and for my beloved:
Each of you supported this fecund, maternal embodiment.
Mothering is my practice. Jai Ma!

—Joani Mortenson

Acknowledgments

This book was gifted to me at a crucial point in my career. I finished my PhD thesis on the erotic maternal and almost immediately started IVF. I was pregnant and green at the gills during my graduation. I submitted my chapter for this book to the original editors, Joani Mortenson and Michelle Walks, days before the heartache and heroics of a difficult birth, a cold stretch of something very close to postnatal depression, and then the intense exultation of that first year with my tiny new soulmate. Eventually, I began to reemerge, blinking in the bright light and wondering who on earth I was. I emailed Joani to find out when publication was due, and she responded by offering me the role of coeditor. Joani, thank you so much for all the time and energy you poured in to the first stages of this book. And also thank you for this gift. It gave me back a sense of my old self—I have felt capable, critical, and clever again for the first time in years.

This book was originally conceived by Michelle Walks. She brought Joani onto the team, and, together, they sent out the call for inspiring submissions, sifted through the thousands and thousands of words sent their way, and began to mould this book into shape. Michelle left the project early on, but in the final stages, she came back on board to assist and advise in the delivery. So to Michelle, I thank you for your vision in bringing this book into being and your valuable guidance in polishing its edges in preparation for birth.

Thank you to the contributors for their gems of knowledge but also for their patience and for enduring my painstakingly detailed editing.

Last of all, thank you to my own mother, Kim Zwalf, who has been my sounding board, my cheer squad, and my coparent; she has played endless hours of "emergency vehicles" to distract my child so I could work. And, of course, as she constantly reminds me, she taught me to read. So, really, it all starts with her. xxx

Holly Zwalf

Cover Artist Statement

Francisca Vanderwoude

Digital video still, "Madonna/Madonna," 2016, 43 minutes
My career in adult entertainment (as a dancer) has tended to stand in direct contrast to my life as a mother. Proceeding through auto-ethnographic and sex-positive feminist frameworks, I have attempted to explore and reconcile my experiences of this binary through an arts-based research practice. Following on from the work of early mother-artist Mary Kelly, I collected video material of myself and my daughter over the course of about three years, filming at home and at work. I approached this as data collection, utilising a variety of camera angles and cinematographic techniques and becoming more reflexive as time went on. Very simple editing techniques such as overlays and time distortion were used to combine and overlap the footage, so as to emphasize the liminal and ambiguous aspects of the imagery. The final work, from which this still is taken, is a kind of extended dreamlike sequence intended for a large-scale, single channel projection. By disrupting the representation of time and space, my aim was to also disrupt assumptions and stereotypes relating to my work as an adult-entertainer, not to mention the "semiotic taboo" of motherhood, which is discussed at length by Andrea Liss in her 2009 publication *Feminist Art and the Maternal* (1-21).

Works Cited

Leiss, Andrea. *Feminist Art and the Maternal*. University of Minnesota Press, 2009.

Contents

Introduction

Mothers, Sex, and Sexuality: A Sexy Book

Holly Zwalf

This is a sexy book for many reasons. It's got the word "sex" blatantly blazed across the front cover, for one, and it's also got some pretty hot pics towards the back. But, mostly, it's sexy because it's bold, brave, and bolshie. *Mothers, Sex, And Sexuality* is a book that talks about things normally not dared spoken out loud. In fact, those three words—"mothers," "sex," and "sexuality"—are rarely even seen strung all together, and for one very salient reason: mothers are not supposed to be sexual. A prevailing madonna-whore and asexual-sexual dichotomy—which has been perpetuated by Christianity, Judaism, and Hinduism, among others, (Cass, Rooks, and Zairunisha, this volume) as a convenient way to contain and constrain women and their bodies—is enforced even today through social pressure and condemnation (Bartlett 59-60; Friedan 46).

At the core of this dichotomy is the dividing of mothers into so-called good and bad ones. The good mother is supposedly entirely fulfilled by her children. She does not need nor is she distracted by sexual desires; she has all she needs met in her children, and she is eternally physically and emotionally available to them (Walks 29-32). She is definitely not pushing her pram in knee-high leather boots, flicking through Tinder while breastfeeding, or, heaven forbid, planning her reentry to the workforce as a sex worker. These are all things a bad mother would do.

Religiosity plays a significant role in defining motherhood, although it is often taken for granted as a cultural norm. The predominantly white writers in this book have at times perhaps taken for granted the fact that

13

Christianity informs our beliefs and moral systems and that it has played a role in perpetuating the madonna-whore dichotomy in Western culture. But I want to acknowledge here in the introduction that this is a reflection of the insidious ways in which Christianity has coloured Western social norms about motherhood and childrearing. Furthermore, the tropes and taboos of the asexual mother are entangled with a celebration of white femininity and heterosexuality that does not apply to mothers across the board. Poor, Indigenous, and Black mothers have been and remain fetishized and hypersexualized, portrayed as irresponsibly promiscuous and seductive as opposed to the modest, chaste white mother (West). In another intriguing inversion white lesbians, who are identified as such by whom they have sex with and who are rampantly sexualized under the male view, magically transform from monstrously deviant to asexual and motherly by virtue of using assisted reproductive technology and other technologies to conceive a child (Longhurst; Thompson).

Recently, the sexual mother has enjoyed a new era of visibility through such cultural tropes as the "yummy mummy" and the "MILF" ("mom I'd like to fuck") in popular porn (and even a niche market of pregnant and lactation porn), sexy maternity bras, and, of course, the famous Demi Moore pregnant shot, which continues to be reworked ad nauseum by celebrities and the general public alike. Yet this celebration of the sexual maternal at times borders on fetishization and should not be misread as an indication that Western society now culturally acknowledges and supports the sexuality of mothers. Sexualizing mothers, though, is itself relatively safe territory and does not disrupt the sexual-maternal divide; indeed, I would argue that the practice of commodifying women's sexuality essentially robs and ignores mothers' agency in sex. It is essential, therefore, to note that the sexual mother herself is not a threat—it is not necessarily sexuality that positions sexual mothers in contradiction to gendered conventions of motherhood (although this is sometimes the case) but rather the unapologetic application of her agency in the expression of her sexuality.

Furthermore, in direct response to these sexy mama tropes, an implied pressure is now placed on new mothers to lose that baby weight, throw away the elastic-sided maternity pants, and get back out there on the sexual objectification catwalk as quickly as possible in order to be (sexually) appreciated. It seems mothers cannot win either way, and as

Vivienne Cass notes in the opening chapter of this book, all of this apparent maternal sexual liberation merely acts as a smokescreen, hiding the fact that in reality not much has changed in our adherence to the asexual mother. Cass describes as an example an online image which begins with the question:

> "*Is your mom self overtaking your sexual self?*" and the image is of a mother in a park exercising to get fit (read: so as to look sexy). Superimposed onto the base of this image is a toddler's face (presumably her child) looking decidedly glum, the inference of neglect plain for all to see. The woman's sexual self is presented as being in competition with her mother self, and the warning of dire consequences should the former win is quite clear. (this volume)

Cass, here, provides an excellent example of the expectations placed on the primary caregiver of a young child to be a martyr—to give up not just her work and identity but also her sexuality in the face of motherhood. Of course, the dichotomy is not technically adhered to; mothers do continue to be sexual beings, exercising their sexual autonomy in numerous different ways. For example, this pressure is played out in the way single moms are perceived when they actively date, in the way pregnant bodies are represented in the media, in the predominantly frumpy maternity wear options available to pregnant people, and in the moral panic around parents who do sex work.

While I was toying around with an image for the cover of this book, I was originally keen on a photo of a heavily pregnant person (myself) in a tight red dress, holding two breast pumps over her breasts in a suggestively seductive pose (now to be found towards the back of this book). Curious as to whether Amazon would allow a cover like this to be advertised on their site, I posted the photo in a women writers' Facebook group to ask for advice and feedback. One writer responded particularly passionately, declaring that the image was inappropriate for the book title. "When I think of mothers and sex I picture a woman on a messy bed, sleeping, in pyjamas; partner on the other side of the bed looking lovingly at her," she tartly retorted. Her point was not just that mothers are too tired for sex. It was that mothers are not, should not, and cannot be sexy.

The titillating title—*Mothers, Sex, and Sexuality*—therefore directs us straight to the core of the book: the taboo of the sexual maternal. It will make some readers uncomfortable, and it will make others curious, but it will also hopefully make all readers question their reactions. What is it about the sexual mother that is so disturbing? Why are people threatened by maternal sexuality, and what does this mean about the structures of gender and power that continue to govern mothers' bodies, even today, when Western society believes itself to be so sexually enlightened? This book puts forward a seemingly obvious and yet very necessary argument: we can be mothers and we can also be sexual—desirable, desiring, desired; we do not have to choose between the two.

It is important to note, however, that arguing for the sexual maternal does not necessarily mean that all mothers should go out there and be hot for it. When I first wrote my chapter for submission to this book, I was eight months pregnant, swollen tight and fit to burst with my first child. My feet were aching from being on stage for three hours during *Engorged—Fucking (With) The Maternal*, a performance night I curated and emceed about motherhood and sexuality (basically all about my pregnant kinky sex life). The show also felt like a celebration of my recently completed PhD thesis on the erotic maternal. I was taking my theory off the page and on to the stage, and it felt good to give it the airing it deserved. Since that time, however, sex and motherhood has not always been the happy union I had hoped for.

As a queer solo parent by choice, sex did not come into my conception story at all, at least not in the traditional sense. I had fertility problems and so had to conceive via in vitro fertilization, a decidedly unsexy, highly medicalized process. I was determined to counteract this lack of sexiness during my pregnancy. Pregnant bodies are erotic, I continually affirmed. I am going to be all over Tinder with my hot, new body. What I did not factor in was morning sickness—four long months of it, relentless, and, again, decidedly unsexy. The second I felt better I was back on Tinder right up until the very end, when I was too big to want to do anything other than wallow in Sydney's Coogee Women's Ocean Baths. And to all the lovers I had accumulated during those last frenzied months, I said "I'll see you on the other side" with a cheery grin and a wink. Oh how wrong I was! The moment my child was born I completely lost interest in sex. I was not just disinterested—I was disgusted. I was like one of those vampires in *True Blood* who watches people eating food—dead, lifeless food—and is repulsed. I felt as though I had transcended the pleasures of mere mortal flesh. Perhaps in some way I finally understood Mary—the virginal one, not the sex worker. She was right—sex and mothers did not mix.

I tried watching porn one day in a vain attempt to recapture my lost self, but all I felt was melancholic nostalgia. *I will never have sex with a hot young queer in a tattoo parlour ever again*, I thought sadly, as I watched the scene on my screen. Not that I had ever had sex in a tattoo parlour, even before the baby came along, but you get the point. This threw my thesis research into doubt. Why did I think the sexual maternal was so important? I genuinely could not remember. It was only during the editing of this book—while preparing for an interview for a podcast titled *Hot Moms—Motherhood, Sexuality, & the Public Gaze* for the feminist website *womenandradio.com*—that I revisited the important question of why the sexual maternal matters. What is it about motherhood and sex that are so incompatible or, more specifically, what is it about mothers' empowered, autonomous expression of sexuality that is so threatening, and why is it so important that we challenge this? My answer slowly rose victorious to the surface—it matters purely because it is denied. As I affirm in my own chapter later in this book, paraphrasing maternal theorist Iris Marion Young, "if the sexual maternal is threatening, we can only assume that this is so because it contains within it the potential to empower motherhood—to free the maternal from its patriarchal constraints."

Motherhood, as currently practiced, is an oppressive institution (O'Reilly 35). Ultimately, if mothers can reimagine mothering as a pleasure, "a mode of sexuality instead of as a substitute for sexuality, as is traditionally upheld" (Zwalf, this volume), I believe this can lead to empowered mothering—by embracing, not denying, pleasure, a reclaiming of the maternal is able to occur. A feminist rereading of desire would take my postbaby asexuality and celebrate it as a refocusing of sensuality onto my relationship with my child (Rooks, this volume). My intimacy was completely fulfilled; I was in an intense romantic and physically sensual relationship. Growing a person inside you, birthing a person, nurturing and protecting them with your body, and falling truly, madly, and deeply in love as you gaze into each other's bloodshot eyes during a 3:00a.m. feed—all of this is all arguably a potential expression of sexuality.

Unfortunately, social constructs regarding appropriate expressions of sexuality, which are also tied up in a moral panic around speaking the words "sex" and "children" in the same sentence, make this kind of correlation intensely problematic, although I would argue that this discomfort extends from a limited understanding of sexuality. I had a delicious conversation with a woman at a queer event recently where she spoke with great ardour about the physical pleasure of being pregnant: "I was almost cumming, all the time, just from stroking my own stomach, or the lace on a piece of lingerie, or from smelling the fruit hanging on trees! Oh yes!" There is nothing dangerous about this expression of desire, no harmful impact on the fruit, the lingerie, or the child. Yet, sadly, this maternal eroticism is frequently denied, which creates great anxiety in some mothers. The most oft-quoted example of this is the American woman several decades ago who had her child taken from her by child services when she rang a parenting hotline to ask whether it was normal to feel turned on while breastfeeding (Perrigo 8-9). Mothers' bodies cannot be switched off and on, to different modes, yet this is unreasonably expected of us. As Amanda Rooks notes, "the language of sensual intimacy has been appropriated by the world of adult sexual and romantic relations" (this volume). Mothers have lost the language they need to talk about mothering, the intimacy and sensuality of it, and the physicality of bearing and nurturing a child.

In this book, therefore, we, the authors, call for a stop to the policing of the maternal body. We make a case for the sexual maternal to be recognized and celebrated and attempt to seek out a new language for maternal sexuality, reimagining pleasure through a feminist lens as separate from patriarchal understandings of desirability and desire. *Mothers, Sex, and Sexuality* continues conversations first started by Simone de Beauvoir in *The Second Sex* in the 1950s and carried forward most notably by Adrienne Rich in *Of Woman Born* in the 1970s. Feminist psychoanalysis has also taken up the call in a vast body of work done largely by Karen Horney, Helene Deutsch, Julia Kristeva, and Nancy Chodorow. Kamala Ganesh and Puri Jyoti have contributed to the topic of mothers and sexuality in Hindi culture, and Black theorists, such as Hortense J Spillers, Dorothy Roberts, and Patricia Hill Collins, have written about the sexualizaton of African American mothers in the United States. More recently LGBTQ+ theorists Julie Thompson, Jaqcui Gabb, and Rachel Epstein have examined lesbian and queer parents in relation to sexuality. With the exceptions of these, however—and of such contemporary feminist theorists as Robyn Longhurst, Iris Marion

Young, Alison Bartlett, and Peggy Kleinplatz—the majority of these writings on this topic are not recent. As Cass notes in her opening chapter, there is a notable silence on the subject in recent literature, research, and in the topics covered in health, anthropology, and sexuality conferences. What this book does is take these largely theoretical discussions and situate them in the contemporary context, examining the sexual maternal in relation to race, class, fatness, kink, sexuality, and, of course, the ways in which mothers navigate parenthood. In current scholarship, sexuality and the maternal are generally issues that are discussed separately, but this book presents a diversity of angles from which the subject of motherhood and sexuality can be discussed as a whole and complete topic in itself.

The authors in this anthology write from a diversity of cultural backgrounds, and their scholarship includes such topics as Hinduism as a prevailing force in modern India, attitudes to sexuality in the Northwestern United States, intersections of sexuality and religion/culture among Indigenous communities in Canada, Southeast Asian and Central and South American migrant labour, as well as relationships to breastfeeding and class in African American communities. This book embraces academic scholarship, autoethnographic writing, and even poetry in its attempts to approach the topic of maternal sexuality; it contains chapters from a variety of disciplines, including psychology, sociology, social work, cultural studies, education, health sciences, and literary criticism. Although some readers may interpret this broad spectrum of content as uneven, we, as editors, feel these interdisciplinary and multimethodological approaches to cultural studies strengthen rather than weaken this body of knowledge.

As editors, we acknowledge that the term "mother" is a gendered term and is consequently limited by gender, and we acknowledge the trans, nonbinary, and gender-queer birthing people who are not represented either by the title of this book or by its content.[1] Despite our desire as editors to widen the frame of "mother" to include gender diversity, in the majority of the works in this anthology, the terms "mother" and "mothering" have been used to refer to cis-gendered women (as opposed to nonbinary or trans parents), and we apologize for this limitation. We are also aware that the majority of chapters approach the topic from a paradigm that assumes whiteness at the norm. I myself have been guilty of this both in my own chapter and in my role as the editor, and I am thankful to our reviewers for so stringently pointing out this shortcoming. Although we have attempted to rectify this limitation by being more critically reflective in our rewrites, this book is still predominantly authored by white writers and is lacking in Indigenous voices and the voices of parents of colour across the world, just as it is also lacking in content from working-class parents. We acknowledge that a stronger commitment to addressing how race and class shape the extent and ways in which mothers can transgress the taboos around maternal sexuality would have made this a more intersectional piece of scholarship, and we apologize for those places where you may find us lacking.

A central theme or thesis of this text is to highlight the cultural, political, psychological, and social binds that mothers are in with regard to sexuality, and to open up safe and sacred conversations about how and why this needs to shift. Included in these chapters are arguments for expansion as well as rich data that illustrate the everyday lived experience of diverse mothers performing sexuality in diverse ways through narratives that run subversive and counter to dominant discourses. Although each submission to this book takes a vastly different and unique approach to the topic, we have organized the content into three categories: sexual mothers, the erotics of mothering, and mothers who disrupt the heteronormative maternal model.

Section I: Some Mothers Do 'Ave It!
Sexual Mothers—Mothers and Sex

In this first section, we approach the question of the sexual mother from a variety of perspectives: the silence surrounding maternal sexuality in health services, the effects of Hinduism and colonization on maternal sexuality, and the ways in which mothers educate their children about sex, pleasure, and sexual health. Cass sets the stage in the opening chapter, "The Myth of Asexual Motherhood," through examining the impact of the madonna-whore archetype on attitudes towards maternal sexuality today, particularly on the assumed asexuality of mothers as perpetuated by health and sexuality professionals. Following in this vein, in "The Sexuality of Mothers in Hindu Life: Myths of Empowerment within Enslavement," Zairunisha exposes the role the veneration of goddesses plays in Hindu culture, which often acts as a smokescreen for the regulation and control of mothers' sexuality.

Although on the surface Hinduism appears to idolize mothers and female sexuality, through case studies of mothers and soon-to-be-mothers from a variety of backgrounds and castes, Zairunisha shows how maternal sexuality is both denied and disallowed in contemporary India. From here, while still focusing on mothers and sex, the book moves away from asexual mothering and towards embracing sexuality. In "Blips of Feminist Mothering: Mothers and Daughters Navigate Taboo Topics Talking about Sex," Lysa Salsbury and Erin Chapman navigate the topic of sex education and analyze the imparting of sexual knowledge from mothers to daughters through a feminist framework. And in closing this section, Angelina Weenie in "Iskwêwiwin: An Autoethnographic Study of Motherhood, Sex, and Sexuality" offers a Canadian First Nations perspective on mothers and sexuality. She provides an important Indigenous voice as she examines the impact her own mother made on her understandings of motherhood and sexuality as well as the effects of colonialization on the maternal body. Through her autoethnographic writing and diary entries, the reader can follow Weenie on a journey of decolonizing and reclaiming her sexuality.

Section II: Babes and Bawdy Breasts: The Erotics of Mothering

Getting to the heart of this anthology, these three chapters embrace the physical erotics of mothering and examine the places where sexuality and motherhood overlap, the pleasures of breastfeeding, and the subversive potential of the powerful matriarchal archetype. This section begins with "Maternal Eroticism and Female Desire in Sue Miller's *The Good Mother*", a delicious textual exploration by Amanda Kane Rooks. Rooks, in perhaps the thesis for this book, puts forward the call for a feminist rewriting or broadening of our understanding of sexuality to encompass, among other things, the sensuality of mothering. This chapter segues into Christa Baiada's "The Scandalous Breast: Confronting the Sexual-Maternal Dichotomy in Toni Morrison's *Song of Solomon* and Susan Choi's *My Education*"—a textual analysis of the erotics of mothering that specifically focuses on breastfeeding as connected to pleasure, romance, and desire, which she then complicates through an enmeshing of the sexual and maternal breast. I deliberated a long time about where to place my own chapter, "Hot Queer Leather

Mamas: Feminist Kink and the Taboo of the Sexual Maternal." The subject matter deals specifically with the erotics of mothering, albeit from a perspective that not only invites but requires a queering of the maternal, which provides a bridge into the final section of this book. This chapter critiques and deessentializes the act of mothering through erotic, childless maternal roleplay; it explores the potential of the maternal as a mode of kinky sexuality.

Section III: Out of Line: Mothers Who Mess with the (Hetero)Maternal Model

This final section looks at those mothers who are situated outside the heterosexual model of motherhood, be it through their sexuality, their bodies, or their intimate relationships with their children's other carers. The section opens with "Identity Shifts: Who Is the Postmodern Queer Mother?," a rousing poem by editor Joani Mortenson, which sets the scene through its addressing of both queer maternal sexualities and the queering of the maternal. Katie B. Garner then examines the psychoanalytic romance between mothers and their nannies—two heterosexual women trapped together in a homoerotic triangulation of need and desire—in "Love Bi the Book: A Chodorowian Examination of the Heterosexual Mother's Love for Nannies in Contemporary Culture." Natasha Pinterics follows with her chapter, "Excessive Maternal Embodiment: The Queer Danger of Desirous Mothers," which defines fat mothers as akin to queer mothers in their disrupting of (hetero)normative maternal bodies. The excess desire of the fat mother, she argues, renders her unacceptable and unworthy in much the same way as with those who shun the heterosexual model of motherhood. The closing chapter, "Engorged: Fucking (with) the Maternal—An Analysis of Antinormativity, Cultural Legitimacy, and Queer Authenticity," by Sam Sperring and Zahra Stardust, provides a deliciously dirty analysis of an erotic maternal performance night. This chapter presents the sexual maternal and maternal sexuality as embodied through performance art, poetry, installations, and comedy, which both facilitates and disrupts queer readings of the maternal through an interrogation of the antinormativity sentiment prevalent in queer culture that labels the maternal body decidedly nonqueer.

There are, as always, gaps in this collection of works—most notably a lack of representation of polyamorous, nonbinary, trans, young, old, or differently abled mothers—but while we regret these absences, we also acknowledge that one book cannot speak for all. We can only hope that this contribution to the scholarship can become a poignant steppingstone in an ongoing conversation and that through this book, we are able to help advance an understanding of, and expand the attitudes towards, mothers, sex, and sexuality.

Endnotes

1. For some texts that do address trans pregnancy (we have been unable to find any academic accounts of nonbinary pregnancy), we can recommend Trevor MacDonald's *Where's the Mother?: Stories from a Transgender Dad* (2016), Syrus Marcus Ware's "Boldly Going Where Few Men Have Gone Before" (2009), Thomas Beatie's *Labor of Love* (2008), and Michelle Walks's dissertation titled *Gender Identity and In/Fertility* (2013).

Works Cited

Bartlett, Alison. "Scandalous Practices and Political Performances: Breastfeeding in the City." *Motherhood: Power and Oppression*, edited by M. Porter et al., Women's Press, 2005, pp. 57-76.

Beatie, Thomas. *Labour of Love: The Story of One Man's Extraordinary Pregnancy.* Seal Press, 2008.

Chodorow, Nancy. *The Reproduction of Mothering: Psychoanalysis and the Sociology of Gender.* University of California Press, 1978.

Collins, Patricia Hill. "Black Women and Motherhood." *Motherhood and Space*, edited by Sarah Hardy and Caroline Wiedmer, Palgrave Macmillan, 2005, pp. 149-159.

Beauvoir, Simone, de. The Second Sex. 1949. Translated by Constance Borde and Sheila Malovany-Chevallier, Alfred A. Knopf, 2010.

Deutsch, Helene. The Psychology of Women: A Psychoanalytic Interpretation. Vol. 2: Motherhood. Green and Stratton, 1945.

Epstein, Rachel. "Queer Parenting in the New Millennium: Resisting Normal." *Canadian Woman Studies/Les Cahiers de la Femme*, vol. 24, no. 2-3, 2005, pp. 7-14.

Friedan, Betty. *The Feminine Mystique.* 2nd ed., Victor Gollancz Ltd, 1964.

Journal of the Association for Research on Mothering, vol. 1, no. 2, 2006, pp. 9-20.

Ganesh, Kamala. "Mother Who Is Not a Mother: In Search of the Great Indian Goddess." *Economic and Political Weekly,* 20-27 Oct. 1997, pp. 58-64.

Horney, Karen. *Feminine Psychology.* New York: Norton, 1967.

Kleinplatz, Peggy. "On the Outside Looking In: In Search of Women's Sexual Experience," *A New View of Women's Sexual Problems,* edited by Ellen Kaschak and Leonore Tiefer, The Haworth Press. 2001, pp. 123-32.

Kristeva, Julia. *The Kristeva Reader,* edited by Toril Moi, Columbia University Press, 1986.

Longhurst, Robyn. *Maternities—Gender, Bodies and Space.* Routledge, 2008.

MacDonald, Trevor. *Where's the Mother? Stories from a Transgender Dad.* Canada Press, 2016.

O'Reilly, Andrea. *Rocking the Cradle: Thoughts on Feminism, Motherhood and the Possibility of Empowered Mothering.* Demeter Press, 2006.

Perrigo, Denise. "Letter." *Mothering,* vol. 63, 1992, pp. 8-9.

Puri, Jyoti. "Concerning 'Kamasutras': Challenging Narrative of History and Sexuality" *Signs,* vol. 27, no. 3, 2002, pp. 603-639.

Roberts, Dorothy E. *Killing the Black Body: Race, Reproduction, and the Meaning of Liberty.* Pantheon Books, 1997.

Rich, Adrienne. *Of Woman Born: Motherhood as Experience and Institution.* W.W. Norton & Co., 1976.

Spillers, Hortense J. "Mama's Baby, Papa's Maybe: An American Grammar Book." *Diacritics,* vol. 17, no. 2, 1987, pp. 64-81.

Thompson, Julie M. *Mommy Queerest: Contemporary Rhetorics of Lesbian Maternal Identity.* University of Massachusetts Press, 2002.

Walks, Michelle. *Gender Identity and In/Fertility.* 2013. University of British Columbia, dissertation.

Ware, Syrus Marcus. "Boldly Going Where Few Men Have Gone Before: One Trans Man's Experience." *Who's Your Daddy? And Other*

Writings on Queer Parenting, edited by Rachel Epstein, Sumach Press, 2009, pp. 65-71.

West, Carolyn M. "Mammy, Jezebel, and Sapphire: Developing an 'Oppositional Gaze' toward the Images of Black Women." *Lectures on the Psychology of Women*, edited by Joan C Chrisler et al., McGraw-Hill, 2004, pp. 237-52.

Young, Iris M. *Throwing Like a Girl and Other Essays in Feminist Philosophy and Social Theory*. Indiana University Press, 1990.

Section I

Some Mothers Do 'Ave It!
Sexual Mothers–Mothers
and Sex

Chapter One

The Myth of Asexual Motherhood

Vivienne Cass

Introduction

Within traditional Christian, Jewish, and Hindu mythology, two distinct types of women are consistently identified. The first, whom we might call the seductress type, is presented as lustful, strong, independent, and having no maternal interests. In modern times, she has been depicted in Western cultures by images that show a strong-bodied woman, scantily dressed with untamed long hair, posing in an alluring manner, and accompanied by symbols of defiance and danger, such as serpents and swords. The second type of woman, the madonna, is quite different. Represented as pure, of high morals, virginal, as well as a faithful and supportive wife (Zairunisha, this volume), she is invariably pictured in both Western and Eastern cultures in the role of mother, who is often looking adoringly and pro-tectively at a child in her arms.

These two archetypes of women are of interest because they represent not only two ends of a motherhood spectrum but also two types of sexual expression. Furthermore, they illustrate the way in which sexuality and motherhood (both as concepts and behaviours) are intricately bound up with one another in the most conflicted of relationships: on the one hand, we have the mothering type of woman who is sexually chaste or asexual, and, on the other, we have the type of woman who lacks maternal interest and carries with her an exotic mix of alluring sexuality and potential danger.

This conflict is, of course, the oft-quoted madonna-whore dichotomy that women experience as they attempt to negotiate their lives around the seeming impossibility of measuring up to the ideal of the madonna while also being comfortable with themselves as sexual beings. For the past thirty years or more, the effect of the madonna-whore conflict on women's relationships and sexual experiences has been recognized in feminist-based sexual therapy as contributing to many of the difficulties that women from various backgrounds (but more typically those involved in heterosexual relationships) experience in their sexual expression (Kleinplatz 125).

Since the late twentieth century, there have been attempts to reconcile these two stereotypes of women. The beginning of this movement can, I believe, be traced to the publication in 1991 of the now iconic photo of a naked and seven-months pregnant Demi Moore (a well-known American actor), which appeared on the front cover of *Vanity Fair* magazine. Taken by the renowned photographer Annie Leibovitz, the bold image cuts straight through the sharp division represented in the madonna-whore dichotomy. Posed with her hands covering her genitals and nipples (but not the full breast) and her arms framing her smooth swollen belly, the image is striking for its open and proud blending of sexuality and motherhood. Not surprisingly, its publication unleashed a torrent of negative reactions, leading to the magazine, on occasion, to be sold in plain paper bags and consigned to the "adult reading" section of stores (Shipps and Caron 95). However, the image also received thunderous applause from many others who were thrilled to see pregnancy released from its traditional prison of voluminous clothing.

Insightful psychological research by Ariella Friedman et al. conducted in the aftermath of the *Vanity Fear* shoot revealed just how much the madonna-whore conflict influenced the thinking of everyday people. In essence, the authors found evidence that both male and female subjects perceived sexuality and motherhood as mutually exclusive. The more sexual a woman was perceived to be, the less she was seen to be motherly. Highly sexual women were characterized as unlikely to be mothers or as "rejecting mothers", who find children a burden and who were perceived as likely to be divorced, single, or widowed. In contrast, nonsexual women were described as lacking enjoyment in sex, although they were prepared to perform it out of a sense of duty. They were assumed not only to be a mother but to be a good mother and married. However, the study found that nonsexual women were also seen as unable to give their children physical or emotional space or to understand their feelings, compared with highly sexual women who were seen to treat their children as equals, to respect their views, and to communicate well with them. Presumably this tapped into the dependent-independent difference that forms part of the distinction between the madonna and seductress types.

Consequently, the sexual/seductress woman is cast as a bad mother and the virginal/madonna type as a good mother. In other words, a good mother is one who is not sexual. It may be concluded, therefore, that early mythology has become transformed into ideology: the ideology of asexual motherhood (Contratto [Weisskopf] 768).

The Modern Madonna Movement

Since the 1990s, there have been increased attempts to break down the mutual exclusivity of motherhood and sexuality, at least in many Western societies. I refer to this as the "modern Madonna movement." Since Moore's 1991 *Vanity Fair* photo, hundreds of copycat pictures have been published by celebrities in a variety of magazines. Everyday women have also replicated Moore's pose and have uploaded their photos to numerous social media sites (and have no doubt added them to their baby albums).

More recently, the modern madonna movement has been extended to include the concept of the "yummy mummy" (Oliver 764; Zwalf, this volume), which encourages mothers to believe that they are sexual beings and can look sexy—a message that is often marketed within a broader framework of good health and wellbeing and, as such, is promoted in women's magazines, gym promotions, and hundreds of Internet articles. At other times, however, this message is distorted to suggest that yummy mummies are mothers who should be and should look sexy. Sometimes this focus is taken even further, portraying sexual acts with a yummy mummy—always from a male heterosexual stance—as something exotic and adventurous. For example, one online banner headline from a website says, "Moms like sex too," which is quite acceptable until you read the small print underneath the banner—"get the dirt!," suggesting something unsavoury is to follow. Taken one step further, this approach gets downright ugly: for those who are successful in reaching the goal of sexy mother, the prize, it would seem, is to be anointed with the title MILF (Mothers I'd Like To Fuck).

Underlying the yummy mummy movement, however, is the same old phenomenon: the ideology of asexual motherhood continues to lurk close to the surface of modern thinking, albeit clothed in a more subtle idiom. One freely available online image begins with the question, "Is your mom self overtaking your sexual self?" and the image is of a mother in a park exercising to get fit (read: so as to look sexy). Superimposed onto the base of this image is a toddler's face (presumably her child) looking decidedly glum, the inference of neglect plain for all to see. The woman's sexual self is presented as being in competition with her mother self, and the warning of dire consequences should the former win is quite clear. In the conflict between these two essentialist selves, the twenty-first-century mother has no more access to a win-win solution than her twentieth-century predecessor.

Thus, for all of the apparent advances made in recent times, the ideology of asexual motherhood continues to influence the way people feel, think, and act. Or to put it another way, motherhood sexuality—the experiencing of sexual feelings and behaviours while a woman is involved in tasks normally associated with motherhood—makes virtually everyone anxious (Contratto [Weisskopf] 767). Unfortunately, two groups who hold significant influence with women in various phases of motherhood have perpetuated these anxieties around maternal sexuality. The first group includes the editorial staff and decision makers of women's magazines, which, as I will discuss shortly, promise much but often deliver little. The second group involves professionals directly engaged in working in the field of sexuality who, as difficult as it is to believe, tend to either avoid the area of motherhood sexuality altogether or approach it with little understanding of the ideological, psychological, and cultural factors involved.

Professional Neglect, Bias, and Ignorance

As long ago as 1945, the remarkable Dr. Helene Deutsch—a medical practitioner, leading psychoanalyst, pioneer of maternal sexuality, and author of the two-volume series *The Psychology of Women*—raised the topic of women who were caught between motherliness and eroticism: "The excitation felt in the genitals can ... disturb the joy of nursing. For the nursing mother can bear almost anything more easily than the confusion of conscious, sexual emotions with the tender, loving action of nursing" (290). Her early insight was remarkable, given the era in which she wrote, but sadly very few today have benefited from it. Researchers, therapists, and educators working in the sexuality field generally show scant understanding of the kinds of tensions between sexuality and motherhood that Deutsch first raised. Nor do they appear to recognize the ideology of asexual motherhood underpinning the indigenous psychologies of many sociocultural environments in which they work. An indigenous psychology is the body of psycho-logical knowledge that each culture holds about human nature and includes all information that is taken to be the truth about mother-hood and sexuality (Cass, "Bringing Psychology" 113). Psychological realities are developed within the boundaries of the indigenous psychology of each specific sociocultural environment, and in Western-influenced cultures, this includes the notion that motherhood and sexuality are mutually exclusive. Unfortunately, research, clinical, and educational professionals working in the sexuality field display little comprehension of the influence these broader epistemological systems have on the way they think. Indeed, they are often the staunch carriers of such cultural beliefs; they possess little awareness of their own socialization processes or of the influence such ideologies may have on the way they approach their clients, patients, or students. It is not surprising, therefore, to find that within the professional literature of sexuality studies, the area of motherhood and sexuality receives little attention, and the attention it does receive is approached from a narrow and reductionist medical perspective. Although some recent pub-lications have pointed to the importance of psychosocial factors, they, nevertheless, still tend to draw from the medical model and to ignore feminist analysis (de Judicibus and McCabe 94; Glowacka et al. 3021; Hipps et al. 2330).

In the twenty-first century, this situation should be viewed as quite untenable. Where are the voices in the so-called sexology movement speaking out against this professional neglect and ignorance? In 2014, I presented a paper at the Asia/Oceanic Federation for Sexology Conference titled "Sexuality and Motherhood," in which I urged sexuality specialists not to ignore this area any longer. I pointed out that I could not recall any symposium or keynote presentation on the issue at any of the sexuality conferences or professional meetings I had attended in the previous forty years. None of the attendees disagreed with this claim. Since then, a small number of papers have appeared, primarily focusing on postpartum sexuality, which is just one phase of motherhood. Nor have sexuality journals shown any serious consideration to addressing motherhood sexuality (see, for example, Latorre and Wu vii, a lost opportunity in this regard).

Examples of professional neglect and their impact are readily available in all of the areas in which sexuality professionals work. In the clinical and educational areas, for instance, research has shown that despite a significant number of women experiencing some kind of sexual difficulty during pregnancy and following the birth of their baby, few raise this topic or ask for assistance from any of their health professionals (Barrett 186; Glazener 330). No doubt there are personal and cultural reasons why some women may not do so, such as feelings of shame about attending to their sexuality in the context of recent motherhood. But of greater interest is why the health professionals themselves did not ask these women whether they had any sexual problems, and why they effectively ignored discussing this important aspect of their lives. Similarly, there continues to be a dearth of educational information given to women (and their partners, where applicable) either during pregnancy or postbirth in regard to possible changes in their sexual experiences during either phase of motherhood (Barrett 186; Foux 271; Grundzinskas and Atkinson 85). An undeclared ideological platform of asexual motherhood appears to pervade the work of a variety of health professionals working with women who are, or hope to be, mothers.

However, it is in the area of sexuality-related research where we truly see a serious lack of understanding of the complex interaction between sexuality and motherhood. Although a relatively small number of studies have been conducted, largely in regard to pregnancy and postpartum experiences, most have significant methodology problems and are of such limited scope that any conclusions must be treated with caution (Buhling et al. 42; Barrett 186; Chang et al. 409; Glazener 330; Rowland et al. 1366). I would like to address some of these issues here because they highlight the deep-seated problems that arise when the ideology of asexual motherhood drives the research focus.

First, it needs to be noted that for many researchers, motherhood seems to be represented solely by the pregnancy and postpartum periods of motherhood. Yet it seems clear to me that there are four phases of motherhood, each of which may involve sexual experiences and difficulties, some unique to each phase:

1. when women and couples are trying to get pregnant;

2. when women are pregnant;

3. the postpartum period (the six month period following childbirth); and

4. living with a baby, then a toddler, and then a small child (that is, the period of balancing motherhood with everything else).

The neglect of the first and last phases is difficult to accept, given that some significant factors arise during these times that may affect mothers' sexual experiences. Let me offer some of my own clinical experiences of women in the first phase, where I have found, for example, that individual women and couples can present with three general areas of sexual difficulty as they attempt to become pregnant:

1. sexual problems preventing pregnancy, essentially an issue for heterosexual couples or those choosing to become pregnant via heterosexual sex (e.g., avoidance of vaginal-penile intercourse, avoidance of sex generally, and a lack of intimacy);

2. sexual difficulties due to the meaning of pregnancy being significantly negative for the woman and/or her partner (e.g., loss of attractiveness, loss of independence, sexual abuse, and avoidance of parenthood); and

3. sexual issues arising from actual engagement in fertility programs (for heterosexual couples this may involve loss of sexual spontaneity, feeling like a "breeder," and reduced intimacy; for lesbians, single women, and others, it may involve reduced intimacy or changed sexual engagement).

Similarly, in phase four, my clinical work has identified a range of sexual difficulties for those parents who engage in sexual activity (whether living with a partner or not), including the existence of many sexual conflicts induced by the presence of a baby, toddler, or growing child (e.g., sexual quality versus quantity; my sexual needs versus yours; being a lover versus being a mother; dating time versus baby time; and sex versus household tasks).

I find it interesting that the two phases that receive attention in the literature—pregnancy and postpartum—are also those which attract the attention of researchers who are keen to document what they consider as sexual dysfunctions in mothers. Or to put it another way: the two phases of motherhood that most obviously reflect the woman-as-madonna archetype have become linked with a serious concern about helping mothers (who are assumed to be heterosexual, monogamous, and coupled) to overcome sexual problems and regain the ability to engage in so-called healthy sex with their partners as soon as possible. Healthy sex is primarily defined in this context by clinical, educational, and research professionals as engaging in vaginal-penile intercourse. These two phases of motherhood are never associated with an interest in positive, nonproblematic sexual experiences, which would, of course, present mothers as sexual beings, once again highlighting the influence of the asexual ideology. It is also of interest that the two phases that attract no research attention (the first and fourth) are those which do recognize mothers as sexual beings. And is it just coincidence that these neglected phases engage mothering issues that have historically been connected with failed mothering, such as an inability to mother naturally or to manage motherhood without stress?

Of course, it is clear that changes in sexual experience do occur for some women (but not all) in the pregnancy and postpartum phases of motherhood, and these may lead to, or be associated with, varying levels of sexual discomfort, pain, and dissatisfaction for some, even many, women (but not for all), which will occur for varying lengths of time. Yet within the literature, little research attempts to differentiate between what may be defined as mild, moderate, and severe sexual changes—or to use varying terms such as "concerns," "dissatisfaction," "complaints," "issues," or "difficulties"—to accurately describe each woman's experiences rather than rushing to pathologize with such terms as "disorder" or "dysfunction." Currently, there exists a bias towards identifying so-called deficits in sexual behaviours without the use of any reference point of what is sufficient, commonplace, usual, expected, or acceptable in women's sexual experience throughout motherhood.

I would argue that recognizing the subtle differences between women and the variations that may occur over time for individual women must surely be an integral part of any research design in order to link these individual differences to both nonsexual and sexual factors. Would it not be more meaningful to study those women who experience no changes at all to their sexual expression during motherhood or those women who quickly resume previous patterns of sexual activity in order to assess which combinations of psychological, sociocultural, and physiological factors may be involved in these circumstances?

At present, sexuality researchers have made no attempt to try and understand the full story of why any woman may experience changes to her sexual experience during the pregnancy or postpartum phases of motherhood. These issues are rarely placed within a broad understanding of sexual, romantic, or relationship behaviours. Nor has there been any attempt to place maternal sexuality within its cultural and social contexts, despite the meaning of both sexuality and motherhood being tightly bound up in the indigenous psychologies of the cultures in which women live and have been socialized. What point is there, for example, in simply identifying an orgasm problem or an inability to become aroused as though these were asocial or acultural activities? And what about a woman who experiences painful intercourse following the birth of a baby but, nevertheless, enjoys a satisfying sex life in all other respects? Such real-life subtleties are not easily accommodated within the medical model, which would simply label her as having a sexual dysfunction.

It is not just the lack of a holistic approach that is at issue here. Those researchers, educators, clinicians, and therapists who adopt such a medical perspective take as their guide the sexual problems listed in the Diagnostic Statistical Manual (DSM) that are specific to women. This list included sexual desire, arousal and orgasm and pain disorders until 2014 when it was changed to orgasm, interest/arousal, and pain/penetration disorders. This approach has led to many other types of sexual difficulties being overlooked, for example discrepancies in sexual preferences, avoidance of sex due to shame regarding body shape, difficulty accepting the self as a sexual being, inability to fully experience sexual passion, sexual inhibition, and so on. The DSM covers just a small segment of the range of possible sexual issues that women can experience, and slavishly following its guidelines leads to many sexuality-related problems of mothers being ignored (e.g., a body image conflict caused by how a woman views her milk-laden breasts, confusion between love for her child and love for her partner, and when a partner, jealous of the woman's attention to the baby, demands more sex).

Another significant methodological problem in assessing research into motherhood sexuality arises from the influence of the prevailing heteronormative ideology, which promotes the idea that vaginal-penile intercourse is the only real sex and all other sexual activity is merely an accompaniment to it. This problem occurs when, for example, sexuality researchers ask their study participants about sex but actually mean vaginal-penile intercourse, a definition they may not make clear. It is also apparent when sexuality researchers use vaginal-penile intercourse as the sole indicator of so-called successful sex or successful treatment. This narrow perspective effectively rules out any research interest in single women, lesbian women, or women for whom intercourse is not the preferred sexual activity; hence, these groups are invariably excluded in motherhood sexuality research. This approach also ignores those women who, following childbirth, are creative enough to engage in sexual acts while suspending intercourse until they feel able to include it in sexual activity without discomfort. Equally ignored are couples who are willing, for a period, to suspend all genitally focused sexual activity in favour of romantic and sensual activities. Since most research protocols tend to ask about engagement in intercourse, anyone who replies in the negative is likely be described as having reduced sexual activity. If associated with difficulties involving desire, arousal, orgasm, or pain the woman will receive the label of sexual dysfunction.

Another significant methodological problem that commonly appears in research design is the lack of questions about a woman's previous sexual or relationship experiences prior to her becoming a mother, which is surprising considering such experiences would seem to be highly relevant to making accurate assessments of a woman's sexual difficulties. For example, perhaps the birth of a child did not create sexual difficulties at all but rather reflected or even reduced sexual problems that existed previously to, and unrelated to, motherhood.

Instead of addressing the complexities I have outlined, research into the effects of motherhood on sex is almost always reduced to simple frequency studies examining how many women in pregnancy and postpartum phases experience the loss of, or reduced, orgasms, sexual interest, and intercourse, and how many experience sexuality-related pain. This is data gathering, but it is at the lowest level—simple bean counting that is of limited usefulness in capturing the depth of human experience.

Let me use the example of orgasm difficulties to illustrate my point: if a study finds that one-third of women have difficulty reaching orgasm postpartum (Barrett 189), what does this say about women who return to orgasm sooner than others, women who are not concerned about their loss of orgasm, women who continue to orgasm but experience it as of lesser quality than prior to motherhood, the meaning given to orgasm by different social groups and cultures, the ways women positively negotiate around this issue in relationships, or the way couples happily accept that their sexual activity does not include orgasm? In other words, the number of women who do or do not have orgasms is a meaningless piece of data if it is isolated from the psychological as well as cultural and other aspects of a woman's life.

There is also the example of breastfeeding and its connection with sexual activity. A great deal of attention has been given to how many breastfeeding women will experience loss of interest and reduced frequency of sexual activity compared to those who do not breastfeed— the primary assumption being that any loss is attributed to hormonal changes in the woman. Even though research results as to whether changes to sexual interest are due to hormones or not have been mixed, researchers continue to look for an answer to this question instead of recognizing that the inconsistency of the results themselves is actually what needs to be addressed. Attending to individual differences and the relative influence of psychological, social, cultural and biological factors would seem to be a good place to start. For example, many women report feeling sexually aroused during breastfeeding (Sydow 27), and one-third to a half of women find breastfeeding to be an erotic experience. However, one-quarter of these women also feel guilty about feeling this way.

To learn more about these experiences, surely it would be more meaningful to try and understand the difference between those women who felt guilty and the 75 per cent who did not rather than treat women as if they were a unified group. Some breastfeeding women, for example, may feel confused when a partner sucks on, or plays with, their breast during sexual, sensual, or romantic times together. Perhaps, they are confused about how to allow both the mother and the lover parts to exist in their life without stress. My experiences tell me that some find this too difficult to do and will avoid sex or physical affection altogether. Hence, the madonna-whore conflict may well be a factor in explaining why some women do not feel interested in sex or cannot become aroused during sex. It is, perhaps, differences such as these that account for research findings being inconsistent, yet these kinds of explanations are rarely, if ever, explored.

Taking a New Approach to Motherhood Sexuality

Clearly, these previous approaches to understanding women's sexual experiences during motherhood are deficient on methodological grounds. However, I contend that the most serious issue is the lack of a multidisciplinary, collaborative, and holistic approach as the foundation for any professional work, whether this is research, education, therapy, or medical treatment. Such a framework must begin with the premise that motherhood is not an illness but rather an experience of life in which sexual experiences ebb and flow and sexual expression is, at times, enhanced and, at times, reduced—an ebb and flow that mothers and their partners will manage in varying ways and with varying degrees of success.

Furthermore, a holistic perspective addresses sexual behaviour, like all behaviour, as the result of multiple interactive variables, which may include factors as diverse as religious expectations, government policies, decision-making processes, power dynamics between partners, and individual differences in level of comfort with physical affection.

This concept of "motherhood-sexuality-as-experience" is not new. In 1976, Adrienne Rich emphasized this approach in her classic book, *Of Woman Born: Motherhood as Experience and Institution,* and two decades later, Judith Daniluk published *Women's Sexuality across the Lifespan: Changing Myths, Creating Meanings.* Though not directly focused on motherhood, the *New View Approach to Women's Sexual Problems* (Kaschak and Tiefer 1) also proposes a holistic framework for understanding women's sexual problems, emphasizing the need to address female sexual experiences in the full context of their lives.

However, the unfortunate reality is that feminist and women's studies literature has had little influence in getting researchers, educators, therapists, or clinicians to base their work in the area of motherhood sexuality within a holistic perspective. To some extent this can be attributed to the many forces that continue to elevate the medical model to its dominant position in the study of sexuality. However, I consider that another key factor weakening the relevance of the holistic approach to motherhood is that it is never embedded within any broader theory of behaviour. As important as sociological, political, and cultural factors are, they are not enough if our work is isolated from the broader context involving links to psychology and physiology. In my own work, published in 1999, I draw upon a constructionist psychology framework that considers any behaviour, including sexual behaviour, to be the result of a complex process of reciprocal interaction occurring between the multiple levels of each individual's psychological capacities and abilities, biological capacities and abilities, the sociocultural environment in which they have been socialized, and the material world around them. I refer to this process as the "dynamic interaction process" (*A Quick Guide* 115).

Such an approach allows us to ask more meaningful and astute questions about motherhood and sexuality than have been asked to date. For example, within the context of the dynamic interaction process, I am interested in how the sexual experiences of a woman (placed against her sociocultural background) are shaped by her experiences of motherhood (directed in varying degrees of influence by her sociocultural background, psychological capacity, and physiology) and vice versa; and how women negotiate a culturally directed conflict between being sexual and being a mother as well as the psychological capacities that may influence these processes. When broad issues such as these are understood then more specific questions can be asked. For example, what interactive combination of psychological, sociocultural, and biological factors lead to a reduction in the quality, quantity, and diversity of a woman's sexual experiences during different phases of motherhood? Also, what interactive combination of psychological, sociocultural and biological factors may buffer a woman against reduced sexual quality, quantity, and diversity during different phases of motherhood? And once these issues are sufficiently understood, further questions pertinent to particular issues may also be asked, such as how the desire to get pregnant effects a woman's or a couple's sexual experiences, or what effects, if any, sociocultural expectations about pregnancy may have on a woman's or a couple's sexual satisfaction following the birth of a child.

Does Popular Literature Trump the Work of Professionals?

Interestingly, popular magazines and online articles that are directed towards women—such as lifestyle, health and fitness, pregnancy, and motherhood publications—are more likely to address motherhood sexuality from the broad context of lived experience than the professional literature. Consider the following titles of articles published in various motherhood, parenting and pregnancy magazines over the past twenty years: "Why Pregnant Women Are Sexy"; Baby Proof Your Sex Life"; "All I Want for Mother's Day Is a Sex Life"; "When Lovers Become Parents"; "Pregnancy Sex Uncensored"; "Giving Birth Won't Spoil Your Sex Life"; "Just Don't Touch My Breasts"; How to Make Love to a Mum"; "Ten Best Ways to Sneak in Sex after Baby"; and "From Motherhood to Bedroom Goddess." A recent analysis of the content of nearly fifteen thousand articles from 1991 (interestingly, the year of Demi Moore's *Vanity Fair* cover picture) to 2010 indicates far less focus on medical dysfunction issues than in the professional literature (Shipps and Caron 103). The authors of this study note that the most common topic was balancing parenting with sexual activity (27 per cent of articles), followed by sexual desire (13 per cent), sexual functioning (11 per cent), looking sexy (10 per cent), sex during pregnancy, sex following birth, birth control and protection (each 9 per cent), and sex and being single (2 per cent).

However, further analysis reveals a picture that is far less rosy than these figures may indicate. Of the nearly fifteen thousand articles examined, just 2.3 per cent actually included serious content on sexuality issues, and of this 2.3 per cent, only one-third were primarily about sexuality. Significantly, the authors found no increase in the number of articles containing sexuality content over the twenty years; rather, there was actually a decrease, created by the deletion of some regular sex columns (an experience I can relate to). In other words, any recognition in these motherhood magazines of mothers as sexual beings was totally superficial and continued to represent motherhood and sexuality as mutually exclusive (Shipps and Caron 111).

In the twenty-first century, the ideology of asexual motherhood continues to mean sexual invisibility for mothers both in the general community and among health professionals. Unfortunately, this also includes sexuality professionals, who I believe should be taking the lead in releasing women from such an onerous ideology. Clearly, it is time that they did so, and I would urge them to work towards this end. The goal must surely be to change motherhood sexuality from a taboo to a visible reality—one that is characterized by a positive acceptance of mothers as sexual beings. However, this cannot occur without engaging in innovative and modern approaches that genuinely attempt to understand the complexity involved in the formation of behaviours relevant to maternal sexuality. The challenge for sexuality professionals is to find new methods for doing this rather than clinging to the old ways. Even more challenging, however, will be the requirement that they first address their own personal ideological bents and biases.

Works Cited

Barrett, Geraldine, et al. "Women's Sexual Health after Childbirth." *Br J Obstetrics Gynaecol.*, vol. 107, no. 2, 2000, pp. 186-95.

Buhling Kai et al. "Rate of Dyspareunia after Delivery in Primiparae According to Mode of Delivery." *European Journal of Obstetrics & Gynecology and Reproductive Biology*, vol. 124, no. 1, 2006, pp. 42-46.

Cass, Vivienne. "Bringing Psychology in from the Cold: Framing Psychological Theory and Research within a Constructionist Psychology Framework." *Psychology and Sexual Orientation: The Meanings we Make – Conversations about Psychology and Sexual Orientation*, edited by Janis Bohan and Glenda Russell, New York University Press, 1999, pp. 106-28.

Cass Vivienne. *A Quick Guide to the Cass Theory of Lesbian & Gay Identity Formation*. Brightfire Press, 2015.

Chang, Shio Ru, et al. "Comparison of the Effects of Episiotomy and No Episiotomy on Pain, Urinary Incontinence, and Sexual Function 3 Months Postpartum: A Prospective Follow-up Study." *Int J Nursing Studies*, vol. 48, no. 4, 2011, pp. 409-18.

Contratto (Weisskopf) Susan. "Maternal Sexuality and Asexual Motherhood." *Signs: Women: Sex and Sexuality*, vol. 5, no. 4, 1980, pp. 766-82.

Daniluk, Judith. *Women's Sexuality across the Lifespan: Changing Myths, Creating Meanings*. The Guildford Press, 1998.

Deutsch, Helene. The Psychology of Women: A Psychoanalytic Interpretation. Vol. 2: Motherhood. Green and Stratton, 1945.

Foux, Rachel. "Sex Education in Pregnancy: Does It Exist? A Literature Review." *Sexual and Relationship Therapy*, vol. 23, no. 3, 2008, pp. 271-77.

Friedman, Ariella, Hana Weinberg, and Ayala Pines. "Sexuality and Motherhood: Mutually Exclusive in Perception of Women." *Sex Roles*, vol. 38, no. 9-10, 1998, pp. 791-99.

Glazener, Cathryn. "Sexual Function after Childbirth: Women's Experiences, Persistent Morbidity and Lack of Professional Recognition." *Br J Obstetrics and Gynaecology*, vol. 104, no. 3, 1992, pp. 330-35.

Glowacka, Maria, et al. "Prevalence and Predictors of Genito-pelvic Pain in Pregnancy and Postpartum: The Prospective Impact of Fear Avoidance." *J Sex Med*, vol. 11, no. 12, 2014, pp. 3021-34.

Grundzinskas, J. and L. Atkinson. "Sexual Function during Puerperium." *Arch Sex Behav*, vol. 13, no. 1, 1984, pp. 85-91.

Hipps Lauren, Lisa Low, and Sari van Anders. "Exploring Women's Postpartum Sexuality: Social, Psychological, Relational and Birth-related Contextual Factors." *J Sex Med*, vol. 9, no. 9, 2012, pp. 2330-41.

Judicibus, Margaret de, and Marita McCabe. "Psychological Factors and the Sexuality of Pregnant and Postpartum Women." *J Sex Res*, vol. 39, no. 2, 2002, pp. 94-103.

Kaschak, Ellen, and Leonore Tiefer, eds. *A New View of Women's Sexual Problems*. The Haworth Press, 2001.

Kleinplatz, Peggy. "On the Outside Looking In: In Search of Women's Sexual Experience." *A New View of Women's Sexual Problems*, edited by Ellen Kaschak and Leonore Tiefer, The Haworth Press. 2001, pp. 123-32.

Latorre, Guisela, and Judy Wu. "Editors' Note: Reproduction, Mother-hood and Sexuality." *Frontiers: A Journal of Women's Studies*, vol. 35, no. 1, 2014, pp. vii-viii.

Oliver, Kelly. "Motherhood, Sexuality and Pregnant Embodiment: Twenty-five Years of Gestation." *Hypatia*, vol. 25, no. 4, 2010, pp. 760-77.

Perel, Esther. *Mating in Captivity.* Harper Collins, 2006.

Rich, Adrienne. *Of Woman Born: Motherhood as Experience and Insti-tution.* W.W. Norton & Co. 1976.

Rowland, Mary, et al. "Breastfeeding and Sexuality Immediately Post-partum." *Can Fam Physician*, vol. 51, no. 10, 2005, pp. 1366-67.

Shipps, Leah, and Sandra Caron. "Motherhood and Sexuality: A 20-year Content Analysis of Sexuality-related Articles in Popular Mag-azines for Mothers." *Journal of International Women's Studies*, vol. 14, no. 1, 2013, pp. 94-112.

Sydow, Kirsten von. "Sexuality during Pregnancy and After Child-birth: A Metacontent Analysis of 59 Studies." *Journal of Psychoso-matic Research*, vol. 47, 1999, pp. 27-49.

Chapter Two

The Sexuality of Mothers in Hindu Life: Myths of Empowerment within Enslavement

Zairunisha

"Prásaṃsanti bhāryāṃ gatayauvanāṃ"
("People praise a wife who is past her youth")

—*Mahābhārata* 5.35.59

Sexual desire is a natural instinct among human beings; however, in Hinduism sex is viewed not as instinctual but rather as spiritual—a sacred act of procreation. In Hindu texts, the Sanskrit word "kama" is generally used to signify desire, pleasure, and love; it is a "science of sensuality" that denotes all kinds of sensual desires, emotional attractions, and aesthetics (Doniger and Kakar 63). The classic text *Kamasutra* defines "kama" as a spiritual act of procreation that maintains the rhythm of the cosmos by amalgamating masculine and feminine sexuality (Thakur). In Hindu culture, the sexuality of a woman as mother is a sacred subject of great reverence. The mother is regarded as an embodiment of the goddess Shakti, who signifies a universal feminine power of procreation and preservation of cosmic order, as well as the destruction of demons and of the universe, in preparation for creation and new beginnings. Hindu society venerates Shakti as the divine mother goddess and as a consort of the male god

47

Shiva. However, there is a vast gap between the idealization and the everyday lived reality of Hindu women's sexuality.

Despite the projection of women's inherent sexual capacity as being sacred in Indian society, it is heavily controlled and regulated by the institutions of marriage and motherhood in traditional Brahmanical (upper-caste Hindu) patriarchal society. Hinduism views the sexuality of the mother as only a means for procreation and not as a representation of desire. Apart from being treated as instruments of procreation, mothers are not viewed as sexual beings. Their sexuality is suppressed and confined to the conjugal relations reserved exclusively for procreation (Cass, this volume). Consequently, the lived experience of the Hindu mother's sexuality is grounded in this traditional patriarchal compass.

This chapter expounds and explores the existing but largely invisible and unacknowledged dichotomy between the symbolic representations of the mother goddess Shakti's sexuality and social constructions of real-life mothers' sexuality in Hindu ways of life. It also considers the manner in which maternal sexuality is devalued and is viewed as nonexistent, immoral, or even as a source of evil. The mother is expected to submit her sexuality entirely to her husband, for his pleasure and progeny alone. Her sexuality is repressed in order to control and confine it exclusively for procreation, and her own desires and needs are neither acknowledged nor validated. Presently, with the availability of mass media, which easily spreads and promotes particular cultural ideologies, Indian Hindu society can now better circumscribe and regulate the sexuality of mothers in order to control their subservient roles in the family. Furthermore, through the deification of the mother's procreative power as the divine mother goddess, Hinduism effectively projects the mother's enslavement as empowerment, a problematic subversion that has strong social consequences.

Methodology

My main field of enquiry relates to the ways in which Hindu women perceive their sexuality in relation to their roles and obligations as a mother. In doing so, I have employed both a feminist framework and a Hindu lens in order to examine the gendered maternal body in Indian Hindu culture. Illustrations have been drawn from the Hindu sacred texts in order to explore and investigate the ways in which traditional

Hindu ideology continues to dominate and restrict the sexuality of mothers in the contemporary world. The aims and objectives of the study were to observe, through interviews, the experiences of women's sexuality before and after motherhood; to discover whether or not mothers view their sexuality separately from motherhood; to identify the wider family's perspective of a mother's sexuality; to analyze the impact of these traditional and socially structured images of mothers on young daughters; and to explore the influence of religious texts on Hindu women.

I studied twenty-two Hindu mothers and pregnant women in Delhi, India, from across the spectrum of caste and class, using purposive and snowballing sampling. These women were from universities as well as organized and unorganized work sectors; they also included housewives and social activists. Apart from personal, face-to-face interviews, I also employed phone interviews for the convenience of some of the subjects, and I audio recorded all my interviews for clarity of data analyzing. The study looked at four different cohorts of mothers: (i) five housewives between the ages of twenty-eight and forty-five, whose primary work was to take care of their children; (ii) six working women between the ages of twenty-eight and forty-six, who divided their time between paid employment and care of their children and their families; (iii) six pregnant women between the ages of twenty-four and thirty; and (iv) five married women between twenty-three and twenty-seven, who intend or hope to become mothers in the near future. These women hailed from both traditional backgrounds and from cosmopolitan areas, and the women lived in a variety of living situations, both with extended and nuclear families. The names of the subjects have been changed to protect their identities. The interviews were held in English however, many women were more comfortable in their regional language and have given their interviews in Hindi which I translated to English later on.

The questions asked during the interviews related to the following key themes. How do women (and their families) experience and view their sexuality before and after pregnancy? Do they feel their sexuality is confined only to the purposes of procreation, or do they also experience (and explore) their sexuality as separate to the act of becoming or being a mother? Do their families value them regardless of whether or not they are mothers? Do they have the freedom to express their sexual feelings, or do they suppress these desires in the name of procreation? Through in-depth interviews and case studies, I engaged with the lived experiences of Hindu women and identified the ways in which the Hindu mother perceives her sexuality as well as her satisfaction and dissatisfaction within the parameters laid down by her religion and culture.

Discourses of the Mother's Sexuality in Hindu Mythological Texts

Ancient Hindu tradition has formed a typology of sex and sensual life (Dhand 96), which is explicitly depicted and articulated in various mythological texts (epics), the *Dharmashastras* (*Manusmriti* and four Vedic [traditional] scriptures), the *Kamashastras* (Kamasutra, ancient text on sex), rituals, symbols, arts, and cultural practices. These texts are primarily written by men and justified as divine sanctions that cannot be questioned by any worldly entities (Roy 156). The *Dharmashastras* declare three primary purposes of Hindu religious life: dharma (ethical norms), artha (means of livelihood), and kama (desires), respectively known as the "trivarga" (Roy 155). The trivarga collectively encompasses the social structure of human beings through its codification (norms and practices), in which kama, governed and legitimized by dharma, represents the sensual facets of life. In Hindu mythologies, káma is associated with the goddess Shakti, who manifests her sexuality in the form of both generative and destructive principles: she creates, preserves, and, if necessary, destroys the universe to make way for new creation.

Vedic scriptures depict two images of the divine mother goddess 'Shakti'—one malevolent, the other benevolent. The mother goddess, in her malevolent form, has a destructive and dangerous sexual energy. She is unmarried and manifests herself without any male consort and appears as both the goddesses Kali and Durga, representing the destruction of evil in order to save her devotees, and the annihilation of the universe to prepare ground for new beginnings. In her benevolent form (as the goddesses Parvati and Lakshmi), the mother goddess is represented as married, as subordinate to her male consort, and as participating with him in the process of procreation and preservation of the cosmos (Apffel-Marglin 40). Although a benevolent goddess has infinite creative as well as destructive powers, these are regulated and controlled by a male god. In this context, Kamala Ganesh explains the implicit unseen male domination and female subordination in Hinduism:

> In popular Indian perceptions of divinity, the dominant image is a male god accompanied by his consort who is his benevolent *Shakti,* the actualizer of his latent power, the embodiment of his grace. Kali and Durga are of course a ubiquitous presence, but the safe domestic mode is represented by Lakshmi—quintessential spouse, symbol of auspiciousness and prosperity. (59)

Images of both benevolent and malevolent goddesses, I would argue, have been constructed in order to represent and also control Hindu women's sexuality. These archetypes act to overcome the threat of women's latent sexual energy, represented in the mythological texts as destructive (a destructiveness, however, that sits in opposition to a goddess's destructive sexual energy) and as capable of disturbing the cosmic order by spreading chaos, disarray, and unrighteousness in society. Ganesh argues the following:

> [There is a] divide between the powerful, "unhusbanded" goddesses (like Kali) whose power is seen as dangerous and destructive, and goddesses who are appropriately married (like Lakshmi) whose power is positive and benevolent, and how this is echoed in social arrangements and evaluations, particularly in the obsessive cultural theme of control and management of female sexuality. (59)

The control over a mother's sexuality is further emphasized through various myths in the sacred Hindu texts in which her uncontrolled sexuality is portrayed as a source of sin.

The myth about the creation of woman in the oldest epic *Mahabharata,* written by sage Krishna Dvaipayana Vadvyasa, provides a clear example of the dichotomous character of woman's sexuality. One of the illustrations shows that women were created by Brahma (the creator of the universe) intentionally for the purpose of perpetrating chaos, disorder, and unrighteousness in the world: "to befuddle humanity, [he] created women" (13.40.7). Brahma provided women the gift of enjoying all kinds of carnal pleasure and to pursue males for the same purpose (13.40.9). At another point, this text says that "in a former creation, women were all virtuous. Those, however, who sprang from this creation of Brahma with the aid of an illusion, became sinful" (13.40.8). In this manner, Brahma himself bestowed contrary qualities in women and divided them into two categories: bad and good. Interestingly, Bernice Lott, in her work *Women's Lives*, argues that both Christian and Hindu traditions present dual conflicting representations of women: there is the motherly maternal woman, who is pure, virginal, holy, and obedient towards her husband, and there is the sexual woman, who is sinful, devilish, and without maternal instinct. These myths show that the woman can either be motherly or sexual, but not both (Cass; Rooks; Zwalf, this volume). In this sense, scriptures and myths expose two opposing views about women and impose strict control over female expressions of sexuality through the institutions of marriage and motherhood.

The classic text *Kamasutra*, traditionally ascribed to sage Mallinaga Vatsayana and compiled between the second and fourth century AD (Bhattacharya 12), discusses the sexual desire and freedom of men and women in greater length, yet it predictably defines women's sexuality as only for male pleasure and progeny (Puri 617). Although the *Kamasutra* elaborates on the sexual relations between men and women as a spiritual act, it also imposes various hierarchical structures on women's sexuality that are channelled and controlled by the social norms of heterosexuality and are confined to being between only a man and a woman. In the *Kamasutra*, women are stratified as maids, remarried women, and courtesans, on the basis of their class and caste. Virgin women of the same caste and class are acceptable for coition in order to have offspring, whereas similar relations with higher caste or remarried women are prohibited. In contrast, coition with women from a lower caste or coition with another man's wife, courtesans, or maids is entirely justified for the pleasure of wealthy men of a high class and caste (Puri 617). Furthermore, violence within coition is both structured and recognized as intrinsic to masculine sexuality, whereas women's anger is only permissible within limits (Roy 160). Women who are unwilling to get married and have children are subjected to intense pressure from their families (Madhavacharya 3.5.2), and a woman is expected to perceive her husband as a god and serve him both physically and socially while also taking care of his extended family (4.1.2). In this way, it can be said that the *Kamasutra* itself is a problematic text in terms of gender, caste, and class hierarchies. It legitimizes the marginalization, objectification and subjugation of women and their sexuality; moreover, it confines and structures the sexuality of women through a heterosexual lens, allowing it only to be expressed for the benefit of wealthy men from a high class and caste (Puri 624).

Similarly, according to the first law book of Hindu religion—*Manusmirti*, written by the sage Manu—although a woman should be respected, honoured, and recognized as a mother and wife, her unrestrained sexuality is hazardous because women are naturally tempted by the desire of carnal pleasure and enjoyment; they will indulge in any unrighteous sexual act without considering its moral consequences and, in effect, disturb the social order (Shah). Manu states that the vulnerability and defencelessness of female sexuality, therefore, needs to be regulated and circumscribed through the evolvement of an elaborate ethical code of conduct. As he instructs, a woman should worship her husband even if she is devoid of virtues. She must be dedicated to her husband all her life, and she has no right to perform any auspicious act without the permission of her husband. She should not do any unpleasant act to her husband, and she should maintain her chastity and not remarry or even approach another man even after the death of her husband (qtd. in Nitisha). Manu stresses the following: "In childhood the father protects her, in youth she is protected by her husband and in old age her sons protect her. A woman does not deserve to be independent" (*Manusmirti*,3:9). In effect, Manu reinforces the claim that Brahma created women purely to support men in the task of procreation and suggests that the most righteous and productive way to shape and control the dangerous power of female sexuality is through her becoming a mother (Shah).

Karen Horney, in her book *Feminine Psychology*, discusses two fundamental reasons for the emergence of procreation myths: first, men's fear of women's sexual power, usually illustrated in various myths and scriptures in which women are depicted with inherent dangerous and mysterious sexual energy, and, second, men's basic envy of women's capacity to give birth, which she calls "womb envy." As a result of such apprehension and subconscious resentment, men consequently hold deep-seated contempt for women, which manifests in an attempt to control women's sexuality through the heavily regulated institution of motherhood. In addition, Horney acknowledges the role society plays in confining and even punishing a woman's sexuality through her role as procreator and mother. However, such feminists as Nancy Chodorow in *The Reproduction of Mothering* and Adrienne Rich in *Of Women Born* claim that the mother's experience of sexuality is not just a personal experience but is institutional—it is constructed and regulated by a patriarchal society.

In Hinduism, it is essential for women to follow their pativrata dharma (uxorial duties) as prescribed in the *Dharmashastras*. In this regard, two ideal women of the sacred Hindu texts— Queen Sita in the epic *Ramayana* (written by sage Valmiki) and Princess Savitri in the epic *Mahabharata*—are presented as great examples of chastity, submissiveness, strength, moral conduct, and dedication towards their husbands and family. Hindu women wish to see themselves in the images of Sita and Savitri, and, therefore, they try to emulate these qualities in their own lives. This process involves a total and uncritical dedication to their husbands and children, regardless of their own desires or needs. As a result, women are reduced to being mothers and wives; in the process losing their own individuality as independent women.

This legacy is passed down from mother to daughter: Hindu daughters are expected to follow the icons of Sita and Savitri and follow their mother's way of life, which prepares them for their future roles as mothers. Young women, while idealizing their mothers, face a conflict between their sexual urges and their mothers' role modelling of a socially constrained sexuality. As Sudhir Kakar states, "The fate of a traditional Indian girl's is a socially enforced progressive renunciation of her erotic needs. The birth of a child does not change this prescription; in fact, maternity often demands an even greater repudiation of a woman's erotic impulses" (97-98). In this way, the sexuality of a mother and her daughter are bound together, but it is not based on true desire but on the expectations of a gendered social structure.

Social demand for the abstinence of the mother is so entrenched in Hindu culture that women in Hindu mythology are sometimes made to pay for its violation with their own lives. The legendary myth of Parshurama and his mother Renuka, in *Mahabharata,* illustrates such a demand. Renuka, mother of five sons, is beheaded by her youngest son, Parshurama, on the order of her husband, Jamadagni, as a punishment for having a fleeting sexual urge. The myth of Renuka shows that women are not even allowed to have a licentious thought, let alone practice the physical act itself. This story is a symbolic representation of modern

Hindu society, where it is still an unacceptable or punishable offense for a woman to even consider her sexuality as separate from her family life.

There are also examples in Hindu scriptures in which women deliberately deny their own sexuality for the sake of their family or husbands, and through these allegiances, also deny their sexuality to other men. The myth of *Panchkanyas* (the Five Holy Virgins) tells the story of five beautiful, intelligent, strong, pious, and supernatural women[1] who either have extramarital relations or take on more than one husband, as dictated by social custom and not by their own choice. All five virgins suffer misfortune in their life and are used by men for social purposes for instance, Ahilya was cursed by her own husband for adultery, Draupadi was the wife of five brothers, Tara was married to her husband's brother and Sita was abandoned by her husband etc. Although they are all married mothers, the five are venerated as holy virgins and are considered as pure and chaste—ideal women to idolize. Despite sometimes being punished for their devotion to these sexual conventions, they do not question their duties and accept as destiny these sexual obligations (sexual obligations are social restrictions that don't allow them to exercise their sexuality beyond social boundaries), the fulfillment of which is essential for both the happiness of their family and for gaining the approval of a society that only serves to further reinforce patriarchal attitudes concerning women's bodies and their sexuality. The above-mentioned examples of various socioreligious myths and ideals all situate the Hindu woman as the obedient desexualized procreator. It is little wonder, therefore, that Hindu women's lives are both limited and regulated by the images of these sacred texts and myths: they simply cannot imagine themselves beyond such ideals.

In more recent times, mass media has become a popular tool through which to spread these traditional ideological myths, as they can reach into the intimacy of the home and influence its viewers swiftly and efficiently. Television, radio, Internet, newspapers, magazines, songs, and literature are all sources responsible for spreading and reinforcing the ideologies of good and bad women. The procreative function of a women's sexuality is variously illustrated in religious films, serials, and speeches. There are many channels available on cable television and Internet sites which telecast mythological narratives and character-based serials, such as *Ramayana, Mahabharata, Shivmahaparan, Mahakali*, and so on.[2] The main aim of these shows, I would argue, is to inspire women to remain true to their religious roots. These programs glorify women's immanence as mothers, and through the guise of religious duties, they attempt to control female sexuality. Perhaps most disturbing, though, is that women tend to accept these prescriptions as their unalterable destiny, barely raising a voice in protest against such gender-based social manipulation. This point will be further illustrated through a discussion of the case studies and interviews I conducted with Hindu mothers.

Case Studies of Hindu Mothers

Findings

The key findings of my research show that Hindu women's sexuality is structured and revolves around traditional religious interpretations of Hindu myths and scriptures. Hindu women's sexuality is primarily associated with their husband's pleasure and progeny. Expressing their sexuality beyond this point is not only socially stigmatized but, as was made explicit in my case studies, becomes a matter of castigation. In response to the interview questions, most of the women stated that for them, the primary purpose of sex in their life was to procreate, which was something they felt obliged to do. Although some of the women were conscious of their sexual desires, they did not or could not see sex as a means for enjoyment due to the social stigma attached to it. Most women felt hesitant to admit to or express their sexuality, even to their husbands. It would seem, therefore, that sexuality and motherhood are directly related in the consciousness of Hindu women.

Sujata—a thirty-seven-year-old, middle-class, and high-caste Brahmin woman—is a school teacher, living with her three children and in-laws in an extended family. She spends most of her day working at the school, and after coming home, she then has to do domestic work for both her children and extended family. She complained that she had a monotonous sexual life not only because of a lack of a personal life but also because of the indifference her husband had towards her sexual urges and needs:

> Before pregnancy, we used to have sex like routine work, not for enjoyment but for having a baby. I had a lot of pressure from my in-laws to have a child as soon as possible. Without a child, I had

no value or status in the family. We could not even think about pleasure—it was just a necessity for us. Now I have to take care of the family and children. Their success is my success, which is more important than any other thing. I don't know, but somehow I feel that I have done what was important.

For Sujata, her sexual life was identical to and indistinguishable from her family life. She was virtually unable to consider her own urges independently from her familial duties—a fact attributed to the traditional values with which she was raised and which were upheld by her own mother.

Another woman, Deboshree—a thirty-two-year-old, high-class, and high-caste Brahmin Bangali mother and housewife—shared similar sentiments. She has two sons with her husband, who is a business man. She never spoke about a lack of satisfaction in her sex life, most likely because Deboshree rarely considered her own needs over those of her family and husband: "I belong to a very traditional Hindu family in which marriage means procreation. For me, my family is my first priority. I always get tense to please my family and husband. I don't want to think about myself. My happiness resides within their happiness, their satisfactions, and dissatisfactions. How can I ignore them for myself!"

Like Sujata and Deboshree, most of the other mothers were indifferent towards their sex lives. These mothers believed that sex for procreation or for the purpose of meeting their husband's demands was their duty. Personal pleasure was not generally something that was even considered, let alone pursued. The interview subjects made it clear that they believed themselves to be performing their duties according to "pativratadharma" (the duties ascribed to a wife). As prescribed in holy texts, the women felt that their role in society was to get married and bear children. Their life goals all centred on their children and their family. Some women did speak about experiencing a loss of sexual urge and also a loss of a sense of their sexual self after having children, but this was ascribed to having heavy family responsibilities. After all, in an extended family, mothers rarely get any privacy, nor do they get much support in their domestic work from other family members.

At the same time, there were women who had experienced some level of sexual self-realization but who were either unable to express their urges or were bound to suppress them due to the fear of attracting the "bad woman" stigma. Janki, a twenty-nine-year-old housewife, belongs to a middle-class Vaishya (third lowest Hindu caste) extended family. Her husband is a cashier in a government bank, and she has a three-year-old daughter. She talked about her feelings of frustration regarding her unfulfilled and suppressed sexual urges:

> I wanted to tell my husband what I want, what my bodily needs are, but how could I say. It would be shameful for me to say such things. I enjoy my sensuality, but if I take an initiative it would not be right. Sometimes I cannot control my desires and think of another man. How sinful it is! He should understand my wishes, my feelings, it should be his side to give value to my desires too, but what can I do? I have to wait only because this is my pativratadharma which I learnt and saw from my childhood in families, TV, and films. I don't want to disobey it.

Any mention of the word "sex" is considered a taboo in traditional Indian society, and for women, there is the additional complexity of protecting their izzat, or honour. Women are torn between their natural urges and their role in society, which is dictated by tradition and by a patriarchal suspicion of maternal sexuality.

Although some Hindu women are, of course, conscious of their sexual desires and (reluctantly) perceive themselves as sexual beings, they are still generally hesitant to express their urges or explore their curiosity regarding sex, since passivity is regarded as a precious virtue. In his book *The Indians*, Sudhir Kakar notes the complex and paradoxical psychology of Indian tradition: "With so many traditional women carrying the baggage of shame and guilt in relation to their (sexual) bodies, with all the images of insatiable women and the notions of sex being an act that drains a man of power and vigour running riot in the male cultural imaginations, the omens for a joyful sexual life in the average Indian marriage are not promising" (93). Hindu women are made to believe that there is something immoral in wanting or enjoying sex, which encourages a sense of fear that society will judge them as bad or selfish if they ever discuss or indulge in sexual activity.

In Indian families, many women cannot even talk to their husbands about taking precautions against an unwanted pregnancy without being accused of contemplating adultery (Pande). For a traditional woman, taking an interest in sex goes against the Hindu ideal of the good mother, who is the image of self-sacrifice, love, kindness, submission, and tolerance. No mother wants to be seen as uncaring or irresponsible, so although many would like to see a shift in attitudes towards maternal sexuality, there is a fear of the consequences. As a result, many women in Hindu culture suffer from low self-esteem and a poor sense of self-worth. They are intensely frustrated and dissatisfied with things the way they currently stand but see themselves as victims of conditions beyond their control.

Looking to the work of maternal theorists outside of India, for a moment, I will refer to a study by the Western theorists Ada Lampert and Ariella Friedman, which highlights the real costs of traditional ways of mothering. According to this study, those women who devote most of their time to care for their children and family have high moral and social status, but they also have low social, personal, and physical self-image. The study indicates the double bind of womanhood—women are forced to choose between being mothers and being sexually autonomous beings. If they refuse a traditional lifestyle, as women seeking an active sexual life tend to be forced to do, then they are strictly castigated from society in much the same way as Renuka and Ahilya. But if they follow traditional ways and values, as allegedly disciplined or good women do, they have to sacrifice their sexual identity (65-81). The same goes for those Hindu women who want to explore their sexuality either before or outside of marriage. This study shows the paradoxical situations women are faced with when considering their choices and priorities in life. However, for most the word "choice" is a misleading word. Most women have no other option but to accept a traditional way of life and at a high personal cost. Additionally, the woman's subjugated and dependent status in the family leaves her vulnerable—like the myths of Sita and Savitri, her social identity and status are linked with her extended family and, of course, her husband. Consequently, the vast majority of women would dare not take any action that could be seen as a punishable offence in the eyes of society.

Pooja—a twenty-three-year-old Hindu upper-caste and upper-class Kshriya woman—works as social activist and is a newlywed, who lives with her husband. She shared her views in the following words:

> Sex is in our nature like hunger, thirst. It should not be wrong for a woman to seek a celebration of her sexuality in the same way as men enjoy doing. But we are a patriarchal society. People

will not say anything to men, yet they will call us a "loose character" woman, searching love for having sex. Nobody would wish to marry that kind of woman. She will have to live alone, without children, lonely in dejected conditions. And when she will feel that sex is not the primary thing in her life anymore, then it will be too late.

Asha, a thirty-three-year-old Hindu Brahmin woman from a low class, was five months pregnant at the time of the interview. She expressed her strong resentment and dissatisfaction with the deep gulf between the way Hindu society celebrates women symbolically and how they are treated in everyday life:

We claim to worship mothers as devi [goddesses] and put them on a pedestal in our mythology. But in the real world, we don't want to worship our women who are also mothers and made to live in the goddess image within themselves. We don't value their feelings, their desires. We always want them to be ever ready for serving their men and families regardless of their own needs, pleasures, and pains. Women also have feelings; they are not just incubators for manufacturing babies.... People are saying that times are changing but I don't think so.... It is the destiny of a Hindu woman to have a male child and unconditionally invest her whole life in that.

A similar case is that of Latika, a twenty-three-year-old pregnant woman who belongs to the lower-caste Dalit community. She lives with her in-laws, and her husband works in a university hostel. Initially, she worked alongside him, but now that she is pregnant, she stays at home. This is her second pregnancy, and she had mixed feelings about it, her situation, and the way she is treated by her extended family:

Since my husband learnt of my having conceived, he has been directed by his parents to avoid any sexual contact with me; he is constantly under pressure from his parents. They think that the child born without such contact will be very fortunate and talented. This they have learnt from the *Dharmashastras*. I fail to understand that ...why can't they think that we (mothers) are also human beings with flesh and blood, having our own wants and natural urges?

Latika has to live with the burden of these traditional prohibitions and prescriptions being forced upon her by her extended family, with no possibility of escape from this repressive environment. Tradition is currently reinforced in various forms by the Hindu cultural revivalists; brutal assaults on women are an important source of fear, insecurity, and vulnerability. In a contemporary social context, the emerging forces of Hindutva,[3] also called Sangh Parivar and Rashriya Sevika Samiti (the Hindu nationalist women's organization), claim to be self-appointed guardians of Hindu tradition and its women iconographies. They profess their commitment to protect the superiority of India's spiritual traditions through the rehabilitation of Hindu women in traditional gender roles as full-time mothers, who are expected to remain subservient to patriarchal domination. Arguably, as a result, there has been an increase of female feticide and rape cases involving young girls, and women face the constant threat of domestic violence, sexual assault, social rejection, and acid attacks in public places, all of which indicate a violently enforced gender hierarchy that understands women as subordinate and men as occupying the superior position in society. Consequently women, and particularly mothers, are constantly under pressure to conceal and deny their sexuality.

It is evident that the real, everyday struggles women face regarding their suppressed sexuality cannot be resolved by a mere veneration of the iconography of the Hindu mother goddess. Ganesh argues that "one cannot 'use' the goddess for finding solutions to contemporary problems any more than one can apply a modernist yardstick of gender equality or hierarchy to measure all cultures at all times. Perhaps the goddess can only remain a source of inspiration, a vision" (63). In a patriarchal society, mother goddesses are often interpreted not as ideals of a women's strength, as initially apparent, but as a symbolic compensation for women's subordination and perceived weakness.

Conclusion: The Paradox of a Mother's Sexuality

The findings of this study confirm that the denial of the split between the mythical asexual mother goddess and the real life sexually desiring mother is a pervasive reality in modern Hindu culture. Hindu communities venerate the mother as a sacred procreator and depict women as life givers and sustainers. Traditional Hindus want to confine a woman's life to the work of procreation alone, which perpetuates a culture in which mothers are not allowed or even able to perceive themselves as independent sexual beings. My research has revealed that in Hindu culture, a woman's sexuality is not seen as distinct from her procreative obligations as a mother. Since women are more valued for their motherhood, sexual freedom and emancipation are almost entirely dismissed as unimportant. Hierarchical and gendered Hindu ideology continues to dominate the social as well as sexual lives of Indian mothers even today. The results of the study show that the ideology of deifying motherhood prescribes women's sexuality as a sacred pro-creative power and, consequently, keeps women enslaved in patriarchal bondage.

Hindu sacred texts classify women into two categories—bad and good—on the basis of their relationship to their sexuality. A woman who expresses her sexual desires is seen as bad. She has to be controlled and regulated by reducing sex to a means of procreation. Sexually active mothers are not seen as good mothers, as they are thought to be less caring, aggressive, selfish, and dangerous for their families. For this, they are castigated and punished by their family and by society in the form of physical and social abuse, shame, abandonment, and separation from their family and their community (Dhand 134, 148). In contrast, the nonsexual mother (or rather the mother who hides her sexuality) has a high moral and social image; she is regarded as caring and as dedicated to her family. Consequently, for traditional Hindus, a woman's sexuality cannot be understood as a source of joy or pleasure (Shah). Women have no value either inside or outside the home, other than as mothers. Once a woman manages to produce a male child, she is expected to invest her life in providing unconditional love and care and at a heavy personal cost. Due to a woman's subordinated and devalued status, if she is unable to have children, society considers it unrighteous for her to explore or even consider her sexuality outside of the conjugal boundary, which is something that men are freely permitted (and even encouraged) to do. And as a result of hiding and suppressing her sexual desires, women are left feeling frustrated, insecure, and fearful of being abandoned.

It is, of course, important to note that changes have occurred in recent times regarding the perceptions and attitudes towards motherhood and sexuality, largely due to the way women in India are breaking social stigmas and barriers. For instance, many women now are more educated and are seeking employment as well as working and interacting with other men outside of the family. However, patriarchal Hindu ideology still prevails in different ways. The ever-increasing reach of electronic media and internet resources has further strengthened the patriarchal desire to control Hindu mothers, both socially and physically. Portrayals and appraisals of mothers are still based on traditional images of the good mother, whose life and sexuality rest in the hands of her family.

To that end, it can be said that the very idea of sexuality in Indian Hindu culture is discursively constructed and rooted in discourses of gender, class, and caste hierarchy; it is further reinforced by various religious texts that still have a strong impact on women's lives even today. In Hinduism, on the one hand, the mother's sexuality is lauded and is projected as a source of power, strength and freedom, whereas, on the other hand, a range of stratified and hierarchical restrictions are imposed on mothers and maternal sexuality. As Joyti Puri aptly points out (in reference to the *Kamasutra*), "That what felt like a sexually repressive culture had actually put out a handbook to enhance sexual pleasure was not only astonishing but also paradoxical." In this way, such discussions of the procreative power of women explicitly show inherent paradoxes regarding sexuality, Hinduism, and Indian culture, and leave the Hindu mother caught in a ceaseless contradiction between the emancipatory projection of her sexuality and its repressive reality.

Endnotes

1. In order to know more about the Panchkanyas women and their stories, please consult the epics *Ramayana* and *Mahabharata*.
2. These serials are, or have been available, on Indian YouTube, various television channels, such as DD National, NDTV Imagine, Star Plus, T-Series, and Colors TV.
3. Hindutva are a group of Hindu nationalists. They understand Hindu tradition from a narrow, sectarian, fundamentalist, and dogmatic viewpoint.

Works Cited

Apffel-Marglin, Frédérique. "Female Sexuality in the Hindu World." *Immaculate and Powerful, the Female in Sacred Image and Social Reality*, edited by Clarissa W. Atlinson, et al., Beacon Press, 1985, pp. 39-60.

Bhattacharya, Narendra Nath. *History of Indian Erotic Literature*. Munshiram Manoharlal, 1975.

Chodorow, Nancy. *The Reproduction of Mothering: Psychoanalysis and the Sociology of Gender*. University of California Press, 1978.

Doniger, Wendy, and Sudhir Kakar. "Introduction." *Kamasutra*, Translated and edited by Wendy Doniger and Sudhir Kakar, Oxford University Press, 2009, pp. 1-68.

Dhand, Arti. *Woman as Fire, Woman as Sage: Sexual Ideology in the Mahabharata*. State University of New York Press, 2008.

Ganesh, Kamala. "Mother Who Is Not a Mother: In Search of the Great Indian Goddess". *Economic and Political Weekly*, 20-27 Oct. 1997, WS, pp. 58-64.

Horney, Karen. *Feminine Psychology*. Norton, 1967.

Kakar, Sudhir. *The Indians*. Penguin Books, 2007.

Lampert, Ada, and Ariella Friedman. "Sex Differences in Vulnerability and Maladjustment as a Function of Parental Investment: An Evolutionary Approach." *Social Biology*, vol. 39, 1992, pp. 65-81.

Nitisha. "Manu's View on the Status of Women." *Your Article Library*, www.yourarticlelibrary.com/political-science/manus-opinion-on-the-status-of-women/40145. Accessed Sept. 20 2019.

Lott, Bernice. *Women's Lives*. Brooks/Cole, 1987.

Pande, Mrinal. *Stepping Out: Life and Sexuality in Rural India*. Penguin, 2003.

Puri, Jyoti. "Concerning 'Kamasutras': Challenging Narrative of History and Sexuality," *Signs*, vol. 27, no. 3, 2002, pp. 603-39.

Rich, Adrienne. *Of Woman Born*. Bantam, 1978.

Roy, Kumkum. "Unravelling the Kamasutra." *Indian Journal of Gender Studies*, vol. 3, no. 2, 1996, pp. 155-60.

Shah, Shalini. *The Making of Womanhood: Gender Relations in the Mahabharata*. Manohar Publisher, 1995.

Thakur, Pallavi. "Kama Sutra: Less about Sex, More about Spirituality." *Speaking Tree*, 2020, www.speakingtree.in/allslides/the-spiritual-side-of-kamasutra. Accessed Apr. 1 2020.

The Kamasutra. Translated and edited by Madhavacharya, vol. 1 – vol. 2, Laxmi Venkateshvara Steam Press, 1934.

The Mahabharata. Translated and edited by J.A.B. Van Buitenen. The University of Chicago Press, 1973–1978. 5 vols.

The Ramayana of Valmiki. Edited by G.H. Bhatt and U.P. Shah. Oriental Institute, 1960–1975. 7 vols.

Chapter Three

Blips of Feminist Mothering: Mothers and Daughters Navigate Taboo Topics in Talking about Sex

Lysa Salsbury and Erin Chapman

In the sociofamilial context of the United States, having conversations about sex and sexuality is often a challenging milestone in the parent-child relationship. Research has shown that open, age-appropriate, and positive communication on these sensitive topics can help lead to healthier sexual outcomes for teens (Kirby 244-45). For mothers who identify as feminist, their relationship with their children is often characterized by a desire for autonomy, self-governance, and self-respect (Green, "Embodied Knowledge/s" 169). However, in a society filled with negative messages around sex, the majority of mothers, unfortunately, often resort to more controlling parental practices and dominant conversation styles (Mauras et al. 467). Shilpa Phadke discusses the quandary faced by feminist mothers in seeking "to expand one's child's boundaries even as one draws other kinds of boundaries—boundaries that will keep them from harm" (101). As she points out, communication about sex and sexuality is frequently mired in tension and discomfort. Feminist mothers face numerous contradictions and conflicts in trying to help their teenagers negotiate the complex choices and challenges of adolescence.

In the rural inland Northwest United States—a region characterized by political, social, religious, and ideological conservatism based in white, traditional Christian values (Pew Research Center)—the sexuality education provided in K-12 public schools is heavily influenced by religious dogma, messages of purity and morality, and narrowly defined gender roles and expectations. Sexuality education programs in Idaho schools must provide "the scientific, psychological information for understanding sex and its relation to the miracle of life" and include "knowledge of the power of the sex drive and the necessity of controlling that drive by self-discipline" (Section 33-1608, Idaho State Legislature). The Sexuality Information and Education Council of the United States (SIECUS) reported in 2018 that less than 5 per cent (4.8 per cent) of Idaho middle schools teach students "all 19 critical sexual health education topics[1] in a required course in any of grades 6, 7, or 8" (7). Given that access to comprehensive, inclusive, and sex-positive sexual health education is systematically denied to most Idaho middle school students, parents and communities that wish to provide their children with this education are left to fill in the gaps.

In this chapter, we discuss findings from a small qualitative study examining communication about sex between self-identified feminist mothers and their adolescent daughters. Respondents participated in a sexuality education program designed for middle-school students and their parents; youths and parents attended concurrent but separate classes using the same curriculum. The program provided a unique opportunity to explore communication between self-identified feminist mothers and their teenage daughters and to examine how these conversations contribute to the teens' development of self-agency and autonomy. Through our analysis, we gained insight into the "blips," or tensions of feminist parenting, and how these are negotiated within mother-daughter dialogue around sex and sexuality.

Background

Mother-Daughter Communication around Sex and Sexuality

Parent-child communication about sex involves complex dynamics and an intricate interplay of age, attitudes, gender, cultural background, social norms, personal beliefs and expectations, faith, sexuality, self-image, demeanour and facial expressions, self-efficacy, and persuasive intentions (Healey 5; Jaccard, Dodge, and Dittus 11-12). Further complicating the process are the components of communication:

the source (e.g., age, gender, trustworthiness, and expertise); the message (e.g., topics addressed and tone—negative, positive, or neutral); the medium through which transmission occurs (e.g., face-to-face, nonverbal, and body language); the recipient (e.g., their developmental stage, gender, knowledge base, motivations, emotional state, and past experiences); and the context in which the communication occurs (e.g., temporal, physical, social, and cultural features as well as privacy and comfort levels of both mother and daughter) (Jaccard, Dodge, and Dittus12).

In this study, we focused on mothers as sources of communication and their daughters as the recipients of messages about sex and relationships. The medium for these exchanges is often face-to-face; however, multiple mechanisms exist by which mothers influence adolescents' sexual behaviour, including direct communication about sex and sexuality as well as, and perhaps more importantly, nondirect transmission of parental beliefs and values (Dittus et al. 1949). The contexts of these interactions are also important to consider, particularly with regard to societal expectations and gender stereotypes, coupled with the emotional states and comfort level of both mother and daughter.

Anecdotal accounts and empirical studies confirm that mothers tend to be the primary parental source of sexuality education. Moms talk to their kids more than dads, and when dads do communicate about sex, they are more likely to direct these exchanges to their sons (see review by DiIorio et al.). The nuanced aspects of communication play an important role in determining the frequency with which these talks occur. Mothers with greater self-efficacy, more confidence in their knowledge base, and a higher level of comfort with sexuality communication are more likely to have these conversations with their children (Guilamo-Ramos et al. 767; Pluhar et al. 287).

The topics mothers typically report conveying to their daughters include messages about menstruation, reproduction, and general information about contraception, sexually transmitted infections (STIs), and sexual intercourse (see review by DiIorio et al.). In discussing these topics, however, Lucia O'Sullivan and her colleagues reported that these talks directed at daughters often include an emphasis on girls' responsibility in avoiding or controlling sexual encounters due to the potentially negative consequences of sex (281). In these exchanges, Erika Pluhar reported that the perceived negative aspects of sex—such as STIs and unplanned pregnancies—tended to outweigh the positive aspects, and mothers frequently conveyed adversarial gender role beliefs to their daughters (183-91). Compared to messages given to sons about sex and sexuality, messages to daughters tend to be more protective and restrictive. As we will explore, these negative messages are in direct contrast to the more sex-positive messaging shared by the self-identified feminist mothers in our study.

It is important to note that the Our Whole Lives (OWL) program actively encourages caregivers of all genders to engage with their children in inclusive sexuality education in a supportive, caring, and nonjudg-mental environment, which directly challenges the norms we discussed regarding mothers as the primary source of education around sex and sexuality. Additionally, unlike other more traditional sexuality education programs, OWL promotes the value that learning is life-long and that knowledge should be cocreated. Along with their children, parents and caregivers are immersed in the OWL curriculum in a parallel learning experience. The authors engaged in studying the experience of participants in the program in an effort to promote the need to continually challenge American norms around limited, abstinence-only, and heteronormative sex education, which falls largely to mothers and women-identified individuals in other caregiving roles (such as teachers) to deliver.

Mothers and Daughters: Discussing Sex, Competence, and Confidence

A sense of autonomy and competence (defined as sexual experiences that are consensual and safe) are viewed as fundamental components to a positive sexual development (Heron et al. 675-677). Increased com-petence and self-agency can manifest as conscious practices of sexual wellbeing—including delaying sexual initiation with a partner or partners until a level of confidence in autonomous decision making is reached, increasing use of protection against STIs, and preventing un-planned pregnancy—when heterosexual sexual activity occurs (Bay-Cheng 133; DiIorio et al. 23). This self-agency also includes increased confidence in negotiating with partners around risk reduction, preven-tion strategies, and alternatives to intercourse, such as outercourse, mutual masturbation, and other forms of sexual stimulation (Widman et al. 737).

Empirical evidence suggests that positive associations between parent-child communication and adolescent sexual behaviours are likely attributed to key mediating elements of the parent-child relationship—namely, a sense of openness, closeness, support, and warmth (Kesterton and Coleman 438). Therefore, the significance of the nuanced nature of the dialogue cannot be underestimated. Nonverbal messages, the atmosphere in which the source and recipient are conversing, and the emotional positions of each party are crucial in the overall process of mother-daughter communication about sex and sexuality.

Mothering as a Feminist Practice

The empowering practice of feminist mothering "offers a way to disrupt the transmission of sexist and patriarchal values from generation to generation" (O'Reilly, "Feminist Mothering" back cover); it provides a "proud defiance of convention" (Glickman 22) that purposefully contravenes stereotypical expectations and structures of motherhood. Feminist mothering involves "dismantling traditional gender social-ization practices" (O'Reilly, "Feminist Mothering" 9) and intentionally opting for nonsexist childrearing strategies. Parents, mothers in particular, can play a crucial role in providing their children with the tools to be autonomous and empowered decision makers around sex and sexuality, which is most effectively conveyed through open and empathetic communication, appropriate role modelling, and helping their children to set their own boundaries. Arguably, the "good mother" norm in traditional, patriarchal, and conservative comm-unities would be to convince children to practice abstinence, perpetuate heteronormative and monogamous relationship norms, and avoid exposing them to any knowledge that may further their interest in sex and sexuality. By actively enrolling their children in a sex-positive and inclusive education program and by participating in the program themselves, the mothers in this study are intentionally pushing back against confining, culturally contextual definitions of what it means to be a good mother.

Feminist mothering values trust and respect (Green, "Developing a Feminist Motherline" 13), and feminist mothers intentionally deploy their role as mothers to challenge patriarchal norms and values within traditional structures of motherhood, creating optimal conditions for parent-child communication on difficult or uncomfortable topics. Our study examined how mothers' parenting practices and communication styles influenced conversations with their teenage daughters around sex and sexuality. We were particularly interested in the tensions that emerged between the desire of self-identified feminist mothers to encourage autonomy (as conceptualized within relational autonomy theory; Mackenzie 146), self-agency, and healthy sexual decision making in their teenage daughters, and the mothers' concerns for their daughters' safety and wellbeing, which were influenced by factors relating both to an oppressive external social environment as well as to the mothers' own early experiences of sex and sexuality.

Procedures and Methods

Researchers

It is important to consider the personal and professional lenses through which this study was conducted. One of the researchers and her teenage daughter participated in the parallel parent-child sexuality education program; their data were omitted from this study. The other researcher was an instructor in the program and taught the teen class. They both identify as feminist and strongly believe in the power of knowledge and communication to empower young people to develop agency regarding their sexual behaviours and relationships. Additionally, the researchers believe that through enhanced knowledge of sex and sexuality, parents can be empowered to openly and honestly communicate with their early teen children about sensitive and taboo (due to American societal messages and socialization around sex) topics. One of the researchers is a faculty member who teaches classes on family and relationships and has a particular passion for and expertise in sexuality education for teens and young adults. She does not identify as religious but rather as agnostic and is not a member of or affiliated with any church. The other researcher is a member of the Unitarian Universalist church where the OWL program in this study was taught, and identifies as agnostic and humanist rather than as Christian. Her interest in this research was influenced by her strong desire to provide a unique and sex-positive educational opportunity around sex and sexuality for her children, which was not available in their local public school system, and by her being both an instructor and the mother of a teenager participating in this program. Together we are the cocreators of a college-level sexual health education forum at our university. As experienced sexuality educators and long-time teachers in the program, they have a strong bias related to the quality of the OWL program and its value in helping young adolescents develop healthy attitudes towards sex and sexuality, characterized by consensual, positive, inclusive, empowering, and mutually pleasurable sexual encounters.

Participants and Program

Participants were recruited from a cohort of mothers and their twelve to fourteen year-old daughters who took part in the coed community-based sexuality education program, OWL, in a small town in the inland Northwest of the United States. OWL is a multilevel series of sexuality education curricula for school-aged children (K-12) through to older adults; this cohort specifically engaged in the workshops and lessons developed for youth between grades seven and nine. The OWL curricula were developed in accordance with the Guidelines for Comprehensive Sexuality Education produced by the SIECUS National Guidelines Task Force (Unitarian Universalist Association [UUA]). The development of the OWL curricula was sponsored by the UUA and the United Church of Christ Justice and Witness Ministries, but the core curricula contain no religious references or doctrine. The content includes extensive discussions of queer sex and sexuality; one of the workshops is dedicated to the topic of consent, and pleasure is a part of the Circles of Sexuality, which undergirds the whole program. Abstinence is presented as an option only. (Please see the UUA's website for a detailed description of the curriculum: *https://www.uua.org/re/owl.*) A companion volume of faith-based content is available for use if desired.[2] The OWL program in this small town is unusual in that it offers a concurrent parent education class, which mirrors the content, activities, and group discussions of the youth class. The class format for the teens comprised one two-hour session every week over twenty-seven weeks. The curriculum content varied from week to week, but it included discussions, activities, exercises, videos, and guest speakers, among others.

All of the mothers who agreed to be interviewed either self-identified as feminist or said that they have values that are in line with feminism. This study did not investigate specifically whether these mothers were taking a feminist approach to sexuality education. Certainly, they were taking advantage of an opportunity for their adolescent children to engage with a secular sexuality education program that "recognizes and respects the diversity of participants with respect to biological sex, gender identity, gender expression, sexual orientation, and disability status" and is "as inclusive as possible of this human diversity" (Unitarian Universalist Association). Additionally, the mothers in the study committed to full participation in a concurrent parent-only OWL session each week. This commitment is indicative of feminist mothering practices, by providing their children with an opportunity to participate in a sex-positive, comprehensive sexuality education program; committing to a parallel journey of education and exploration; and being open to having mutually vulnerable conversations with their daughters about sex and sexuality.

Each of the mothers interviewed had experienced a wide variety of formal and informal, as well as positive and negative, sexuality education during their own adolescence. All were employed outside the home; their occupations included health educator, physician, psychologist, librarian, student affairs professional, yoga instructor, and nurse. The mothers' ages ranged from thirty-three to fifty-three. All had daughters in the program who were either in the seventh or eighth grade. In total, seven mother-daughter dyads were interviewed; however, only the interviews with the mothers have been used in this chapter. Although OWL is a program for youth of all genders (and this specific OWL group did include boys in the youth class and fathers in the parent class), our focus for this chapter is on the data obtained about the mothers and their daughters. We plan to continue to analyze the interviews we conducted with the teenage girls for future research papers, and future research also warrants exploration of father-son, father-daughter, and mother-son dynamics.

Procedure and Data Gathering

Prior to conducting the interviews, we received approval from our university for research on human participants via the Institutional Review Board. Consent was obtained from all of the participants individually, including the teens. In addition, the mothers also consented to their daughters participation. One daughter in the group declined to be interviewed, and one mother had two daughters who both agreed to participate. Mothers and daughters were interviewed separately; pseudonyms are used for the purpose of confidentiality in reporting. Each of the semistructured interviews with the mothers was audio recorded and then transcribed verbatim, resulting in seventy-nine single-spaced pages of data for analysis. Each participant was asked the same open-ended questions, pertaining to, among other topics, their self-described feminist identity, their own experiences with sex education as children, and how they address topics relating to sex and sexuality with their teen daughters. Opportunity was also given for the conversations to take a natural course; the interviews followed the lead of the interviewee, providing ample space for the mother's voice and experiences to surface. Each interview lasted for roughly half an hour.

Findings and Discussions

As we analyzed the interview data, three main themes emerged: (1) feminist mothering as a personal lived experience; (2) a desire for enhanced communication around sex and sexuality between mother and daughter; and (3) mothers' perceptions of daughters' development of autonomy and self-agency in sexual decision making. These themes reflected our positionality and specific interests for the study, and they have been examined within the larger body of literature around patterns and processes of communication, sexuality education, and feminist mothering. A fourth theme, centered around the tensions that surface in feminist mothering practices, emerged as an observable phenomenon within each of the three previous themes, and is detailed in its own section. Within each of these themes, we identified a number of topics common to the mothers' experiences, as detailed below.

Theme One: Feminist Mothering as a Personal Lived Experience

Feminist mothering seeks to challenge patriarchal structures of motherhood that are oppressive to women and redefine maternal practices as "a site of empowerment, a location for social change" (O'Reilly, "Feminist Mothering" 3). Some of the mothers in our study had grown up in conservative and/or religious family environments and explained that their decision to parent with feminist principles was due in large part to a growing questioning of the values of their own upbringing as well as a desire to interrupt the cycles of sexism within their own family traditions: "I looked around at the church I was going to, and it's men up in the front, it's male deities, it's ... all the Children of Promise are men, and I just said, 'How can I sit here and let them be brainwashed into this even more than society in general does?'" (Charlotte). Many had made conscious efforts to raise their children in a nonsexist home environment and to actively challenge gender roles within the family structure: "I do my best to have a division of labour in the household that doesn't reflect gender lines. I've tried to teach both of them skills that might traditionally be considered masculine or feminine." (Janet)

Some expressed why they had consciously chosen feminist mothering as a parenting paradigm: "Feminism I think probably is the lens through which I parent. I use it as a way to encourage—especially my girls—to strive for things that I wouldn't have done as a child, because I didn't believe I could" (Jackie). The mothers stated that they had made a conscious choice to move away from traditional expectations that their mothering role would designate them as the primary sex educator, opting for what Andrea O'Reilly describes as "a counternarrative of motherhood" (*From Motherhood to Mothering* 10). They emphasized wanting a mothering experience that was more supportive of their own individual mothering practices and one that was free from the pressure and judgment of socially constructed and gendered parenting norms; they wanted an experience more responsive to the specific needs of their children. These decisions often led to tensions between wanting to provide more comprehensive education for their children and negotiating aspects of the spiritual and social traditions of their upbringing (Weenie, this volume).

Theme Two: Desire for Enhanced Communication around Sex and Sexuality

All of the mothers interviewed enrolled their children in the OWL program based on a strong desire for them to receive accurate sexuality education inclusive of diverse identities and experiences. Some mothers, like Jackie, felt strongly that sex and sexuality should be demystified and presented as normal and natural topics for discussion: "I believe that all of those things are natural processes and natural to our body, and therefore I want to talk about them equally." Others, like Jill, were adamant that their children should benefit from more rigorous education than they themselves received: "I would really consider it a failure on my part if they ended up being pregnant and unprepared for it. I want them to have all the information and be as comfortable as they can be with sex, because it's a big part of life." Some of the mothers credited the structure of the parallel parent-child education classes with helping to communicate with their teen around sex and sexuality: "I think it makes parents an ally, like, 'You're there with me, I can talk to you about these difficult things'" (Janet). Such a finding was not unexpected, as the mothers were all seeking this type of educational experience for their children. Interestingly, one mother, Jackie, expressed that her participation in the OWL program had hindered communication with her children:

> By having it be dual, I think ... [the OWL program impacted] our ability to talk about the class, like, right afterward... because they had just gone through it and I had just gone through it. And I think there was an awkwardness about it for them. So I think they felt ... a little bit exposed. It made them feel like they couldn't then share with me the pieces they actually wanted me to know about.

Although this was the opposite experience articulated by the other mothers—who felt the OWL program enhanced their communication with their teens—Jackie's experience is congruent with past research and may indicate a need to address fundamental communication skills (a "How to Talk to Your Teens about Sex" section) within the parent education class (Pluhar et al. 289).

Theme Three: Teens' Development of Self-Agency in Sexual Decision Making

The mothers' aspirations for their daughters' gradual development as informed and empowered sexual decision makers was the third theme: "I'm not that worried that they're going to be pressured into something that they don't want to do. They seem pretty... they're like, 'Oh, Mom. Don't even worry about that. Why would we do that?'" (Charlotte). Many of the mothers were gratified at the way in which the OWL program normalized sex and sexuality as a healthy and satisfying part of adult life. The program also allowed for an unprecedented (from the mothers' point of view) level of comfort regarding discussing sex in a coed environment and in a state that often segregates sexuality education by gender: "They are able to talk about a lot of stuff that I would never have dreamed of talking about with boys in my classes or whatever when I was a teenager" (Janet). The mothers' narratives also contained strong messages of self-empowerment for their daughters as autonomous and independent decision makers: "In my house, I don't force too many issues. If they really object, we'll talk about it, and most of the time, I accommodate their wishes" (Janet). These mothers discussed inspiring agency and autonomy in their children as an important parenting goal. As mentioned previously, research suggests that the attitude of the mothers, their tone, warmth, openness, and their supportiveness emerge as more important to their children than the specific information shared (Kesterton and Coleman 446; DiIorio et al. 17).

Within each of the above-listed themes, we noticed a phenomenon we dubbed the "blips of feminist mothering." All of the mothers articulated tension or conflict within the following three areas: (1) a desire to encourage their daughters' freedom of choice and personal autonomy alongside their responsibility as mothers to assist them in negotiating boundaries that will keep them safe in a society that supports and promotes sexual objectification; (2) a desire to provide comprehensive information around sex and sexuality alongside the mothers' own comfort levels around openly sharing details of their personal intimate experiences; and (3) their experiences as self-identified feminists engaged in the practice of mothering, in a society that is often unsupportive of sexuality education or feminism. We explore these blips in the following section.

Theme Four: The Blips of Feminist Mothering

The first blip or tension that we identified revolved around the pressure mothers felt to have "the talk" with their children. Given that conversations around sex typically fall to mothers (Blitstein et al. 47; see also review by DiIorio et al.), many of the women expressed a feeling of awkwardness and discomfort around the social expectation that they are largely responsible for their children's sexuality education (Fox and Inazu 347) and that this conversation had to be framed as an intimidating or embarrassing sit-down talk (Guilamo-Ramos et al. 767). Indeed, Tina Coffelt emphasizes that the complexity of talking about sex is such that it "does not function as an isolated birds-and-the-bees conversation" (118), which was a sentiment echoed by Jill: "You know, it's not what I hear other people talk about, this huge discussion, we're having 'the talk,' or whatever." Another mother, Kara, reiterated Jill's feelings: "I don't hesitate to explain things, but it's hard for me to sit somebody down... I don't think I've done very much with sitting my girls down and saying, 'I need to talk to you about some things.' I wouldn't say that I'm very assertive about initiating conversations with them."

These mothers expressed wanting to be a source of accurate information for their children, but they felt pressured and also inauthentic when addressing the subject matter in a stereotypical "one-shot deal" (Guilamos-Ramos et al. 767-68). Although the OWL program provided an opportunity for ongoing conversations, prior research has suggested "simply instructing parents to talk with their children is not enough; parents need concrete strategies for navigating conversations about sex" (Maurus et al. 476). The mothers in our study were already open to teaching their children about sex; however, the OWL program provided a welcome structure for framing these conversations and to bolstering their own knowledge on certain topics.

Another blip that emerged involved mothers' desire for their children to be well informed about sex in an age-appropriate way, yet they had concerns about transgressing boundaries, set by both themselves and by other mothers. Several of the mothers expressed anxiety about their children's friends being exposed to information about sex and sexuality that their own parents may not have been sharing as freely: "I had a complete book of pregnancy and childbirth that interested the kids, and that got a lot of use in our house. And that was one that I think Emma liked to show her friends, but, um, I remember thinking, should I be telling the parents that that's [how] they spent the afternoon?" (Kara). Charlotte articulated the tension of wanting to be able to discuss sex openly with her daughters while maintaining appropriate boundaries regarding how much personal information she should share: "So, I mean, that part, I haven't been as free, you know, where I don't say, 'Well, you know, your dad and I do this or that in bed.'"

Another prominent blip that emerged from the data involved mothers' fears for their daughters' physical and emotional safety as well as the social implications of their knowledge and behaviour around sex and sexuality versus their desire to help their teens develop autonomy and self-agency. As mentioned earlier, traditional patterns of communication between mothers and daughters regarding safety are typically more restrictive and protective, and focused on limit setting, than they are for sons (Mauras et al. 473).

Jill talked about deciding when it was appropriate for her daughter, Sally, to start dating, but also setting limits on her future potential intimate relationships: "When she turned fourteen, I told her she could date, she can, um, see people, and I tried to leave it gender neutral 'cause who knows, but she can't date anybody more than two years older than her." The tension here between facilitating autonomy and making rules regarding (perceived) safety is clear—despite living in a socially conservative climate, Jill is open minded enough to concede that her daughter may pursue a same-sex relationship. However, she is concerned that if she goes out with anyone significantly older than her, there will potentially be a power imbalance and even possibly legal ramifications. She is caught between wanting to free and control her daughter, and within this contradiction, the clearest example of the blips of feminist motherhood becomes evident.

Both Jackie and Charlotte mentioned struggling with wanting to concede their daughters' autonomy and self-determination in their clothing choices, yet they also feared for their health, wellbeing, and personal safety in a sex-obsessed yet often sex-negative society. For example, Charlotte expressed frustration at the hypersexualization of girls' apparel, the influence of her daughters' peers, and the limitations regarding the lack of clothing choices available to them as consumers.

> I'm just like, "Can you just buy a dress that's not mid-thigh and strapless for any occasion whatsoever?" You know, it just seems like ... that's what's available and... looking around, you do see that okay, this is what everyone's wearing; it wouldn't be that they [her daughters] were out of the norm. I mean, I have to accept some of that as just ... the styles, which is okay, but I think if anything, that's something where I'm kinda like, you know... "Are you sure that's what you wanna be wearing?"

Jackie emphasized how important it is to her that her children are able to make their own choices and that she provides gentle guidance without smothering them, but she also admits she sometimes struggles to know where to draw the line:

I'm very sensitive to somebody else's autonomy and their right to choose for themselves on certain things, but as a parent, there's a line there…. When my oldest daughter … wanted to start wearing high heels, I was just, like, "You're twelve … probably not." In my head, I was, like, "All right, well, (A) there's a need to learn to walk in them so you can be safe and not sprain an ankle, and (B) what is this doing about sexual objectification?"

These women provide vivid examples of how self-identified feminist mothers experience tension between the desire to empower their daughters to be independent decision makers and their need to protect them from the gender-based violence and sexual objectification that permeate their social reality. In rural, conservative America, the mere act of enrolling one's children in a comprehensive, inclusive sexuality education program outside of the public school system could be considered a radical act of empowerment. Compared to other more progressive regions and nations, this may not seem like much, but for the geographic location and political climate in which this study took place, this is significant. It is important to keep in mind the differences between attitudes, policies, and educational programming in the majority of the United States, compared to those in Canada, Australia, and many European countries.

There are no clear paths to negotiating these blips of feminist mothering. Feminism in many ways remains oppositional to traditional parenting paradigms, and we must acknowledge this tension at the same time as we seek to find ways to challenge it. What is apparent from these interviews is that feminism provides a starting place to enter into these typically difficult conversations with greater awareness, sensitivity, and insight. By exposing their children to this type of education, these mothers hope to challenge patriarchal ideals of both motherhood and sexuality education, creating increased possibilities for their daughters' autonomy, self-agency, and healthy sexual identity. However, as illustrated through these mothers' narratives, efforts to engage in mothering with feminist values are frequently complicated by oppressive gendered norms as well as by the struggles of navigating a hypersexual and sexist society. These blips of feminist mothering are tangible reminders of the social and political realities that women and girls continue to face in the United States.

Conclusion

The OWL program offered an ideal environment in which to identify and interview mothers who parented with self-identified feminist values and who had a strong interest in providing their daughters with a solid foundation of comprehensive and inclusive sexuality education. Our analysis revealed that OWL, though not specifically marketed as a feminist curriculum, served as an effective conduit for open and honest communication for most of the mothers and their daughters. For the purpose of this chapter, we focused solely on the mothers' perspectives; future research will explore the daughters' experiences of OWL and their opinions of the parallel parent-youth classes. Compelling further study could also investigate how the teens' participation in OWL strengthened or enhanced their growing sexual self-awareness and agency. One suggestion for improving the OWL parent class in a way that could potentially enhance parent-child interactions includes addressing skill building and practice, specifically around positive, supportive, and nonjudgmental communication techniques regarding how to talk to children about sex and sexuality (Feldman and Rosenthal 147).

Feminist mothering endorses channels of communication that are open and empathetic, which can be challenging between mothers and daughters when sex and relationships are the topic of conversation— topics that generally still remain taboo in most regions of the United States. This situation is further complicated by the contextual nature of the dialogue and the prevailing social norms that tend to place expectations and limitations on the discourse. We speculate that the dissonance between feminist mothering and the social conditions in which the mothers are engaging in their maternal practices is what, at least in part, causes the blips or tensions identified in this study.

Endnotes

1. The nineteen critical sexual health education topics as identified by the Center for Disease Control (CDC) are (1) communication and negotiation skills; (2) goal setting and decision-making skills; (3) how to create and sustain healthy and respectful relationships; (4) influences of family, peers, media, technology, and other factors on sexual risk behaviour; (5) preventative care that is necessary to

maintain reproductive and sexual health; (6) influencing and supporting others to avoid or reduce sexual risk behaviours; (7) benefits
of being sexually abstinent; (8) efficacy of condoms; (9) importance
of using condoms consistently and correctly; (10) importance of
using a condom at the same time as another form of contraception
to prevent both STDs and pregnancy; (11) how to obtain condoms;
(12) how to correctly use a condom; (13) methods of contraception
other than condoms; (14) how to access valid and reliable information, products, and services related to HIV, STDs, and pregnancy; (15) how HIV and other STDs are transmitted; (16) health
consequences of HIV, other STDs, and pregnancy; (17) importance
of limiting the number of sexual partners; (18) sexual orientation;
and (19) gender roles, gender identity, or gender expression (Center
for Disease Control, 2016).

2. The OWL curriculum has an optional religious supplement titled
Sexuality and Our Faith, which is only available for use by trained
facilitators within the United Church of Christ and Unitarian Universalist congregations. This supplement was not used with the cohort in this study because the program was open to the community,
and many participants were not members of either church. The
OWL program can be and is frequently used in nonreligious (secular, community, and public school) settings with appropriately
trained facilitators.

Works Cited

Bay-Cheng, Laina Y. "Ethical Parenting of Sexually Active Youth:
Ensuring Safety While Enabling Development." *Sex Education,* vol.
13, no. 2, 2013, pp. 133-45.

Blitstein, Jonathan L., et al. "Repeated Exposure to Media Messages
Encouraging Parent-Child Communication About Sex: Differential
Trajectories for Mothers and Fathers." *American Journal of Health
Promotion,* vol. 27, no. 1, 2012, pp. 43-51.

Center for Disease Control (CDC). "School Health Profiles 2016:
Characteristics of Health Programs Among Secondary Schools."
CDC, 2016, www.cdc.gov/healthyyouth/data/profiles/pdf/2016/
2016_Profiles_Report.pdf. Accessed 16 Oct. 2019.

Coffelt, Tina A. "Is Sexual Communication Challenging Between Mothers and Daughters?" *Journal of Family Communication* 10 (2010): 116-130.

DiIorio, Colleen, Erika Pluhar, and Lisa Belcher. "Parent-Child Communication about Sexuality: A Review of the Literature from 1980–2002." *Journal of HIV/AIDS Prevention and Education for Adolescents and Children*, vol. 5, no. 3-4, 2003, pp. 7-32.

Dittus, Patricia J., James Jaccard, and Vivian V. Gordon. "Direct and Nondirect Communication of Maternal Beliefs to Adolescents: Adolescent Motivations for Premarital Activity." *Journal of Applied Social Psychology*, vol. 29, no. 9, 1999, pp. 1927-63.

Dougherty, Debbie S. "Sexual Harassment as (Dys)Functional Process: A Feminist Standpoint Analysis." *Journal of Applied Communication Research*, vol. 29, no. 4, 2001, pp. 372-402.

Feldman, S. Shirley, and Doreen A. Rosenthal. "The Effect of Communication Characteristics on Family Members' Perceptions of Parents as Sex Educators." *Journal of Research on Adolescence*, vol. 10, no. 2, 2000, pp. 119-50.

Fox, Greer Litton, and Judith K. Inazu. "Mother-Daughter Communication about Sex." *Family Relations*, vol. 29, no. 3, 1980, pp. 347-52.

Glickman, Rose L. *Daughters of Feminists*. St. Martin's Press, 1993.

Green, Fiona Joy. "Developing a Feminist Motherline: Reflections on a Decade of Feminist Parenting." *Journal of the Association for Research on Mothering*, vol. 8, no. 1-2, 2006, pp. 7-20.

Green, Fiona Joy. "Feminist Motherline: Embodied Knowledge/s of Feminist Mothering." *Feminist Mothering*, edited by Andrea O'Reilly, SUNY Press, 2008, pp. 161-76.

Guilamo-Ramos, Vincent, et al. "Parent-Adolescent Communication about Sexual Intercourse: An Analysis of Maternal Reluctance to Communicate." *Health Psychology*, vol. 27, no. 6, 2008, pp. 760-69.

Healey, Gwen. "Inuit Parent Perspectives on Sexual Health Communication with Adolescent Children in Nunavut: 'It's Kinda Hard for Me to try to Find the Words.'" *International Journal of Circumpolar Health*, vol. 73, no. 1, 2014, pp. 1-7.

Heron, Jon, et al. "Social Factors Associated with Readiness for Sexual Activity in Adolescents: A Population-Based Cohort Study." *Archives of Sexual Behavior* 44, 2015, pp. 669-678.

Jaccard, James, Tonya Dodge, and Patricia Dittus. "Parent-Adolescent Communication about Sex and Birth Control: A Conceptual Framework." *New Directions for Child and Adolescent Development*, vol. 97, 2002, pp. 9-41.

Kesterton, David, and Lester Coleman. "Speakeasy: A UK-Wide Initiative Raising Parents' Confidence and Ability to Talk about Sex and Relationships with their Children. *Sex Education*, vol. 10, no. 4, 2010, pp. 437-48.

Kirby, Douglas. "Increasing Communication Between Parents and their Children about Sex." *BMG*, vol. 336, 2008, p. 206.

Mackenzie, Catriona. "Feminist Innovation in Philosophy: Relational Autonomy and Social Justice." *Women's Studies International Forum*, vol. 72, 2019, pp. 144-51.

Mauras, Carrie B., Wendy S. Grolnick, and Rachel W. Friendly. "Time for 'The Talk'... Now What? Autonomous Support and Structure in Mother-Daughter Conversations about Sex." *Journal of Early Adolescence*, vol. 33, no. 4, 2012, pp. 458-81.

Miles, Matthew. B., and A. Michael Huberman. *Qualitative Data Analysis: An Expanded Sourcebook*. 2nd ed. Sage, 1994.

O'Reilly, Andrea, ed. *Feminist Mothering*. SUNY Press, 2008.

O'Reilly, Andrea, editor. *From Motherhood to Mothering: The Legacy of Adrienne Rich's Of Woman Born*. Albany: SUNY Press, 2004.

O'Sullivan, Lucia, et al. "Mother-Daughter Communication about Sex among Urban African American and Latino Families." *Journal of Adolescent Research*, vol. 16, no. 3, 2001, pp. 269-92.

Pew Research Center. "Religious Landscape Study." *Pew Forum*, 2014, www.pewforum.org/religious-landscape-study/compare/political-ideology/by/state/. Accessed 16 Oct. 2019.

Phadke, Shilpa. "Feminist Mothering? Some Reflections on Sexuality and Risk from Urban India." *South Asia: Journal of South Asian Studies*, vol. 36, no. 1, 2013, pp. 92-106.

Pluhar, Erika I. *Family Communication about Sexuality: A Qualitative Study with African American Mothers and Their Adolescent Daughters.* 2001. University of Pennsylvania, PhD dissertation.

Pluhar, Erika I., Colleen K. DiIrio, and Frances A. McCarty. "Correlates of Sexuality Communication among Mothers and 6-12 Year-old Children." *Child: Care, Health and Development,* vol. 34, no. 3, 2007, pp. 283-90.

Sexuality Information and Education Council of the United States (SIECUS). "State Profiles, Fiscal Year 2018—Idaho." *SIECUS,* siecus.org/wp-content/uploads/2019/03/Idaho-FY18-Final-1.pdf. Accessed 16 Oct. 2019.

Unitarian Universalist Association. "Our Whole Lives: Lifespan Sexuality Education." www.uua.org/re/owl. Accessed 22 May 2018.

Widman, Laura, et al. "Sexual Communication Between Early Adolescents and Their Dating Partners, Parents, and Best Friends." *Journal of Sex Research,* vol. 51, no. 7, 2014, pp. 731-41.

Chapter Four

Iskwêwiwin: An Autoethnographic Study of Motherhood, Sex, and Sexuality

Angelina Weenie

"Dreams die hard as we watch them erode
But we cannot be denied
The fire inside."

—Bob Seger, "The Fire Inside"

Introduction

L ittle has been written about motherhood, sex, and sexuality from the perspective of First Nations women. I am a Plains Cree woman from Sweetgrass First Nation, Saskatchewan, Canada. Cree is my first language, and I am a fluent Cree speaker. Language and culture are an integral part of who I am and it informs, in part, this autoethnographic study on iskwêwiwin. The Cree term for motherhood is "ka ocawâsimisihk" (Waugh, LeClaire, and Cardinal 365), which means bearing or having children. The Cree word for womanhood is "iskwêwiwin," and it reflects the everyday experience of mothering and being a woman. I begin by using these terms as a way of framing the concepts of motherhood, sex, and sexuality from a First Nations perspective.

Autoethnography is a research methodology, which can be understood as autobiography as well as the study of self within a cultural context. Caroline Ellis states that autoethnography is "research, writing, story and method that connect the autobiographical and personal to the cultural, social, and political" (xix), and Clive Seale describes auto-ethnography as a research method wherein "researchers used their own experiences and responses to events as sources of evidence about social processes" (108). Characterized as a "social and cultural research practice influenced by constructionist epistemologies," this method is grounded in the notion that knowledge is socially constructed (108). Sharlene Nagy Hess-Biber and Patricia Leavy write that in auto-ethnography, "researchers use their own thoughts, feelings, and exper-iences as a means of understanding the social world, or some aspect of it" (xxix). Heewon Chang explains further that the method "is not about focusing on self alone, but about searching for understanding of others (culture/society) through self (48). These theoretical notions will be used to write my story and my lived experience of motherhood, sex, and sexuality.

September 26, 2010

I received a woman's pipe on September 23, 2010, at Island Lake First Nation. I have more to learn. This is a spiritual journey.

I have learned to listen for messages in my everyday life in order to make meaning of my life experiences. One day I was listening to a sports broadcaster who quoted the words of the song, "The Fire Inside," by Bob Seger. I wrote those words down because they reflect what my journey has been about. Despite the adversity and the hardships associated with being a woman, I will not be denied the fire inside. I had a dream of being in a relationship in which a mother and father work together to raise their family as true partners, but that dream has long been shattered. I have never been married, and I have two sons which I have always supported. The full support of my mother has helped me throughout.

bell hooks maintains that "the act of writing one's autobiography is a way to find again that aspect of self and experience that may no longer be an actual part of one's life but is a living memory shaping and inform-ing the present" (*remembered rapture* 84). I have thought deeply about why and how I should write my story because I will be reliving painful memories and reopening old wounds, especially regarding my sexual history. The benefit of historical self-reflection can be viewed as a way of learning from our past and moving forwards. O'Reilly-Scanlon writes that "As we analyze our past through the process of memory-work, we begin to see the power of the past and its connection to the way we are living our present lives. With this increased understanding we have an ability to make changes- to live our lives more consciously and deliberately" (84). I have come to understand writing as cathartic, and it is through writing and journaling I have been able to heal and put things into perspective. According to Claudia Mitchell and Sandra Weber, through struggling "for self-knowledge and identity" (2), we can reinvent ourselves and others can learn from our experience. It is, primarily, from this standpoint that I share my story.

January 3, 2011

Being alone and being happy. To take each day as it comes. All is well really. Turn my will and my life over to the care of God, each day. Being alone is tough though. I have often thought about writing my story. I have come to understand that exploring my inner and personal world of relationships is a way of feeling, dealing, and healing. It is sometimes a sordid one but it is my story and the life that I have lived, and it has not all been pretty.

Yesterday, I experienced yet another deep disappointment, and it surprised me about how hurt I can feel about things and still cry. So perhaps it is time to write it all out and lay it all out, first, for myself, and then, perhaps, others may learn from my story. In the process, I hope to come to arrive at some deep truths about myself. I have been told that telling about our wounds is, ultimately, about helping others.

My astrologer tells me that I have never been in a real relationship, and I believe that to be true also. So how does it come to be that at fifty-six years old, I still cannot be flippant about sex, love, and relationships? I hurt, and I cannot get over things so easy. Is it my constitution? As I have gotten older, I have attempted to safeguard my heart and stay away from those who are likely to hurt me. But I have much more to learn about affairs of the heart. I search in myself for defects and answers to how I allow myself to be led to such unhealthy and hurtful situations at fifty-six years old. It was not as easy as I thought to be so glib about personal relationships. You see that I am sharing a very deep and intimate part of myself with another. I am naïve about affairs of the heart.

I have learned that for writing to be compelling and authentic, we, as writers, need to share our innermost selves. In the process, we make ourselves vulnerable to the world. I am also conscious of the ethics of telling my story. I do not want to implicate others. With these considerations in mind, I will use memories, personal writing, journals, and reflections to represent the social, political, and cultural terrain of First Nations motherhood. This is my story, and it is not inferred that my experience will be the same as other women, First Nations or non–First Nations.

My Identity

I am a mother and grandmother. In Cree, "iskwêw" means woman, and the word for "fire" is "iskotêw." And when "iskotêw" is broken down, it means woman's heart—"iskwêw otêh." An Elder taught us the meaning of this word at an educational culture camp, and it helped the students and me to understand that we must be like the fire and let nothing deter us from achieving our dreams and goals in life. He also taught us that we are life-givers and that we are responsible for tending the home fires and taking care of our families.

Motherhood

My boyfriend had beaten me up, so I went back home to the reserve to live with my parents. This was during the summer of 1972, and I was eighteen years old. I did not know that I was pregnant. I was often irregular with my menstrual cycle, and I experienced pain. For that reason, my mother thought that I would not be able to bear children. I was sleeping a lot, and I do not recall who sent me to see the doctor, but I found out that I was three-months pregnant. This was hard to believe because I probably should have miscarried. My boyfriend had been brutal with me. He had punched and kicked me repeatedly.

I went and found my boyfriend, and I stayed with him because I believed that I should be with the father of my baby. I got an apartment, with the help of social services, in Saskatoon, Saskatchewan. My mother counselled me on how to take care of myself. I was not sure what to expect about delivering a baby. One day, I was experiencing back pain. I was at home alone when I felt a sudden gush of water. I phoned my sister, and she drove me to the hospital. I was in pain for about five hours, and then I delivered a nine-and a half-pound boy on May 5, 1973.

As a young mother, I felt quite inept. I was uncomfortable taking my son out in public because I worried that he would start crying and I would not know how to handle things. My mother would often come to babysit for me, and she taught me how to care for a baby.

Things did not go well for me and my boyfriend. It continued to be a physically abusive relationship. I lived common law with him for seven years, thinking that I was obligated to be with him because he was the father of my son. I used alcohol to numb the pain and to forget the misery. I witnessed domestic violence in other Aboriginal women's lives, and I started to feel that it was normal for Aboriginal women, in general, to be mistreated and abused and that somehow this was also my destiny in life. This was a shock to me in many ways, as I came from a sheltered home and I could not understand why I was being beaten regularly. I felt I was somehow to blame for how I was being treated.

My mother's experience was different. She never drank in her life. What I remember about her is that she was independent, strong, and courageous. My mother worked in the city at a time when it was unheard of for an Indian woman to live and work off-reserve. I believe that in her own way, she was a true feminist by seeking to "transform those realities that compromise[d] women's well-being and human rights" (Larocque 57). She did not let racism, or any other barriers, prevent her from seeking a better life for herself and her family.

I believe I am now very much like my mother. She would get up early in the morning to get the fire going and start heating water for the laundry that needed to be done every day. She would cook and take care of her family, and it seemed to be an all-consuming task. From her, I learned to be a hard-worker.

My mother went to a residential school, where she stayed until she was twenty-one years old. I was told that she did a novena and prayed for two weeks in order to decide whether she should become a nun or marry my dad. Her deep belief in and acceptance of what the nuns taught her was ever present in her life. It likely hurt her a lot when I became an unwed mother at nineteen years of age. One of my friends stayed in a home for unwed mothers when she became pregnant. She later gave up her child for adoption. When I was in the hospital, the lady who gave birth at the same time as me also gave up her child for adoption.

But it never crossed my mind to give up my child. My mother gave me her full support and never once did she advise me to get married. She told my sister and me that we did not need to get married. Instead, we should get an education, travel, and be happy.

November 5, 2015

It has been twenty-six years since my mother passed away. She is in my heart and in my thoughts always. Whenever I am struggling, she comes to me in my dreams. I know that she is with me in spirit.

Even though I was living in a bad situation for a long time, I did go back to school, and I completed a teacher education program. I understood that education would help me to build a better life for myself and my son. Once I found a job, I moved away and broke up with my boyfriend. I soon became involved with another man, and I had another son. I lost my baby, who was stillborn, on May 10, 1981. I had another son on June 8, 1983. This marked ten years of tumultuousness. Much of it involved learning from the mistakes and bad choices I made. I was simply living through these life situations as best as I could.

May 10, 2010

On May 10, 1981, I lost my son, Bryant Joel. I remember and pray for him today. I am in Victoria, British Columbia, and am trying to find healing and solace by being near the ocean. I have slept a lot during the weekend. I scared myself when I almost fell asleep at the wheel last week. I want to breakdown. Is it so hard to let go of a dream? Perhaps I am too bitter. I travel and try to find peace and happiness wherever I am.

As a mother, I followed what my mother had told me. I am now a single mother of two grown sons and a grandmother of two boys. My mother said, "When you bring children into this world, you need to take care of them." When I was in the hard world of alcoholism, this was not always the case, but, nevertheless, I have always worked and tried to take care of my children. I am a teacher by profession, and I was able to support myself and my sons. I never left them. I am thankful to my mother and my sister for taking care of my sons when I was not healthy. Today, I devote my life to giving back and helping my sons and grandsons in whatever way is necessary.

December 25, 2010

I prepared Christmas dinner and spent it with my sons and grandsons. We have accepted that it is only us now. My grandson said the prayer. This is our family, with no father present for my sons. I do not understand it, but it is what it is. We have lost many close family members, and we miss them. I felt like crying when I heard "Oh Holy Night." My dad and several others would sing Cree hymns at Midnight Mass. They believed so strongly in what they had been taught in residential school.

It was hardly ever an issue that I was not married and that I was a single mother, even in my chosen profession. This may be due to the changing attitudes in society, in which living common law and single parenting have become more accepted. I remember when my first son became ill and my mother and sister helped me to bring him to the hospital. The nurse asked if he had a father. My mother replied, "Of course he has a father. How could he have been born?" That was the end of that conversation. I always remember how my mother stood up for me. Her response helped me to feel more accepting of my status as an unmarried mother.

Discussion

My parents were devout Catholics, and I believed that I had I disgraced my family when I became pregnant at the age of eighteen. Because I was not married and had a child out of wedlock, I thought that I was not a good Catholic, and I did not go to church for a long time. Overall, I felt unworthy as a person, and I chose to escape the reality of my life through alcohol. I was a binge-drinker, and the turning point of my life was when I joined a twelve-step program and found sobriety. I was counselled by a priest who helped me to believe in a loving God. The main thing was that I had to learn to forgive myself.

May 29, 2010

In the summer of 1995, I came to terms with life. How different it was then. I remember carousing and not caring how I looked or acted. I was chasing a dream. I had to find out for myself and see things for myself. Some truths have come to light. Today, I take care of myself. If someone loves me they will treat me right. I am here in Toronto. I am here by myself. I am following the path set for me by the Creator, the Creator at work in my life. I still hope and dream for love, companionship, and friendship, but it not so driving anymore. I am preparing myself for a better life to come. How much better could it be? I have life, breath, and health. I have finished my doctorate, and I am fifteen years sober now.

Sex and sexuality were not talked about openly when I was young. I had thought at one point that this was part of our culture. However, when I read the works of Michel Foucault, a French philosopher and critical theorist, I started to gain a better understanding of how and why sexuality was repressed. Foucault maintains that the history of sexuality was founded on Victorian principles, wherein "it had first been necessary to subjugate [sex] at the level of language, control its free circulation in speech, expunge it from the things that were said, and extinguish the words that rendered it too visibly present" (17). These were the religious teachings my mother learned when she went to residential school. Any talk of sexuality was silenced. During my childhood, I was made to understand that sex and sexuality were sinful and dirty. Because sex and sexuality were to be repressed and denied, it affected the choices I made in life. As Carlos G. Prado states, "Regulation involved inculcating attitudes, imbuing values, shaping desires, orienting inclinations, enabling sexual identities, and classifying all sorts of interests, appetites, and acts" (94). This statement encapsulates the way that I have experienced sexuality, and it has required a lifetime to come to terms with my sexuality and to see it as natural and healthy.

December 29, 2010

It is getting closer to the end of the year. Show me the way, God. I pray for guidance, strength, and direction in my life. My neighbour gave me a ride to bingo last night. He is nice to me. We can be friends. Just be myself.

I have had to heal from my past, and this has led me to search for cultural understandings of sex and sexuality. I now have a newfound awareness of my own relationship to sex and sexuality based on language and culture. In Cree, the term used for sex is "iskwêwiwin," which means female or womanhood. "Wicehtowin" is the term used for "the act of having a partnership or friendship: spousal; unity" (Waugh et al. 227). It is common to use the term "e-wicehtotcihk" to signify two people are together or they are a couple. Related to these terms is the word sex appeal, "kâkâwâtitohk" (Waugh et al. 539), which is to be attracted to, or have a crush, on someone. Being physically attracted to that person can lead to a more intimate, close, or sexual relationship. These words show that sex and sexuality are part of our humanness; thus, I have become less conflicted about being a sexual person.

I looked and saw the green eyes, seemingly for the first time. I had talked to you and seen you before, but somehow you looked different today. Or was it me seeing with new eyes and a new awakening of mind, body, and spirit? The smile and the green eyes caught my attention today. It made me consider that I can look good and attract someone if I like, at least I used to. Or perhaps it is me being foolish. I talked to a friend and she said, "You're alive." Maybe that is all it is.

In June 2013, I was part of an Indigenous education culture camp at Sturgeon Lake First Nation, Saskatchewan, Canada. Elders shared about various aspects of traditional knowledge during these camps. For one of the sessions, Elder Terry Daniels shared about the four aspects of a relationship: ê-nitawi-nitistawêyimat, ê-nisitawêyimat, ê-nayîst-awêyimat, and ê-sakaskêyimat. Before anything sexual occurs, one needs to begin with ê-nitawi-nitistawêyimat, which means that you have to go and find out about that person. You spend time with that person getting to know him or her. Following this, ê-nisitawêyimat means that you know only that person, and ê-nayîstawêyimat means that you now know only that person. Once you have made a commitment to that person, there is the aspect of ê-sakaskêyimat, which means that you are now attached to that person. Once these four aspects of a relationship have been fulfilled, then the couple is ready for making a stronger commitment to each other. It is through these four aspects that lifelong relationships are formed. After hearing these teachings, I realized that these traditional teachings need to be central to our understandings of sex and sexuality, as they can help youth to form healthy sexual identities and work to alleviate the type of emotional turmoil and confusion that I lived through.

Today is January 29, 2012. I am at Rankin Inlet, Nunavut. I am spending the night here, and tomorrow I will be travelling further north. The Arctic is a place of cold and harshness, but it is a good place for me to be right now, as I work through personal issues and relationships.

I have related my journey as a single mother as well as the beliefs I have learned about motherhood, sex and sexuality from both a Western and First Nations viewpoint. As part of coming to terms with my life, I have also been drawn to the work of feminists, such as bell hooks, who have helped me to understand that women do have personal power. This idea has helped me to move beyond having a victim mentality. For the most part, however, my experience has been about working through the confusion, pain, and frustration without having a clear articulation and understanding of sex and sexuality as well as gender violence and oppression.

In graduate school, I started to learn about colonization and decolonization, and I published a paper on postcolonial healing and recovery (Weenie). While I was writing this paper, it dawned on me that what I was experiencing could be attributed to living in a system imbued with racism, sexism, patriarchy, and colonialism. I saw how decolonization could be related to my life. I wrote that the decolonizing of self was "analogous to extricating oneself from an abusive relationship. One must break through the denial and begin the process of recovery and healing. It means unlearning what we have been taught about ourselves and learning to value ourselves" (Weenie 65). I discovered that as a woman, on an individual and collective level, I had agency and I could change my life.

January 21, 2014

I am listening to Writers and Company on CBC radio, and I am fascinated by these authors. I want to be a writer, too. When I retire, I want to write more. These are the words I hear, and I stop and write them down in my journal: "the ability to forgive is in our power;" "we are never free from what has happened to us;" "hanging on to our pain and our grievances;" and "forgive and move on."

With further reading and study, it became clear to me how First Nations women became part of the larger assimilationist plan (Milloy). Martin Cannon states that "Even prior to Confederation and the emergence of the first statute entitled the *Indian Act* of 1876, the colonial enterprise in Canada had virtually enforced a system of Eurocentric policies, beliefs and value systems upon First Nations." (2). First Nations women were particularly affected, as it was thought that "motherhood was the most formative socializing element" (Milloy 40); thus, girls were taught to be civilizing mothers when they attended residential schools. My mother was part of this educative process, and, to a great extent, she followed their religious teachings. However, her refusal to be bound within a certain space and way of being reflected her strength of spirit. Her example has shown me that I do not have to feel compelled to follow the dictates of society and that I can be strong in my own right.

Christmas 2014

I spent Christmas Eve alone at home. I did my laundry. I thought of going to mass, but I was tired, so I decided to relax and stay at home. I made sure my place was neat and clean.

Today is Christmas Day. I have decided that it is okay to journey alone. I have been lonely, and I have prayed many times for someone special to come into my life. I have yearned for companionship, love, and friendship, and it comes in different forms. Perhaps, I have not acknowledged those things when they were there. I will live and let live. I have decided to write. I live by the river, and I can see the hoar frost on the trees. It is a beautiful scene, truly a sight to behold. I like to think that I have put all my demons to rest and I am ready for better things.

The sun is shining today. God has created this perfect day, a day to take joy in. I have decided that I will go and visit my relatives on the reserve and I will be happy with them. It will not be a visit of forced gaiety, as family gatherings often are, but one of quiet peace and serenity. Things are the way they are meant to be today.

My writings reflect my own experience of motherhood in relation to my experiences of sex and sexuality. I have used ideas from literature on sexuality with which I can best identify. I am now at a place that is filled with a sense of hope, understanding, as well as a feeling of acceptance of how my life has unfolded. My journal entries reflect my knowledge and understanding of womanhood, of iskwêwiwin. When I think back to the physical abuse, I understand it within the context of men believing they must be in control. hooks writes, "Men who oppressed women did not do so because they acted simply from the space of free will; they were in their own way agents of a system they had not put into place" (*Communion* 34). I was not at a place to fathom or articulate such an idea when I was experiencing domestic violence. I have come to see, however, that this notion reflects the social conditioning that we were all a part of. It seems that men had to live up to colonial expectations to rule "their" women. It did not occur to me that this was the reason for the violence; I saw myself as a victim and that I was somewhat to blame for my circumstances. At the time, and for most of my life, I thought that as women, "Our value, our worth, and whether or not we can be loved are always determined by someone else" (*Communion*, hooks xv). This idea was certainly true for me for a long time. In the struggle of coming to terms with such issues, I was able to transform my life. I no longer accept abuse, and I am comfortable with being alone. I have learned self-acceptance, and I am building a meaningful life as an academic, a mother, a grandmother, and a woman.

I spend a lot of time on the road. It is not unusual for me to drive eight hours in a day. I listen to music, to the radio, to sports games, or just drive in silence with nothing but my own thoughts and take in the scenery. I have come to enjoy the ride. I learn a lot by listening to radio talk shows. I have learned from the ride. In many ways, it has been my saving grace.

Works Cited

Cannon, Martin. "The Regulation of First Nations Sexuality." *The Canadian Journal of Native Studies*, vol. XVIII, no. 1, 1998, pp. 1-18.

Chang, Heewon. "Autoethnography." *Autoethnography as Method*. Left Coast Press, 2008, pp. 43-57.

Ellis, Caroline. *The Ethnographic I: The Methodology Novel about Autoethnography*. AltaMira Press. Print.

Foucault, Michel. *The History of Sexuality*. Random House, Inc. 1990.

hooks, bell. *remembered rapture. the writer at work*. Holt Paperbacks. 1999.

hooks, bell. *Communion. The Female Search for Love*. New York, HarperCollins Publishers, 2002.

LaRocque, Emma. "Métis and Feminist. Ethical Reflections on Feminism, Human Rights and Decolonization." *Making Space for Indigenous Feminism*, edited by Joyce Green, Fernwood Publishing, 2007, pp. 53-71.

Milloy, John S. *A National Crime: The Canadian Government and The Residential School System. 1879 to 1986.* University of Manitoba Press. 1999.

Mitchell, Claudia, and Sandra Weber. *Reinventing Ourselves As Teachers. Beyond Nostalgia.* Falmer Press, 1999.

Nagy Hesse-Biber, Sharlene, and Patricia Leavy, eds. *Emergent Methods in Social Research.* Sage Publications, 2006.

O'Reilly-Scanlon, Kathleen. *She's Still on My Mind: Teachers' Memories, Memory-Work And Self-Study.* 2000, University of McGill, dissertation.

Prado, Carlos. G. *Starting with Foucault. An Introduction to Genealogy.* Westview Press, 2000.

Seale, Clive, ed. *Researching Society and Culture.* Sage Publications, 2006.

Seger, Bob. *The Fire Inside.* Capitol, 1991.

Waugh, Earle, Nancy LeClaire, and George Cardinal. *Alberta Elder's Cree Dictionary.* The University of Alberta Press, 1998.

Weenie, Angelina. "Post-Colonial Recovering and Healing." *Learn in Beauty. Indigenous Education for a New Century,* edited by Jon Reyhner et al., Northern Arizona University, 2000, pp. 65-70.

Section II

Babes and Bawdy Breasts:
The Erotics of Mothering

Chapter Five

Maternal Eroticism and Female Desire in Sue Miller's *The Good Mother*

Amanda Kane Rooks

*T*he *Good Mother* portrays a new kind of conflict for the growing number of single mothers in the Western world in the late twentieth century; tracking the fall from grace of newly divorced "good mother", Anna Dunlap. The struggles and adversities that Anna faces expose the persistent disavowal of mothers as sexual beings in the late twentieth century, despite the alleged freedoms won for women in the wake of the feminist and sexual liberation movements. In this essay, I argue that *The Good Mother* has continued relevance for modern readers, as it broadens the debates around the persistent ideology of asexual motherhood in its presentation of mothering as an erotic experience, one that shares a number of parallels with sexual eroticism and desire. I reveal how Miller's novel provides a provocative disruption of the borders between mothering and sexuality in a way that brings to light the issues that silently sustain many of the cultural anxieties surrounding both of these aspects of female experience. I argue that in challenging the cultural requirement of suppressing the component of eroticism in the mothering role, Miller's novel calls for an alternative, expanded understanding of both sexuality and motherhood—one that considers the difference in construction, representation, and experience that may occur if sexuality, eroticism, and motherhood were considered through a maternal lens.

There is not yet a language around the erotic and sexual components of mothering that is accepted as part of popular discourse. The understandable taboos existing around these issues no doubt impede our ability to speak about maternal sexuality and maternal eroticism without assumptions or anxieties around the prospect of immoral, abusive, and illegal behaviours. In her book, *Erotic Attunement: Parenthood and the Ethics of Sensuality between Unequals*, Cristina Traina offers some useful definitions for "eroticism," "maternal eroticism," and "maternal sexuality" in terms of establishing an appropriate discourse through which to examine this fraught area of investigation. According to Traina,

> *Eroticism* is a quality of attraction to another person that desires intimacy with her on multiple levels: physical, emotional, spiritual, and intellectual. Eroticism can include what we think of as genital, sexual desire, but if it does, this is a subset of the larger category…. *Maternal eroticism* is holistic, specifically maternal attraction to—and desire for intimacy with—her child…. *Maternal sexuality* specifically includes, but is not limited to, the sexual subset of erotic feelings, desires, and attractions that may emerge in motherhood, and the ways in which mothers incorporate these into their relationships and behaviour. (7)

Traina's understandings challenge the widespread moral conviction that relationships between parents and their children are entirely and necessarily disconnected from sexuality and eroticism. Her definitions of eroticism and maternal eroticism in particular are deployed herein in order to examine the form and significance of the parallels and convergences between sexual and maternal experience constructed in Miller's novel.

The depictions of Anna's relationship with her child and her relationship with her lover in *The Good Mother* fuse discourses of maternal, sexual, and erotic love. Anna takes immense pleasure in Molly's body, noting that her daughter's skin "gleamed white as a dream as she jumped around naked" (6). Of her daughter, Anna reflects that she "never tired of looking at her" and that it is almost as if she "were taking something from her by loving her so greedily" (4). When her daughter is away from her, Anna "imagined her compact and smooth body … how she smelled, how her thin straight hair felt on my cheek" (165). Anna's passion for her daughter's physical form echoes the physical desire and longing characteristic of sexual attraction towards an adult lover. Indeed, the novel's depiction of Anna's physical attraction towards her actual lover, Leo, involves an allusion to her child: after their first sexual encounter, Anna admires Leo's body as he sleeps, including "his hands [which] rested, curled slightly near his face," hands that Anna notes are "like a child's, like Molly's" (107). Just as Anna reflects that during sex with Leo she "lost track of the boundaries between us" (11), so too is her intimacy with her daughter characterized by a sense of physical union and oneness: "She leaned against my breast while I read, and her head moved slightly with my every breath, as though she were still part of my body" (8). These juxtaposed images of maternal and sexual longing and desire suggest the shared characteristics of these two forms of human intimacy. Miller constructs maternal passion and adult sexual passion as rooted in the same desire for sensual and loving union with another person, as conditions both stemming from what Daphne de Marneffe calls "the same kind of integrating delight" (302).

This sense of "integrating delight" finds its definitive expression in the novel when Molly comes to her mother's bed for comfort, just as Leo and Anna are making love:

> He had come into me from behind ... when I heard her shuffle in the hallway ... I stilled myself and that stopped his motion. Together we lowered ourselves and, as the bedroom door swung open, I turned towards the little halting figure.... I held the covers up to welcome her, and she clambered in and lay down next to me.... I held her in the curve of my upper body and smelled the damp sweetness of her hair and skin.... Leo moved sometimes, and then lay still. I can remember feeling a sense of completion, as though I had everything I wanted held close, held inside me; as though I had finally found a way to have everything. We seemed fused, the three of us, all the boundaries between us dissolved; and I felt the medium for that. In my sleepiness I thought of myself as simply a *way* for Leo and Molly and me to be together, as *clear*, translucent (124).

The celebratory tone of this passage—as well as its rejoicing in the sense of satisfaction and fulfillment Anna experiences over having her child and her lover in close proximity to her own body—trumps any misgivings the reader may have regarding the idea of a child in bed with two adults engaging in sexual intercourse. The reader presumably shares Anna's implicit understanding that this episode contains no trace of the exploitative, that it is a tender moment of comfort and loving intimacy and that Molly, in her innocence and naivety, is too young to experience it as anything otherwise. A sense of the ease and rightness of the relationship between Anna's mothering and sexual roles is also conveyed via her earlier observation:

> I felt I'd never been so happy, and perhaps I never was. Our lives seemed magically interpenetrated, commingled, even as we each separated into all the day's complicated activities. I had never expected it to seem so graceful and easy, but Molly's seemingly complete comfort with Leo was like a benediction on all aspects of the relationship, even the sexual. (123-24)

Both passages point to the crossovers and parallels of sexual and maternal relationships, at least in terms of the idea that the qualities of nurturance, physical intimacy, emotional connection, and individual gratification are essential to the healthy functioning of such relationships.

Anne Ferguson addresses these crossovers and parallels via her notion of "sex/affective energy." According to Ferguson, the energy of human sexuality is generally "emotional and affectionate," and its key objective is "emotional incorporation with others" (11). Hence, because she desires "emotional incorporation" with both her lover and her child, Anna derives pleasure and gratification from looking at and touching her child in ways that sometimes mirror her intimacy with her lover. As Ferguson explains, "bodily pleasure," both a related desire and by-product of the desire for union with another, can be derived just as sufficiently through "simple touching, as in hugging" as through orgasm with an adult partner (11). Much like Miller's celebratory depiction of the relationship between Anna's maternal and sexual intimacies in *The Good Mother*, Ferguson's observations call for an expanded understanding of the sexual and the maternal—one that in placing maternity and sexuality on a continuum of human intimacy and connection allows that two things can be analogous (i.e., intimacy with a child and intimacy with a lover) without necessarily being identical. As Traina might have it, the novel's depiction of the parallels and crossovers between Anna's maternal intimacies and her sexual intimacies points to the essential and "inevitable erotic potential of all human relations" (94).

Despite its innocuous nature, however, the episode in bed between Anna, Leo, and Molly will ultimately see Anna lose custody of her daughter in family court. Anna's ex-husband Brian initiates custody proceedings in response to what he alleges is an episode of sexual abuse perpetrated by his ex-wife's lover against his daughter. The episode in question involves Molly entering the bathroom while Leo is in the shower. She proceeds to ask him questions about his penis and asks if she can touch it, which, disturbingly, Leo allows her to do. Although Leo's actions are extremely inappropriate, it is quickly established at the court hearing that Leo and Molly's encounter was an ill-judged attempt on Leo's part to follow Anna's lead in terms of her concern for dispelling any potential hang ups her daughter may develop about the body and sexuality. In Leo's words, he was trying to "be as relaxed, as natural with Molly, as she [Anna] was. About her body and that kind of thing" (178). Hence, although he felt "a little uncomfortable about it," Leo had "seen how relaxed Anna was about it all, and ... didn't want to screw that up or anything" (177). With Leo's innocence quickly established, the focus of the custody suite swiftly turns to what is perhaps the real source of Brian's misgivings: his inability to control or suppress his ex-wife's sexual activity.

When Brian takes the witness stand, there is an implicit acceptance on the part of the court that he maintains some kind of entitlement over Anna's sex life. Brian's testimony is dominated by the topic of Anna's postdivorce dating experiences, including the fact that his ex-wife would "get calls from different men" at her apartment and that there is evidence of a man living at her apartment—"a razor, a can of shaving foam ... a man's hiking boots" (244). Despite his (wrongful) accusations against Leo, Brian cites Molly's "being exposed to ... [Anna and Leo's] sex life" as the "major disruption" in his daughter's life, not the sexual abuse that he alleges has been occurring (249). When objections are made by Anna's lawyer, they are sustained but always with a sardonic grin from the judge, who is frequently described through this episode as "smiling" and having "smiled" (244, 245). Moreover, when Leo takes the stand, he is required to divulge how long he had known Anna prior to the sexual consummation of their relationship (256). Although the sexual relationship between Brian and his new wife is deemed irrelevant to Brian's fitness as his daughter's potential primary guardian and, thereby, does not warrant a mention in the court proceedings, the suggestion that Anna may be sexually promiscuous or may be living with a lover is used as evidence of her alleged incompetence as a parent. A sexual woman, it seems, cannot also be a fit mother.

When Anna is eventually required to disclose to the court the details of the aforementioned episode where Molly enters her bedroom when she is making love to Leo, Brian's victory in the custody proceedings is assured. Brian's lawyer, Fine, constructs the episode as one of sexual depravity:

> "Mrs. Dunlap, is it true that on at least one of the occasions when Molly came down the hall and got into bed with you, you had intercourse with Mr. Cutter while she was in that bed?"
>
> "We were having intercourse when she came in, yes."
>
> "And you continued to do so, isn't that the case?"
>
> "Mr. Cutter stayed inside me."
>
> "Which is what we define, I think, as intercourse. It will do for me anyway."
>
> There was muted laughter here and there in the room, and Fine's lips curled slightly, as though to acknowledge it. (263)

Fine centres the remainder of the proceedings around what he claims is Anna's "*bad judgement* around ... sexual issues with her daughter," including nudity in the house (270). He asserts that Anna is "psychologically absent" on account both of her relationship with Leo and of her working two part-time jobs, which "has meant that she's had to put her child into day care full-time" (271, 270). Again, Brian's relationship status and working life (which also finds him away from his daughter for the most part) is irrelevant. In Fine's public estimation, Anna's circumstances have left Molly "traumatized" and suffering from a sense of "abandonment" (271). As the final verdict approaches, Anna is rendered silent and incapable of defending herself against the court's gendered expectations around parenting, sex, caregiving, and work: she is overwhelmed by "an impulse to stand up and shout out some truth, to begin this again from the start, to change the vocabulary. But the pipes hissed. The judge listened carefully. The lawyers made their pitches. And then it was over" (273).

Fine's deliberate obfuscation of the significance of the episode in bed between Anna, Leo, and, in particular, Molly, as well as Anna's inability to "change the vocabulary" around this episode, implicate the way the language of erotic intimacy has largely been appropriated by the realm of adult sexuality (273). Iris Young observes that in Western cultures, notions of sexual feeling and erotic intimacy are predominantly considered synonymous with heteronormative sexual contact, representations of which tend to be fixated on intercourse as "the true sex act" (194). Traina adds that the perniciousness of this exclusivity of association is compounded as a result of the tendency to narrowly define sexual eroticism itself in terms of "the more powerful person's penetration of the other" and to characterize it as a "cycle of intense, dangerously irrational attraction-desire-release" (12, 91). As Traina points out, under this vision of power and sexuality, where eroticism is assumed to present a perpetually "grave temptation," the "eroticism of maternity" is presumed dangerous or "unlimited by any moral boundaries except forbidden sexual pleasure" (12). Hence, the court fails to conceive of the intimate episode between Molly, Leo, and Anna as disconnected from notions of power, exploitation, and abuse. Ultimately, the court proceedings ensure the preservation of traditional patriarchal categories: women's sexuality should be contained within marriage. Moreover, motherhood should be preserved with childhood—a category that should have no trace whatsoever of the sexual or even the erotic.

The predominantly male courtroom attendees appear to take great pleasure in the public exposure and degradation of Anna's sex life. When Brian's lawyer, Fine, first raises the subject of Anna and Leo's sexual relationship, Anna notes that his voice suddenly becomes "sharp, cheerful" and that it is actually the "first time" she has "seen him smile" (256). Fine's expression of prurient enjoyment is mirrored by the judge, who, as previously mentioned, smirks as he sustains the objections of Anna's lawyer to Fine's questions about his client's sexual encounters (244, 245). Anna's recollection of the events as a form of "forced intimacy" implicates the sense of a symbolic collective violence being perpetrated against her (130). Even Anna's lawyer, Muth, is eventually exposed as complicit in his client's degradation. After the custody verdict has been delivered, Anna observes the affable interaction between Muth and Fine and recalls their earlier "muted, somehow conspiratorial greeting in the echoing courthouse hall [and] their laughter coming out of Mrs. Harkessian's office together" (272-73). Not only is the exposure of Anna's postmarital sex life exploited as a source of individual voyeuristic enjoyment, but it also acts as a conduit for toxic male bonding, in which camaraderie is achieved via the shared contempt and degradation of female sexuality.

Anna's experience serves as a cautionary model and reveals that even well into the late twentieth century, to be a woman—particularly a mother—and sexually free remained a punishable offense. In her examination of the role of women and mothers in particular in the late twentieth century, E. Ann Kaplan observes that the changing status of the nuclear family, women's increasing sexual freedoms, and the separation of women's sexuality from the desire to have children sparked hostilities, at least in conservative quarters, in relation to the alleged threat posed by the so-called liberated woman, whose sexuality must be contained and controlled lest it become "dangerously unleashed" (Kaplan 412). Ferguson likewise observes that although various changes since the nineteenth century have ensured the weakening of "the patriarchal control of individual men over women and children in families ... the power of men to control women and children through wage labour, the state and sexual liaisons" was actually strengthened in the twentieth century—a distinction Ferguson refers to as nineteenth century "husband patriarchy" versus twentieth-century "public patriarchy" (12). The appropriation of Anna's sexual and erotic experiences in the family court suggests the failure of the alleged progressive ideals of the sexual revolution to allow for women's sexual and erotic freedoms and pleasures. Although Anna is free to divorce her husband and live independently with her child, her experience of degradation, humiliation, and eventual loss in the family court attests to the authority of "public patriarchy" in the late twentieth century, in which motherhood and women's sexuality continued to function as key sites of patriarchal oppression.

Anna's experience of attending a women's group meeting prior to her divorce also implicates the limitations of the alleged relaxation in standards of sexual morality in the late twentieth century, at least where women were concerned. Anna recalls the rather desperate, overstated declarations of sexual freedom from the women at the meeting, including one woman who "talked about whole evenings spent in solitary erotic play; who loved to taste herself on her own fingers, who'd ... bought a vibrator to increase her pleasure" (84). Another woman—whom Anna describes as "one of the most sexually charged women [she'd] ever met" (84)—divulges the details of her promiscuous sex life, yet she admits to having never experimented with sexual self-pleasure at all. The stories of alleged sexual adventure and daring at the women's group leave Anna feeling not only uninspired but also resigned to the idea that she "simply didn't have erotic feelings" at all (83) and to the notion that "That's just sex ... I mean *everyone* does that ... That's the whole point of the sexual revolution" (110).

The hollow declarations of sexual freedom at the women's group, alongside Anna's assumption of her own sexual frigidity (which she later realizes was a mistaken assumption) implicates the cruel offshoot of the late twentieth century insistence on sex as pleasure as distinguished from nineteenth-century patriarchal conceptions of sex as reproduction. As Ferguson observes, this distinction did not automatically grant women freedom over their bodies and their sexuality; it merely created a shift in "the way men use sexuality ... to control the production of sexual pleasure for themselves" (15). Although the experience of bodily pleasure and sexual intimacy without moral regulation and judgment is undeniably worth fighting for, the uninspiring stories of alleged sexual adventure shared at the women's group suggests the sexual revolution did not necessarily extend such freedoms to women.

The novel's depiction of Anna's adolescent sexual encounters similarly suggests the failure of conventional conceptions of sexual freedom to see beyond male-defined and male-centric notions of sexuality. Anna recalls the pressure to engage in sexual activity in her adolescence at parties, where "I didn't know what to do, and so did nothing while a whole series of boys ground groaning against me, their eyes shut against seeing me, their hands on my breasts, and finally in my blouse, up my skirt" (52). Anna recollects that her response to these encounters was consistently one of detachment and even self-loathing: "I felt nothing, less than nothing" (52). What Anna refers to as her "willed passivity" in these sexual encounters is mirrored in her memory of her mother's displays of sexual indifference towards her father (50). Anna recalls that the "withholding cool quality" of her mother was "the very thing" that her father "played to, the thing which spurred him on" (47). Years later, Anna's mother attempts to engage her adult daughter in a spirit of solidarity in relation to her sex life: "Her posture was as one sufferer to another. She half-pridefully complained of my father's ardour" (128). These experiences suggest the normalization of a form of male sexual pursuit that holds scant regard for female pleasure or desire. As is the case in Anna's courtroom experience, the novel's depiction of Anna's adolescent sexual encounters illustrates a disturbing phenomenon whereby the denial and degradation of female sexuality are exploited as fodder for male pleasure.

Although *The Good Mother* depicts as unjust the family court's perception of the episode in which Molly seeks comfort from her mother while Anna and Leo are making love, the novel still shows that the line between maternal eroticism and adult sexual eroticism must be firmly drawn. Indeed, the novel's idyllic depictions of the mingling of Anna's sexual and maternal roles coexist alongside far darker promptings in the narrative. One episode sees Anna draw a disquieting association between her child and a pornographic photograph she finds in her lover's apartment: the image of the "woman on her hands and knees, her open cunt, ass towards the camera, her head staring upside down at the photographer from under her dangling breasts" triggers Anna to "remember abruptly the posture Molly had assumed one night, after her bath" (161). This stark, unsettling juxtaposition of the child and the world of pornographic adult sexuality indirectly points to the justifiable concerns inherent in any consideration or theorization of the shared erotic characteristics of adult sexual relationships and relationships between adults and children. The sense of skirting dangerously close to taboo, of the danger of crossing a line, is also suggested via Anna's jarring interior observation when she embraces her daughter after having made love to Leo one morning: "When I bent to kiss her, ... my tongue touched the little ridges my teeth had made on the insides of my lips when I sucked Leo off" (127). Anna's unsettling observation suggests that perhaps she, too, grapples with the manner in which her sexual and mothering roles may appropriately coexist.

Anna's self-doubt regarding the appropriateness of her maternal attachment, as well as her fear of overstepping boundaries and of taking too much from her child, is also presumably related to cultural pressures on women to perform a sacrificial and self-abnegating form of motherhood. Anna worries that she is "too bound up with her" daughter, whom she fears she might love too "greedily" (80, 4). Although the reader does not doubt that she is indeed a good, caring mother, Anna struggles with how to "love her [daughter] without damaging her ... not too much, not too little. Is there such a love?" (80). Anna is unable to be entirely at ease with the sensual pleasure and gratification she obtains through her child. As Young would argue, Anna's anxiety points to the importance of allowing and "affirming a kind of love in which a woman does not have to choose between pursuing her own selfish, insatiable desire and giving pleasure and sustenance to another close to her, a nurturance that gives and also takes for itself" (200). Young's observation and its application to the undeserved unease with which Anna experiences the pleasures she derives through her intimacy with her child points to the importance of challenging the sacrificial motherhood ideal, including an acknowledgment and celebration of the mutual erotic pleasures inherent to the mother-child dyad.

The allowance that women's erotic pleasures are not necessarily confined to heteronormative, male-centric sexuality is further evidenced in the novel's intermittent flashback narrative, centred on Anna's pregnant young aunt, Babe. Whereas the rest of the family views Babe's out-of-wedlock pregnancy as a source of shame and disgrace, the adolescent Anna is in awe of her aunt's pregnant body. When the young Anna stumbles upon her aunt naked, she observes that

> Babe was beautiful. She had been beautiful even at my age, but now she looked like a woman to me.... a kind of heaviness seemed to pull her belly lower so it had a curve downward, and her thick fleecy hair seemed tucked underneath it. But her breasts were what most stirred me. They were still smallish, but they seemed fat, and the nipples were flat and wide as poker chips.... Babe, beautiful anyway, and now lush, standing in a pool of discarded clothing, representing a womanhood I felt was impossible for me; and me, all acute angles, caught on the edge of pubescence, gaping at her in amazement. (42)

Anna's reaction is presumably in part a sexual one: she is described as being "stirred" and "aroused" by the spectacle of her aunt's body, a sensation that leaves her feeling at once "stunned, appalled and thrilled" (41, 42). Lacking a language through which to speak about or reflectively experience her erotic and sexual feelings in response to the beguiling vision of her pregnant aunt, Anna is rendered at once "silent [and] embarrassed" (42). Babe, by contrast, is able to express and celebrate the erotic power of her procreant body: she looks "down at herself with satisfaction" (42), tells Anna that pregnancy is a "wonderful" feeling, like being "ripe and full" (42) and invites her niece to touch her body:

"She stepped towards me, reaching for my paralyzed hands, and raised them to her breasts. Her skin was softer even than it looked.... Her voice was excited, telling me—what? I can't remember. She moved my hands down her waist, then to her abdomen. I felt her fur brush against my fingertips, dry, and yet soft" (42). Babe's pregnancy facilitates a moment of erotic sharing between aunt and niece, as they express their mutual pleasure in the sexual power and beauty of the pregnant female body. Much like the aforementioned episode in bed between Anna, her lover, and her child, this intimate moment between aunt and niece exposes the potentially diffuse nature of female eroticism and, in this case, female sexual desire more generally.

This episode of triumphant tenderness and sharing between Babe and Anna attests to the existence of varied and nonphallic-oriented forms of eroticism, through which women can experience emotional and physical connection and pleasure. In a society where, as Young observes, nonphallic pleasures are frequently considered "either deviant or preparatory" (194)—as foreplay in preparation for the main event—the nature of Babe and Anna's episode of erotic sharing challenges the limited view of human sexuality and eroticism as synonymous with genitally focused, orgasm-oriented, and potentially threatening or exploitative behaviours. The interaction between Babe and Anna clearly occupies a different space—one where erotic and even sexual feelings are not necessarily a precursor to sexual contact or release and where the dark associations of sexuality and eroticism with shame, fear, and insatiable bodily appetites is substituted with the life-affirming associations of intimacy, mutual pleasure, sharing, and connection.

The novel's destabilization of male-defined and male-centric notions of human sexuality is further reinforced via the depiction of Anna's sexual relationship with Brian prior to their divorce. Anna describes the sex between them as "always so ... nothing. So terrible" (12). Despite Brian's alleged experimental approach to sex, and his apparent focus on sexually pleasuring his wife, Anna is left feeling indifferent and unfulfilled: "He was enthusiastic and experimental. But to me the positions he tried felt just like that: positions ... with Brian I felt ... absurd ... He would lie next to me, his face buried between my legs, licking and licking ... for the most part, I was neutral towards the whole enterprise" (84). Anna's sexual dissatisfaction with her husband is also mirrored in her friend, Ursula's complaint: "All my boyfriend ever wants to do is go down on me ... it makes him feel at home, like he's being a good boy and cleaning his plate" (86-87). Anna and Ursula's mutual dissatisfaction supports Lynda Marin's suggestion that women's emotional and physical pleasures are constrained by the widespread conviction that a woman's sexuality is "securely organized around her genitals and directed toward her adult sexual partner" (12). Although the female pleasure potentially offered via cunnilingus is obvious, Anna and Ursula's shared disappointment in their sexual partners' efforts suggests the more polymorphous and less regionalized nature of female sexuality; mere physical stimulation and arousal are not necessarily sufficient to elicit female desire and pleasure.

Helene Cixous explores this phenomenon in her essay *The Laugh of the Medusa* "Though masculine sexuality gravitates around the penis, engendering that centralized body ... under the dictatorship of its parts, woman does not bring about the same regionalization which serves the couple head/genitals and which is inscribed only within boundaries. Her libido is cosmic, just as her unconscious is worldwide" (889). Cixous's insistence on the variance and complexity of female sexuality relative to male-defined norms is also reflected in the work of fellow French philosopher, Luce Irigaray. In *This Sex Which Is Not One*, Irigaray claims that

"*Woman has sex organs more or less everywhere*. She finds pleasure almost everywhere ... the geography of her pleasure is far more diversified, more multiple in its differences, more complex, more subtle, than is commonly imagined—in an imaginary rather too narrowly focused on sameness" (8). Cixous's and Irigaray's shared concept of the complex and diversified (or "cosmic") female libido dislodges female pleasure and desire from phallocentric sexuality and eroticism. Moreover, in elevating female sexuality to a quantum scale of holism and integration, the notion of a "cosmic female libido" implies a direct correlation between women's experience of sexual desire and pleasure as well as their position or capacity for freedom and agency under patriarchy. The pleasure Anna derives from the form of eroticism experienced with her aunt, Babe, and later with her own child, and the contrasting parallel lack of pleasure she experiences in the rigid single mindedness of her husband's (and—as her experience at the women's group may indicate—her culture's) notion and performance of sexual eroticism attest to the link that Cixous and Irigaray observe between male oppression and women's performance of and capacity for erotic and sexual pleasure and desire. In a male-defined and male-centric world, female eroticism and sexuality are inevitably thwarted.

In Miller's novel, it is motherhood or the maternal state that best facilitates the potentially diffuse, polymorphous nature of female eroticism and sexuality. Given its reliance on the erotic and sexual capital of Babe's pregnant body, the episode of erotic sharing between Babe and Anna defies the patriarchal demand that the mother role be strictly disconnected from the sexual or the erotic. The picture postcard of the Madonna and child that Babe sends to Anna later in her pregnancy similarly refutes the cultural tendency to split female sexuality and eroticism from motherhood. The postcard depicts a Renaissance-era image of the Madonna with breasts bared, embracing a naked baby Jesus—"a fat, real, mischievous boy, penis and all" (43). This image challenges the late Christian appropriation and celebration of the Virgin as a symbol of female purity and compliance. Much like Anna's response to Babe's pregnant body (and also the sensual pleasure she later derives through mothering her child), the postcard's depiction of the sensual blessed intimacy between mother and child suggests the virtue of the maternal erotic and acknowledges that, as Amber E. Kinser argues, mothering inevitably occurs on "some place on a spectrum of sensuality that implicates bodies and desires and the erotic" (120).

It is, perhaps, this inevitable association between the maternal state and female sexuality and eroticism that accounts for the repulsion Anna's father later feels towards her pregnancy. Whereas Babe's pregnant body is depicted as a celebratory expression of female sexuality and fecundity, Anna's recollection of her own pregnancy by contrast reveals how pregnancy can be experienced as a source of shame and disgust. The aversion Anna's father holds towards Anna's pregnant state is made obvious in Anna's recollection of the day she witnessed a bird fly into the patio wall at her parent's home. The narrative associates the bird's fragile state, as it lay on the ground, stunned from the impact, to Anna's physical vulnerability in pregnancy: "I bent over the bird. Its wings beat the ground at my approach, and then it stilled. One wing was hanging limply off its body. It fluttered its good wing again, moving about a foot over the ground; then collapsed, its small bright eyes seeming to watch me. I stood up. I remembered feeling a sense of vulnerability and fragility because of the pregnancy" (28). The association drawn between Anna and the struggling bird is cast in a decidedly unsettling light when her father enacts an ostensive mercy killing via a series of blows from his shovel: "He raised it over his head and brought it down on to the bird. I turned away quickly but I could hear the dull thumps, and under them, the repeated click of the bird's bill against the metal. Three, four times he raised the shovel and brought it down" (28). The narrative further associates this overzealous assault on the bird and the disgust Anna's father feels towards his daughter's maternal body: "When he stopped, I turned to him. He looked quickly down at my belly and then away, a flicker of disgust having momentarily touched his face. I looked down too as I tried to pull the bathrobe shut. My belly protruded in the diaphanous nightgown, the extroverted navel like an obscene gesture" (28).

According to Colin McGinn, "disgust belongs in the area of human experience most protected by taboo and hedged with euphemism" (3). Disgust is, inevitably, tied to and influenced by social prohibition, yet regardless of how persuasive the societal taboos that demand asexual motherhood may be, the pregnant body persists as a powerful and unsettling symbolic reminder that the mother woman is inevitably the sexual woman. Much like the sneering degradation of Anna's sexuality in family court, the extreme aversion Anna's father feels towards his daughter's pregnancy (not to mention his violent symbolic castigation of the same) implicates the male fear and loathing of such a notion.

In the novel, it is mothers who pay the greatest price for the delimitations placed on female eroticism and sexuality under patriarchy. Much like Anna and her castigation at the hands of the family court, Babe is punished for attempting to exercise her sexual freedom outside the patriarchal institution of marriage. Shunned by her family and sent away to Geneva, Babe is forced to spend her confinement in isolation and to give her baby up for adoption. Babe's experience renders her wretched and isolated, precipitates her descent into alcoholism and mental illness, and, ultimately, leads to her tragic suicide by drowning. In this way, Babe's tragic trajectory aligns her with a long line of infamous literary heroines, including Chopin's Edna Pontellier, Flaubert's Emma Bovary, and Tolstoy's Anna Karenina—all of whom attempt to exercise their sexual freedom, subsequently fall into social disrepute and decline, lose their children, and, eventually, take their own lives.

Miller's situating of Babe's tragic demise early in the narrative signals that Anna's story, though resonant of the plight of past literary heroines, will somehow be different. Indeed, Anna reflects that "Babe and her life," ultimately, became "less a model to me than a cautionary tale" (43). The tension between women's desire for freedom and self-fulfillment and societal conventions and expectations of female sexual conduct is resolved in the stories of Babe and her literary forebears via their deaths. Anna's admission (prior to her aunt's death) that Babe "made everyone nervous, and we were all just as happy, in truth, to have her gone" reflects the anxiety that the stories of particular tragic literary heroines of the past both represent and elicit in their readers as well as the concomitant sense of relief that their (self) destruction potentially incurs (40). Although these stories highlight the impossibility of being a woman, particularly a mother, and sexually free, they fail to imagine a resolution to this tension beyond female self-destruction. Through Anna's story, Miller's novel experiments not only with offering its central heroine an alternative fate (one that refuses to violently dispose of her) but also with foregrounding the mother-child dyad—a relationship that is largely marginalized in the stories of Anna's literary predecessors.

In recovering the mother-child relationship from the margins, Anna's story explores the damage done not just to women and mothers under patriarchy, but also to the child and, in this case, to the mother-daughter relationship. In her engagement with the neo-Freudian notion of the Electra complex, Julia Kristeva observes that patriarchy demands the daughter align herself with the father: "The daughter ... is rewarded by the symbolic order when she identifies with the father: only here is she recognized not as herself but in opposition to her rival, the mother" (152).

The novel's depiction of Molly's relationship with her parents captures this sense of the child's rivalry against the mother in complicity with the father: "She turned to Brian. She had a brave coquettish smile on her face, and she said, 'I really hate my mom, don't you? We hate her, right?'" (24). Although Anna has a closer relationship with their daughter, she recognizes Molly's allegiance to her father: "If she had to choose between us, she'd pick Brian, the one she didn't see enough of, the one she yearned after. I was just the medium she lived in, as familiar to her, as taken for granted, as air and food" (24). Molly's passion for her father and concomitant animosity towards her mother is mirrored in Anna's earlier attitude towards her own parents in her childhood. Despite her father's lack of emotional availability—the fact that "she was never very real to him" (47)—Anna reflects that "she hated her" mother and that it was her father she "yearned to know ... better, if only to justify somehow the passionate love ... [she] felt for him" (37, 35). As psychoanalyst Juliet Mitchell would argue, the depiction of Molly's and Anna's shared girlhood allegiance to their fathers despite their closer bond with their mothers enacts the Electra complex, whereby the girl shifts her first love for her mother to a compensatory love for her father as a means of gaining access to the detached father and, by extension, the symbolic order from which she is otherwise excluded (4).

Molly's hostility towards her mother is particularly evident in response to any sign or expression of her mother's sexual agency or appeal. When Anna dresses up and attempts to look her most physically attractive, she observes that "Molly looked at me critically ... Then she turned to Brian. 'She's not pretty,' she said emphatically. 'She's mom'" (103). Then later, Molly watches Anna looking for her purse and keys, and says "I hate when you have a *date* ... Stupid Mom" (109).

Molly's reproachful fascination provides an illustration of the way, according to Mitchell, the daughter's renunciation of the mother involves both her enthrallment with, and repudiation of, the prospect of the mother's autonomy, particularly as it manifests sexually: "Let *jouissance* be forbidden to the mother: this is the demand of the father's daughter, fascinated by the mother's *jouissance*" (152). As Kristeva observes, the daughter's "sublimated sadistic attacks on the mother" are essentially self-mutilating; they inevitably entail "censuring herself as a woman" (152). The tragic price the daughter must pay for her (compulsory) collusion with the father in opposition to the mother's sexuality is the inevitable and eventual parallel denial of her own.

Although Anna's story enacts the misfortune and tragedy that potentially befall mothers (and their daughters) under patriarchal sexual morality, the novel's final note is arguably one of optimism. The closing passage finds Anna and her daughter reunited after the final court hearing:

She ran into my embrace ... and I picked her up, held her tight. Her hands rose to my face, stroked it, patted it, as though this were part of her way of seeing me, as though she were blind.

I swallowed hard not to cry, and said her name over and over. Then her hands, smelling of sweat, of soap, covered my eyes.... She laughed and brought her face up to mine. In the secret dark circle of her hands, her breath was warm and sweet on me. She kissed me, carefully, daintily, lips pursed—four, five, six times—exactly on my mouth.

I held her tight for a long moment in our unseeing embrace. It seemed the same, her smell, her touch, the wiry density of her limbs.... Her dress was rucked up in back, her hair wispy and wild from our embrace. Everything was familiar, and also unknown (310).

The embracement of the body and its pleasures evident in this final passage constructs a celebratory vision that resurrects the power and virtue of the maternal erotic. With Anna "hearing some kind of music" in her head and musing, "Ah *yes ... this is how it begins*" (310) in the final line, the novel ends with a sense of hope—of new beginnings arising from an acceptance and celebration of this form of eroticism. There is a sense that, in complicit relation with her daughter, Anna will attempt to create a new future, one where she refuses to be made taboo to her child and where she will strive to resolve the tragic self/other tension experienced by daughters and mothers under patriarchal morality.

Anna's tragedy, as enacted in the family court episode, draws our attention to the ways in which patriarchal conceptions of sexuality and eroticism tarnish and degrade mothers' sexuality and maternal eroticism. Miller's novel challenges the cultural expectation of asexual motherhood and confronts the sequestering of eroticism to the realm of adult sexuality, where it is drawn up predominantly in service of men. Through its celebratory depiction of maternal eroticism, *The Good Mother* offers a hopeful prescription for how to alter those moral conceptions of maternal, sexual, and erotic experiences that perpetuate the notion of asexual motherhood and that potentially harm relationships between mothers and their children. Moreover, the novel's celebratory vision of maternal eroticism—alongside its depiction of sexual relationships between men and women characterized by frustration, exploitation, and discontentment—holds implications that reach far beyond the mother-child dyad. In highlighting the broadly erotic nature of the mother-child relationship, *The Good Mother* implies, as Traina argues, that eroticism is "integral" not just to sexual relationships but also, ideally, "*all* thoughtful, generous, nurturing relationships" (my emphasis, 6).

Works Cited

Cixous, Helene. "The Laugh of the Medusa." *Signs*, vol. 1, no. 4, 1976, pp. 875-93.

Marneffe de, Daphne. *Maternal Desire: On Children, Love, and the Inner Life*. Little, 2004.

Ferguson, Ann. "Motherhood and Sexuality: Some Feminist Questions." *Hypatia*, vol. 1, no. 2, 1986, p. 3.

Irigaray, Luce. *This Sex Which Is Not One*. 1977. Translated by Catherine Porter. Cornell University Press, 1985.

Kaplan, E. Ann "Sex, Work and Motherhood: The Impossible Triangle." *The Journal of Sex Research*, vol. 27, no. 3, 1990, pp 409-425.

Kinser, Amber E. "Embracing the Tensions of a Maternal Erotic." *Mothering in the Third Wave*, edited by Amber R. Kinser, Demeter Press, 2008, pp. 119-25.

Kristeva, Julia. *The Kristeva Reader*, edited by Toril Mo. Columbia University Press, 1986.

Marin, Lynda. "Mother and Child: The Erotic Bond." *Mother Journeys: Feminists Write About Mothering*, edted by Maureen T. Reddy, Spinsters Ink, 1994, pp. 9-21.

McGinn, Colin. *The Meaning of Disgust*. Oxford University Press, 2011.

Miller, Sue. *The Good Mother*. Bantam Doubleday Dell Publishing Group, 1986.

Mitchell, Juliet. *Psychoanalysis and Feminism: Freud, Laing, Reich and Women*. Vintage Books, 1975.

Traina, Cristina. *Erotic Attunement: Parenthood and the Ethics of Sensuality between Unequals*. The University of Chicago Press, 2011.

Young, Iris M. *Throwing like a Girl and Other Essays in Feminist Philosophy and Social Theory*. Indiana University Press, 1990.

Chapter Six

The Scandalous Breast: Confronting the Sexual-Maternal Dichotomy in Toni Morrison's *Song of Solomon* and Susan Choi's *My Education*

Christa Baiada

In 1990, feminist philosopher Iris Young wrote that "Breasts are a scandal because they shatter the border between motherhood and sexuality" (199). Powerful as this statement is, it requires qualification, since the border perseveres in the cultural imagination. Breasts do have the potential to shatter the cultural separation between motherhood and sexuality, but the maternal breast, most readily manifested in the lactating breast, has instead been vigilantly disciplined to avoid such a cataclysmic challenge to our cultural constructions of women's bodies, identities, and behaviour.

Breasts in Western culture are prime symbols of not only sexuality but also, if secondly, idealized maternity. Breastfeeding occasions the intersection of these two conflicting associations of breasts and, threatens the realization of Young's shattering of this foundational cultural dichotomy. Thus, breastfeeding is an act in which the border between maternal and sexual is most rigidly disciplined. Studies by Pam Carter and Cindy Stearns both find that nursing mothers who negotiate complex codes of privacy and decency and anticipate social monitoring and judgment vigilantly police their own breastfeeding practices in order to present an acceptable maternal body—one that is nurturing and asexual. As Stearns writes, "To transgress the precarious boundaries of the good maternal body is to risk being labeled a bad mother and/or sexually inappropriate or deviant" (322). Nursing breasts must be desexualized in order to accommodate the discourses of motherhood[1] that demand selfless attention to children's needs. Sexuality asserts desire, which then becomes need. So-called good mothers assert no needs of their own.

Yet an embodied experience of mothering does not deny body. Mothering for most women is intimate and physical. As Noelle Oxenhandler has written, "To feel the erotically charged nature of the parent-child relationship—the thousand small intimacies that weave parent and child together—is to feel that one is breaking a taboo" (9). This is the case whether one breastfeeds or not; nonetheless, breastfeeding has the potential to intensify physical and bodily intimacy but also anxiety, as the same breast a child nurses at is an erogenous zone from which women derive sexual pleasure and which has been experientially formed by our cultural eroticization of breasts.

Although such pleasure is by no means universal among nursing mothers, it is, nonetheless, common[2] but difficult to openly discuss. The intense physical pleasure a woman may experience in breastfeeding is not sexual in the way generally understood, and it would appear that a language does not yet exist to discuss such an expansive view of the sexual. The experience is not necessarily genital or orgasm oriented, but it is inevitably a sensual act in which two bodies engage intimately; one gives to the other, and there is a release (of oxytocin, other pleasurable hormones, and, of course, milk). Sexologists and scholars of the maternal who focus on similar physiological responses have proposed a reconceptualization of female sexuality that incorporates bodily maternal experiences from childbirth to breastfeeding, but they have failed to make a marked impact on discourses of female sexuality, which are still dominated by a patriarchal construct of sexuality.[3] To suppress or deny the sensations of such meaningful physical contact experienced by large numbers of women instantiates the cultural denial of female sexuality outside the constraints of phallic sexuality and reinforces the binary of sexual and maternal bodies. As Cristina Traina argues in *Erotic*

Attunement, "establishing the normalcy of mothers' erotic experience involves embracing biological, psychological, and social science research on the multidimensionality of women's sexuality including its links to maternity, which in turn unsettles traditional moral descriptions of sexuality" (3-4).

Artistic depictions of breastfeeding traditionally reinforce the social and cultural agenda of an elevated form of motherhood—selfless and sacrificial—in the service of child, family, and society. In literature, Steinbeck's Rose-of-Sharon nursing a starving man at the end of *Grapes of Wrath* exemplifies this. Scholars have analyzed the representation of breastfeeding in public policy and advocacy campaigns, television shows, and magazines, and have shown how these depictions can illuminate cultural conflicts about mothers' practices, subjectivity, and authority (Blum; Hausman; Kukla). More specifically in relation to maternal sexuality, scholars have found that popular cultural representations of breastfeeding deny, reject, or sanitize sexuality in mothering. Although this is the norm, it is not necessarily the rule.

In this chapter, I examine two contemporary American novels that reject the dichotomy between the maternal and the sexual by blurring the boundary at the potentially scandalous breast. With rare significant attention to lactation and strikingly unusual scenes of breastfeeding, Toni Morrison's *Song of Solomon* (1977) and Susan Choi's *My Education* (2013) force readers to confront the cultural discomfort caused by an intersection of the maternal and the sexual as well as question their own assumptions about mothers, bodies, and sexuality.

Song of Solomon: The Maternal Is Sexual

The protagonist of *Song of Solomon* (1977) is Macon Dead III, known in the novel and hereafter in this chapter as Milkman. Milkman's mother, Ruth, is the motherless daughter of the only "Negro" doctor in town. Ruth is "pressed small" (Morrison 124) and assimilated into white bourgeois values by her haughty and overprotective father, who is her only companion until she marries Macon. Submissive to first her father and then her husband, Ruth is ill-suited to be a culture bearer or teach her children self-love (O'Reilly, *Toni Morrison* 76-77).

The relationship between Ruth and her husband, Macon Dead, is as cold as their surname. Macon resents and is suspicious of Ruth's relationship with her father,[4] and his hatred for his wife permeates the family. Deprived of touch for over ten years, Ruth is "desperate to lie with her husband and have another baby by him, the son she bore was first off a wished for bond between herself and Macon, something to hold them together and reinstate their sex lives" (13). However, the new baby fails to resuscitate relations with Macon, which makes him even more angry and resentful. Ruth, instead, turns to the intimacy of mothering to provide her with the "balm, a gentle touch or nuzzling of some sort" (13), which she needs to get her through the day. Ruth co-opts and prolongs nursing, deploying it not so much as a selfless maternal act but more for her own survival to sate her human need for touch.

Once or twice a day, Ruth summons her toddler son to her sewing room, where she nurses him. This routine continues until Freddie, her husband's lackey, comes to the house on an errand, peeks through the study window, and sees Ruth nursing Macon. He is tickled by the sight of the young boy at his mother's breast and runs into the house to find them and exclaim his glee. Interestingly, Freddie docs not initially view the scene as sexual or Ruth as a sexual being. Issues of race and class figure larger in rendering the tableau surprising and comically ironic to Freddie. Breastfeeding has particular resonances for African American women, who have historically been dehumanized and consequently excessively sexualized by white culture and excluded from the category of sacred motherhood; their maternal bodies were exploited instead through their work as mammies (taking care of white children, at the expense of their own) or later vilified as welfare mothers or emasculating matriarchs.[5] Freddie notes the contrast between Ruth's bourgeois assimilated persona and the racialized associations of breastfeeding, especially extended breastfeeding, with lower classes and Black women of the South. Looking at Ruth, he sees the ultrarefined, bourgeois, and lemony-skinned Ruth Foster Dead—a doctor's daughter and wife of a wealthy landlord—nursing a dark-skinned boy, like a poor Southern mammy in a play of reversed racial coding. He laughs at her, and in this moment, she becomes an object of ridicule and is knocked off her lofty pedestal.

Freddy sees nothing sexual until his gaze shifts to the boy, at which point Ruth is marginalized and the child becomes the driving actor of the scene: "His eyes were on the boy. Appreciative eyes that communicated some complicity she was excluded from.... 'A milkman.

That's what you got here, Miss Rufie. A natural milkman if I ever seen one. Look out, womens. Here he come. Huh!'" (14-15). Though only a child, Macon is, here, rechristened with the name he will hitherto be known by and is given agency and attributed sexual precociousness. He is initiated into the world of male-centred sexuality in collusion with Freddie. Freddie's response indicates not only a culturally inscribed interpretation that insists upon gendered notions of sexual agency (coded masculine) but also one that either is ignorant of or in denial of the possibility of female bodily pleasure.

Milkman's memory of this scene is triggered by his father's stories of Ruth's inappropriate relationship with her own father, proffered as justification for Macon's striking her. Milkman is confused by the idea that his mother nursed him beyond infancy: "My mother nursed me when I was old enough to talk, stand up, and wear knickers ... when there was no reason for it, when I also drank milk and Ovaltine and everything from a glass" (78). Breastmilk is not a nutritional necessity for a four-year-old who can talk, walk, and drink independently, and although some children do still enjoy nursing at this age, it was not the case for Milkman. So what other purpose could there have been? Any pleasure for Ruth, if not rooted in selfless maternal devotion, is assumed to be perverse. Likewise, literary scholarship has tended to reinforce a similar interpretation of Ruth's extended nursing.[6] J. Brooks Bouson, who addresses extended breastfeeding briefly in his study as one of the Deads' "shameful family secrets," suggests that Morrison positions readers voyeuristically to witness "a taboo, oedipally-tinged scene" and, in doing so, risks eliciting a response of shame and disgust (83). This disgust seems to derive from some literary critics' internalization of dominant discourses of good motherhood that include selflessness, exclude sexuality, and presume Black female sexuality and maternity to be suspect.

Ruth's practice transgresses the boundary between the maternal and sexual breast, but on a close reading, any interpretations that claim incest or pathology are not actually supported by the text. Any discomfort experienced by the reader can be attributed more to their own prejudices and socially constructed ideas regarding breastfeeding practices than to the text itself, which perhaps is Morrison's point. Morrison's language describes most plainly Milkman's boredom and Ruth's pleasure:

When he came in to the little room she unbuttoned her blouse and smiled. He was too young to be dazzled by her nipples, but he was old enough to be bored by the flat taste of mother's milk, so he came reluctantly, as a chore, and lay as he had at least once a day each day of his life in his mother's arms, and tried to pull the thin, faintly sweet milk from her flesh without hurting her with his teeth.

She felt him. His restraint, his courtesy, his indifference, all of which pushed her into fantasy. She had the distinct impression that his lips were pulling from her a thread of light. It was as though she were a cauldron issuing spinning gold. Like the miller's daughter—the one who sat at night in a straw-filled room, thrilled with the secret power Rumpelstiltskin had given her: to see golden thread stream from her very own shuttle. And that was the other part of her pleasure, a pleasure she hated to give up." (13-14)[7]

Morrison conveys vastly different experiences from both the child's and mother's perspective, but neither perspective indicates harm or perversion has occurred. The boy is uninterested, dutiful, and courteous (demonstrating the most consideration for his mother the reader sees until the end of the novel), but he is in no way compromised. There is nothing sexual, for him, in this interaction. Ruth experiences a diffuse pleasure in his attention (his restraint and courtesy) as well as in the "felt" touch she feels as Milkman suckles her nipple. The pleasure is undeniably sensual and definitely erotic, perhaps sexual, but not in the commonly understood sense of sex as hetero-orgasmic. The bodily pleasure suggests a steady, tingling sensation of the nipples and is cast as a glowing sense of peace and contentment. As noted earlier, breastfeeding involves the stimulation of nipples (an erogenous zone) and the release of relaxing hormones, such as oxytocin, as well as milk, which Ruth fantasizes as a golden thread being pulled gently through her nipple. The physiological sources of this pleasure are natural and inescapable, so perhaps it is Ruth's acknowledgment and embrace of this pleasure that is so dangerous, especially as a Black woman.

Such a welcoming of pleasure offers a glimpse of potential maternal eroticism, with which we, as a culture, are not comfortable. How do we talk about pleasure separate from sex? About eros that is not erotic? Or eroticism that is not sexual in the limited ways we tend to think of sexuality (genital and orgasmic)? Ruth's pleasure unnerves because we have yet to account for the reality of the female body or for maternal intimacy with a child, which is both sensual and physically pleasurable. Traina notes that "Opening the door the slightest crack to erotic pleasure in breastfeeding does not inevitably lead, in women's experience ... to pursuit of inappropriate orgasmic pleasure with children" (42). But as responses to Ruth's prolonged nursing both in the novel and in literary criticism demonstrate, no concept of female sexuality exists that can accommodate the kind of maternal eroticism Morrison opens the door to.

Edith Frampton—one of the few critics to positively interpret Ruth's breastfeeding, and most radically so[8]—explains that Ruth's pleasure comes from a sense of power in her own body: "By means of lactation, Ruth ... feels in possession of a 'secret power' that is as valuable as the ability to spin 'golden thread.' With her own body, 'her very own shuttle', she is able to create a seemingly magical substance. Her sense of empowerment, such an excruciatingly tenuous commodity in her life, is a profound 'pleasure she hated to give up'" (148). Frampton offers a much needed corrective to the predominant analyses that disparage Ruth's actions, and she shifts the discourse on the nursing scenes from pathology to empowerment. However, even Frampton stops short of acknowledging the simple pleasure derived from breastfeeding. Although Frampton's argument concerning Morrison's oeuvre, in general, recognizes the importance of body, breast, power, and pleasure in Morrison's treatment of mothers, in relation to Ruth, she only locates pleasure in the power of the lactating body. She shies away from directly addressing the bodily pleasure inherent in breastfeeding and takes recourse to the theoretical idea of there being pleasure in power—a political pleasure. Perhaps, she fears evoking the spectre of incest she is so strongly arguing against, but I would argue that Ruth's physical pleasure needs to be concretely addressed in order to acknowledge the potential intervention Morrison is making in discourses of maternal, and even female, sexuality.

Motherhood for Ruth never conforms to the ideal model of the sacrificial, selfless mother. And although it is arguable that Ruth using her young son's touch to fulfill her needs is troubling, it is not troubling because of the pleasure she experiences in breastfeeding. Her act is problematic because it is selfish and, therefore, unethical. The ethical responsibility lies upon the parent to consider the needs of the child and requires what Oxenhandler and Traina call "erotic attunement"—that is, "constant motion between self-awareness and attentiveness to the other" (Traina 140). Ruth does not engage in such attunement with the young Milkman, whose indifference and sense of obligation she ignores. However, I will reiterate that the reader also does not see him suffer harm, humiliation, or coercion from his mother's nursing. Any sense of shame comes not from the experience itself but from the external meaning imposed on the practice by Freddie, the sexual implications of the name "Milkman," and Ruth's response to being discovered, which suggests an anticipated censure.

Although it is possible to identify sensual pleasure as the motivation for Ruth's behaviour, I argue that such pleasure is natural and even often unavoidable, as opposed to being perverse or deviant. Extending the nursing to prolong the pleasure also need not be problematic, provided the increasing boredom of the young Milkman had been taken into account. Through Ruth, Morrison insists upon a sensual experience of mothering that is both practical and political. Ruth's body is not merely entangled in power structures of race and gender; it is also a body, a sensory organ, and a site of pleasure and pain, much of which she experiences through the physical act of mothering, but which our cultural constructions of the breast and female sexuality cannot comfortably accommodate.

Morrison ultimately invites the reader, through Milkman, to see Ruth's actions in a more empathetic light within the context of her unmet needs for intimacy and human connection. For the majority of the book, Milkman fails to consider Ruth as a person in her own right. However, with the insight and experience he gains through his journey, by the end of the novel, Milkman is able to reflect compassionately about his mother: "The best years of her life, from the age of twenty to forty, had been celibate, and aside from the consummation that began his own life, the rest of her life had been the same.... His mother had been able to live through that by a long nursing of her son, some occasional visits to a graveyard. What might she have been like had her husband loved her?" (301). Milkman not only sympathizes with Ruth but also empathizes with her. With this as the final word on Ruth's nursing practice, he and, I believe, Morrison are asking the reader to consider whether this denial of Ruth's body and bodily pleasure, rather than Ruth herself, is what is truly deviant.

My Education: The Sexual Is Maternal

Whereas Morrison confronts her readers with the sexual that is present in the maternal, Choi forces her readers to engage the maternal in the sexual. Although both authors approach the question of maternal sexuality from two different directions, they both assert the uncomfortable truth that the sexual and maternal bodies are one and the same. If in *Song of Solomon*, there is a cultural attempt to suppress and vilify this truth, in *My Education*, the sexual maternal is challenged by the narrator's insistence on denying and forcing a separation between the two, which is, again, represented most significantly in lactating breasts.

My Education (2013) is the story of graduate student Regina Gottleib's intense love affair with her professor's wife, a new mother and professor herself. Although Regina is initially infatuated with the renowned and raffish Nicholas Brodeur, her fascination blossoms into a passionate obsession with his wife, Martha Hallett. Narrated retrospectively by Regina, the driving force of the novel is this all-consuming affair that upends both their lives as well as Regina's naïve belief in the transcendence of real-life impositions. As a wife, mother, academic, and lover, Martha's various identities, demands, and desires seem to be in conflict. She wants sexual passion, scholarly prestige, and a maternal bond with her son, but these goals do not seem compatibly realizable. Martha ends her already troubled marriage and neglects her academic pursuits to spend time with Regina. However, she remains committed to her infant son, Joachim, who is an impediment to the unimpeded unity and attention Regina desires. Halfway through the novel, time leaps forwards fifteen years to Regina as a married mother herself. Regina's retrospective perspective of Martha is both nostalgically gilded and gently critical—the criticism reserved largely (though not exclusively) for her "imperfect example of motherhood" (237).

The relationship between Martha and Regina, primarily sexual and graphically so, unsettles (most) readers' presumptions about maternal identity through both Martha's bisexuality and Choi's insistence upon Martha's body as simultaneously maternal and sexual, exemplified in scenes that prominently feature Martha's lactating breasts. Although both Morrison and Choi affirm an existence of maternal sexuality that cannot and should not be denied, Choi—writing in an era of greater, though still limited, acceptance of female sexual freedom and diversity—

begins with a bolder challenge to the location of female and maternal sexuality within heterosexual marriage than Morrison. Whereas Ruth accepts that without intimacy from Macon she is destined to live untouched and resorts to intimacy in mothering as her only "balm," Martha is dissatisfied with her sexual relations with Nicholas and refuses to repress her sexual needs to conform to dictates of wifely fidelity. She follows her desire wherever it leads her and where it leads is variable, further challenging the norms by rejecting heteronormativity, despite her position as wife and mother in a heteronormative nuclear family.

Choi presents not only a sexually assertive and autonomous mother who acts outside the dictates of proper femininity and domesticity but one who also opposes the heteronormative "mark" of motherhood.[9] However, this challenge is neither comprehensive nor sustained. Martha is not without ambivalence, an ambivalence that seems to begin with her becoming a mother. She is susceptible to the influence of discourses of good motherhood in her own eyes as well as those of others. And, ultimately, the novel realigns with discourses of restrained maternal sexuality and heteronormativity. Regina makes an unannounced visit to Martha, who has moved to the country with her now teenage son, and then arranges, without Martha's knowledge, for her to be reunited with an old (male) love interest. Why Regina assumes Martha would want to be paired with him is not clear, particularly after Regina and Martha, still powerfully attracted to each other, make love once again. Nonetheless, the final scene depicts a smiling Regina peering in on Martha, this man, and Martha's son, who are seated at a table as a potential nuclear family; she then returns home to her own husband and son. This ending suggests a general allegiance to the discourses of good motherhood as an essentially heterosexual institution. Or, at the very least, it hints at the great difficulty of countering these entwined cultural institutions of motherhood, disciplined female sexuality, and heteronormativity.

Martha's lactating breasts punctuate the discourses of good mother-hood—asexuality and sacrifice—and disrupt the demands for propriety placed on the maternal body. Following her first passionate interaction with Regina, Martha meets with her to insist there will be no further relations. Martha calls upon her age, profession, and, most insistently, her familial status as wife and mother to support her declaration:

"I'm married. That's what marriage is about; you work this crap out. Recommit. I have a child. In fact I have to go now" (65). As Martha speaks, a wet mark on her blouse spreads, punctuating the proprietary call of her child. Perfectly ignorant of the mark's meaning, as she is not yet a mother herself, Regina interprets the growing spot in romantic and symbolic terms. She notes that "in the course of [Martha's] words, her heart had started to bleed" (65). Martha, becoming aware of the stain, though, proffers it as of evidence of her case and dashes away in embarrassment: "She felt it, and her hand went to cover the spot. '"You see,' she murmured but her voice had sunk and its low roughness thrilled me. 'You see, I have to go.' ... *You see, the glance said, my body tells the truth, if you think that I don't*'" (65-66).

This scene demonstrates Martha's difficulty in rejecting discourses of good motherhood; the primacy of maternal duties and the infant's needs coincides with an attempt to free desire from predetermined scripts. Martha's body literally pulls her back from temptation; it physically and visually marks her as a mother. And Martha's parting comment is more complex than it seems. As is insinuated by the desire, regret, and embarrassment in her voice, the "truth" of Martha's body is double voiced: it expresses both maternal embodiment and a sexual desire she is struggling to suppress.

Martha's resolve is short lived. When she later calls Regina to apologize for her abrupt departure, she initiates a series of phone calls of increasing intimacy that quickly give way to a full-blown affair. Unable to concede to the demands of asexual maternity, Martha, instead, tries to keep her sexuality and her mothering separate. The strategy is impossible to maintain for various reasons, one of which being the physiology of lactation. Breastfeeding intrudes repeatedly on their time together and represents Martha's more mature lifestyle and subsequent responsibilities, which Regina cannot either comprehend or accept. Breastfeeding a newborn requires the mother and child to be physically proximate every two to three hours, day and night. Martha has chosen to breastfeed exclusively, and this commitment restricts her movement and freedom to the point that she is unable to be away from Joachim, her infant, for extended periods of time.

Of course, this level of commitment is untenable for many mothers and has resulted in the manufacture of the breast pump, which makes a rare literary appearance in *My Education*. To better accommodate the competing demands of her sexual romantic relationship with Regina and her maternal relationship with her child, Martha purchases a pump and takes it with her on evenings out at bars with Regina, which allows Martha to spend more time with her lover, but she must, as a result, retreat to the car to pump at times.[10] The maternal body—particularly the lactating one—will not be ignored and cannot be escaped or put aside.

Regina seeks not so much a separation between Martha's sexual and maternal selves as an erasure of Martha's maternity. For the most intense period of their relationship, Regina is willfully oblivious to Martha as mother. Her willful blindness is partly youth and naïvete and partly defiance. She is irritated by any imposition on their relationship and jealous of the power Joachim has over his mother's time and also her body. Desire is paramount for Regina; duty, insignificant. (And duty is the only way she can conceive of the claims of motherhood on Martha until she herself has a child.)

In the most striking breastfeeding scene in the novel, where the reader witnesses Regina suckling on Martha's breasts, the impossibility of a separation between the maternal and the sexual is once more apparent. After making love at Martha's home, Martha leaves Regina in her room to tend to Joachim's evening routine, but Regina attempts to assert the demands of her sexuality by descending to the kitchen and intruding upon the domestic scene of mother, nanny, and child. At first, Martha is angry, as she is unable to nurse an unsettled Joachim and is forced to unconvincingly introduce Regina to her nanny as a research assistant. Martha then retreats with Regina to the privacy of the outdoor pergola. When Regina embraces Martha, however, Martha winces in pain, and, again, her shirt is drenched with milk. Her engorged breasts are hard and hot, a physical manifestation of the disrupted mother-child relationship, and Regina rebelliously attempts to restore Martha's body to its sexual state by suckling at her breast, against Martha's initial wishes:

> "No!" she repeated, and now I felt what she must have, over-
> powering me at the start of our day, when she shuddered and
> capsized, emanating a guttural, helpless, admonishing moan as I
> sucked on the nipple until with a shocking mechanical sudd-
> enness, like a shower head being turned on, her hot milk filled
> my mouth. It queasily tasted of vegetation, and of her, but mostly

and sickeningly like itself, but I was so hungry for the taste it obscured, of her flesh, that I gulped it down just to get past it, and past it, and past it, until her soft breast moved and squelched, deflated, underneath the harsh probes of my tongue, and she'd groaned in relief and then grabbed my head literally by the ears, and forced the other hard breast in my mouth.

"You sick thing," she gasped when I was done. (86)

As I have discussed elsewhere, Regina's disgust for the messy, leaking maternal body is undeniable. She is repulsed by both breast and milk and strives to "get past" the maternal to a singularly sexual breast, which she describes as Martha's "obscured ... flesh," but this is, of course, impossible. The maternal and the sexual breast are one and the same (Baiada 8). Young describes this as the "functionally *undecidable* in the split between motherhood and sexuality" (198). Regina acts to reestablish the strict maternal-sexual divide with which society is culturally comfortable, but she does so in a way that evokes discomfort in readers by transgressing the line between the two. In contrast, when Martha latches Regina to her other breast, she is refusing to allow this disentangling of the maternal and sexual, instead insisting on her need and desire for both to exist in that moment. Whereas Ruth Dead's pleasure evokes the sexual in the context of the maternal, the description of Martha's orgasmic pleasure at Regina's suckling affirms the presence of the maternal in the erotic. Martha's pleasure is both sexual and maternal: it results from both the erogenous nipple stimulation as well as from the release of hormones and a relief of pressure in her hardening, milk-filled breasts.

Martha's final words—"You sick thing"—give the scene a kinky twist. This flippant dismissal of her pleasure recasts it as all Regina's doing, deflecting the blame of this transgressive desire away from herself and on to her lover. Martha relishes in the experience of simultaneity but deems it perverse, thereby again reestablishing a maternal-sexual separation. The force of this rare depiction of the potential synchronicity of the sexual maternal experience fails to expand the way society defines and confines mothers.

In acknowledging those pleasurable and sexual desires which do not conform to a socially sanctioned version of female sexuality or of motherhood, Martha, nonetheless, accepts the norms in one more sweeping compromise. She catastrophically ends her relationship with Regina rather than go public with it, but she will not go back to her husband either. Martha, as the reader later learns, does not remain part of a traditional family and continues to have lovers, both men and women, but all transient. Instead, she withdraws from society and centres her life on her son, perhaps because of the difficulty of ordering her sexual desires with the options and identities available to her as a mother.

Conclusion

By acknowledging the physical pleasure of breastfeeding as normal, natural, and socially acceptable, we can counter the damaging consequences of the patriarchal logic that asserts male ownership of the female body and that disciplines it, at least in part, by insisting upon a rigid separation of motherhood and sexuality, which effectively creates a disembodied experience of motherhood as the norm. Morrison's Ruth and Choi's Martha experience sensual pleasure in suckling—a natural physical response that is culturally repressed because it blurs the comfortable distinction between the maternal and the sexual body. Both characters make a bold move by inviting readers to acknowledge and accept a woman-centred experience of their breasts.

However, the manner in which each author refutes trite cultural scripts of maternal sexuality ultimately diverge. *Song of Solomon* makes a modest but firm call for the recognition of maternal sensual pleasure as something that should not be denied. Ruth's desire for love and the right to be touched, acknowledged in Milkman's newfound empathy for his mother, remains steadfast in its challenge to the limited concepts of maternal erotics. *My Education*, in contrast, begins with an excitingly daring transgression of the boundaries of maternal sexuality—asserting both a sexual agency as well as a desire to refuse to conform to heterosexual imperatives. It ends, nonetheless, with Regina's attempt to reinstate Martha in a heteronormative family structure. Even though Choi abjures from definitively resolving Martha's fate,[11] this ending emphasizes not the ability to reimagine maternal identities and sexualities but rather the prodigious social pressures that push back against such reimaginings.

Acknowledgment

I would like to thank the PSC-CUNY for the grant funding my work on this essay and Michael LaCombe and Jennifer Lemberg for their invaluable feedback on earlier drafts.

Endnotes

1. I use the word "motherhood," in the tradition of Adrienne Rich, to refer to the patriarchal institution of motherhood, as opposed to the experience of mothering that is female centred and potentially empowering (O'Reilly, *Mother Outlaws* 1-4).

2. A 2000 study in the *Journal of Midwifery and Women's Health* (see Avery) noted that 41 per cent of nursing mothers in a group of over five hundred urban, white American first-time mothers self-reported experiencing sexual arousal during breastfeeding.

3. For a thorough and incisive review of the literature on breastfeeding and sexuality, see Christina Traina.

4. Macon is uncomfortable with and threatened by Ruth's excessive attentiveness to her father. He is disgusted that her father delivered Ruth's daughters and claims to have discovered her naked in bed with her father's deceased corpse sucking his fingers—an occurrence left deliberately ambiguous in the text.

5. For a discussion of the resonances of the legacy of intersectional racial and gendered oppression and exploitation of African American women on contemporary rates of and attitudes toward breastfeeding, see Patricia Hill Collins and Linda Blum.

6. The characterization of the nursing occurring in the novel as being extended is itself problematic. The age of weaning deemed appropriate rests upon culturally specific standards and varies widely throughout time and place. In contemporary America, while private nursing through toddlerhood may be accepted in particular social groups, public displays, most notoriously the May 10, 2012, *Time Magazine* cover featuring a mother nursing her three year old son, tend to elicit indignation and mother bashing. Of course the *Time* cover, associated with a story addressing the "extremes of attachment parenthood" (connoting transgression of conventional limits) seems likely designed, in its details, to encourage such a response.

7. Morrison identifies "the first part" of Ruth's pleasure as deriving from the room where the nursing takes place, formerly her father's study, and now sparsely furnished with a rocker, footstool, dress dummy, and sewing machine, which are all clearly hers—the space all her own.

8. Others here include Andrea O'Reilly and Marianne Hirsch. Hirsch argues that through her act of nursing, Ruth reclaims Milkman, "repossessing him from the symbolic, connecting him to her with a stream of milk" (85), whereas O'Reilly interprets it primarily as an act of defiance against the assimilatory discourses that shape Ruth's life—"of a culture that demands clear division between women's reproductive and sexual selves" (*Toni Morrison* 143).

9. Jeffner Allen in "Motherhood: The Annihilation of Women" writes that "Stamped, firmly imprinted on women's bodies, is the emblem that our bodies have been opened to the world of men … From conception to abortion, acts which are biologically different yet symbolically the same, our stomachs are marked MOTHER" (322).

10. It is interesting that Choi here co-opts the traditional use of the breast pump as enabling breastfeeding mothers to continue to participate in the workforce the same as men, instead using it to provide her character with the social and sexual license afforded to men, who are generally largely unimpeded by parenthood.

11. For a more developed analysis of the ending of Choi's novel in relation to maternal sexuality and the female story of development, see Christa Baiada.

Works Cited

Allen, Jeffner. "Motherhood: The Annihilation of Women." Mothering: Essays in Feminist Theory, edited by Joyce Trebilcot, Rowman and Littlefield, 1984, pp. 315-30.

Avery, M. D., et al. "The Experience of Sexuality during Breastfeeding among Primiparious Women." *Journal of Midwifery and Women's Health.* 45.3 (2000): 227-37.

Baiada, Christa. "Contemporary Stories of Female Development and the Outer Limits of Maternal Sexuality in Susan Choi's *My Education* and Amy Sohn's *Prospect Park West." Critique: Studies in Contemporary*

Fiction, vol. 61, no. 1, 2019, pp. 26-39. doi: 10.1080/00111619. 2019. 1665491.

Blum, Linda. *At the Breast: Ideologies of Breastfeeding and Motherhood in the Contemporary United States.* Beacon, 1999.

Bouson, J. Brooks. *Quiet as It's Kept: Shame, Trauma, and Race in the Novels of Toni Morrison.* SUNY Press, 2000.

Carter, Pam. *Feminism, Breasts, and Breastfeeding.* St. Martin's Press, 1995.

Choi, Susan. *My Education.* Penguin, 2013.

Collins, Patricia Hill. *Black Feminist Thought: Knowledge, Consciousness, and the Politics of Empowerment.* Routledge, 1990.

Frampton, Edith. "'You Just Can't Fly on Off and Leave a Body': The Intercorporeal Breastfeeding Subject of Toni Morrison's Fiction." *Women: A Cultural Review*, vol. 16, no. 2, 2005, pp. 141-63.

Hausman, Bernice L. *Mother's Milk: Breastfeeding Controversies in American Culture.* Routledge, 2003.

Hirsch, Marianne. "Knowing their Names: Toni Morrison's *Song of Solomon*." *New Essays on* Song of Solomon, edited by Valerie Smith, Cambridge University Press, 1995, pp. 69-92.

Kukla, Rebecca. "Ethics and Ideology in Breastfeeding Advocacy Campaigns." *Hypatia*, vol. 21, no. 1, 2006, pp. 157-80.

Morrison, Toni. *Song of Solomon.* 1977, Penguin, 1987.

O'Reilly, Andrea. *Mother Outlaws: Theories and Practices of Empowered Mothering.* Women's Press, 2004.

O'Reilly, Andrea. *Toni Morrison and Motherhood: A Politics of the Heart.* SUNY Press, 2004.

Oxenhandler, Noelle. *The Eros of Parenthood.* St. Martin's, 2001.

Stearns, Cindy A. "Breastfeeding and the Good Maternal Body" *Gender and Society*, vol. 13, no. 3, 1999, pp. 308-25.

Traina, Christina L. H. *Erotic Attunement: Parenthood and the Ethics of Sensuality between Unequals.* University of Chicago Press, 2014.

Young, Iris. "The Breasted Experience: The Look and the Feeling." *Throwing Like a Girl and Other Essays in Feminist Philosophy and Social Theory*, Indiana University Press, 1990, pp. 189-209.

Chapter Seven

Hot Queer Leather Mamas: Feminist Kink and the Taboo of the Sexual Maternal

Holly Zwalf

"Damn, I wish I was your lover
I'd rock you till the daylight comes
Make sure you are smiling and warm
I am everything
Tonight I'll be your mother
I'll do such things to ease your pain
Free your mind and you won't feel ashamed."

—Sophie B. Hawkins

"Gillian, if you weren't my mother I would make you my wife."

—The Waifs

In keeping with the long-established and culturally imposed madonna-whore dichotomy that prevails in predominantly white, Western Christian-based societies, the maternal body continues to be subjected to intense public scrutiny and is heavily censored and regulated, particularly in relation to sexuality (Bartlett 59-60; Friedan 46). Although countries such as Australia, Canada, and the United States are officially secular, religion still plays an influential role in their legal systems as well as in their social morals. In her work on the maternal figure, feminist theorist Iris Marion Young notes that the Catholic Church has relentlessly promoted the virgin mother as both the height of femininity and the ultimate feminine power (albeit controlled and restricted by the patriarchal constraints of the Church), who is exalted and favoured by God yet who forsakes her sexuality in an act of martyrdom for her child. This story is, of course, the origin of the age-old madonna-whore dichotomy, which haunts women to this day, as it depicts the archetypal mother as gentle, completely absorbed by the child in her arms, and, most importantly, chaste.[1] The good mother, thus, is positioned as mutually exclusive from the "whore"—the sexual woman who is promiscuous and immoral.

This chapter explores the sexual-maternal dichotomy, as well as the problem of maternal essentialism, through a study of queer women, trans men, and nonbinary leather Mommies. Leather Mommies are people who engage in dominant maternal role-play in a BDSM (bondage, discipline/dominance, submission/sadism, and masochism) context and who, in effect, eroticize the omnipotent and nurturing force of the mother. Through an ethnographic study of the San Francisco leather Mommy community, I have observed the leather Mommy's ability to (re)negotiate the interplay between maternal expression and sexuality, feminism, and queer politics. Furthermore, I contend that by transgressing the taboo of the sexual maternal, the leather Mommy offers a fresh critique of essentialism by challenging the way we, as a society, currently define and limit the maternal. At the same time, this chapter also explores the limitations of queer kink and its ability to subvert long-established social norms; it raises the question of whether the leather Mommy is able to succeed in disrupting dominant maternal discourses or, as a product of patriarchal systems of desire, whether she,[2] too, ends up simply reinforcing essentialist ideals.

Despite a long history of feminist engagement with motherhood as an institution, an essentialist definition of the maternal prevails in popular social discourses. These essentialist discourses are both scientifically invalid and theoretically untenable, yet they operate to circumscribe social expectations of women, restricting not only mothers but also those who are excluded from the maternal, such as trans women, trans men, cis-gendered men, nonbinary people, and childless women. For centuries, women in Western cultures have been anchored to the home, to childrearing, and to an eternal commitment to sacrifice everything for the benefit of their families, the ramifications of which are still reflected in the domestic expectations placed on women today. This containment of the maternal is further played out through employment in relation to both race and class with Indigenous women, women of colour, and working-class women caring for the children of families from higher social classes (Colen 78, 86-87). In addition, motherhood is upheld as peak femininity, and, historically, a (heterosexual) woman's worth has been firmly situated in notions of mothering and the family (Zairunisha, this volume). As Ann Oakley summarizes: "Motherhood represents the greatest achievement of a woman's life: the sole true means of self-realization" (186).

With the emergence of feminism, the maternal became a recurring problem, which successive feminist theorists saw as important to address. In the late 1940s, ahead of her time, Simone de Beauvoir forged the path for second-wave feminism, identifying motherhood as a key component of women's oppression—a concern that Adrienne Rich examined in her mid-seventies ground-breaking work *Of Woman Born*. At the heart of the feminist furore is the problem of the so-called ideal mother, who embodies a catalogue of unrealistic (and mostly undesirable) criteria that serve to control women's actions and decisions, regulate their desires, and reinforce a patriarchal definition of the maternal. Included in this list is the expectation that the mother be selfless, provide nourishment, shelter, unconditional love, and endless support to her child, put her child's needs before her own career, sex life, and mental health, and, of course, be joyful in all of these sacrifices (Rich).[3] These sentiments are echoed repeatedly in both maternal theory and contemporary writing on motherhood (O'Reilly; Giles; Ruddick; Bartlett; Longhurst; and Young) and continue to constitute the maternal bench-mark today. Any woman who deviates from this path, feels unfulfilled by motherhood, prioritises her needs ahead of the child's, or (gasp) identifies as queer and/or overtly sexual is deemed a bad mother. She is criticized and condemned in the public eye.

As Young expounds, women are split into two opposing sides: the good, who loves (her children) on a spiritual level and is, therefore, devoid of eroticism or bodily sin, and the bad, who is sexual, selfish, and seeks physical pleasure (87). It is important to note that this silencing of sexuality is not imposed on the paternal—there is no evidence to suggest that a sexual father is restricted or rejected in the same way. Sexual limitations and restrictions are continually placed on the maternal body through systems of approval and disapproval, the good versus bad mother dichotomy, and gendered and economical distributions of parental labour, which see far more women than men continuing to be physically confined to the home.

Consequently, lesbian mothering is also a no-no because of its association with sex: "Lesbians tend to be constructed as bad mothers because, like gay men, they are associated in the popular imaginary, with sexual activity" (Longhurst 126), which clearly conflicts with the virginal madonna ideal. It follows, therefore, that the good mother is also heterosexual (O'Reilly 36). In *Mommy Queerest*, a book further exploring the double bind of lesbian sexuality and asexual mothering, Julie M Thompson makes the following point: "While lesbians are excluded from legitimate maternity because of their ostensibly reprehensible erotic desires and practices, heterosexual mothers are excluded from the enactment of a non-procreative sexuality lest such activity be construed as immoral" (6). If it is subversive for a lesbian to become a mother, then a queer woman role-playing as a mother without even having a child is a two-fold slap in the face of the maternal ideal. In effect, the queer leather Mommy says of the maternal: "I can be this regardless of who I fuck; hell, I can even be Mommy if I don't reproduce."

Considering the role that sex plays in heterosexual reproduction, motherhood has, ironically, for a long time shared a complicated and uneasy relationship with sexuality. In the past ten to twenty years pregnant women have started to sex up their maternity clothes and mommy images in a seeming defiance of the compulsory demure, asexual maternal body (Longhurst 51, 72; Cass this volume). However, with the exception of several recent phenomena such as the yummy mummy, the MILF (Mom I'd Like to Fuck), and the emergence of a new genre of soft erotica patronizingly dubbed "mommy porn"[4] (sparked by E. L. James's *Fifty Shades of Grey*), mothers are generally told by the media, by their peers, and by people on the street that the maternal and sex do not mix.[5] The white, middle-class maternal body is expected to be asexual, in keeping with the long-established and culturally imposed madonna-whore dichotomy (Bartlett 59-60; Friedan 46). Yet the inverse of this is true of Black mothers and poor mothers, who are overly sexualized and also heavily judged (West; Pinterics and Baida, this volume). Either way, the mother and her sexuality are constrained by notions of appropriate maternal behaviour.

The sexual maternal is threatening because it has the potential to empower motherhood and to free the maternal from its patriarchal constraints (Young 84-89). People are, at best, uncomfortable with a sexual maternal body and, at worst, aggressively censorious (Newby 48; Longhurst 67–80). Women are labelled bad mothers if they have casual sex, date multiple partners, or work in the sex industry ("Mother and a Whore"; Dodsworth 100)—in other words, if they share their physical body with someone other than the baby (Longhurst 103). Although it is obvious that women who are mothers are, or can still choose to be, sexually active, what is not openly discussed is whether a mother is able to exercise her sexual agency—that is, to actively desire and, most crucially, to derive a private, intimate pleasure from her maternal labour.

The notion of a sexual mother seems to elicit a level of queasiness in many, as highlighted in the musings of the author of *Real Stories of Motherhood*, a light-hearted mommy memoir:

Most people are strangely uneasy about the combination of mothers and sex—my husband doesn't even like me to utter the two words in the same sentence, especially if I'm talking about his mother. It seems to have escaped his notice, at least in the bedroom, that I am now a mother. I sometimes wonder if it would be the end of our sex life if he put two and two together. (Newby 48)

Disappointingly, this attitude is not restricted to the heterosexual world. In a published conversation between queer femme activists Barbara Cruishank and Joan Nestle, they discuss an event they both attended where there were lots of lesbian moms present:

BC: It was so unsexy.

JN: You just can't combine babies and sex. (114)

This exchange reflects a common attitude in the queer community: as far as sex appeal goes, once you have a baby, you are no longer of any interest. Even though the maternal and the sexual constantly touch and merge, new mothers still feel the pressure to transform from a sexual to a maternal being (Bartlett 59-60).

Thus, I embarked with great interest on my study of queer women, trans men, and nonbinary leather Mommies. Before examining the gender politics at play in the leather Mommy community, it is useful to first look at who or what, exactly, a leather Mommy is. A leather Mommy is a dominant top, who is likely to be, at different times, nurturing, caring, authoritarian, and disciplinary. A Mommy scene consists of role playing between consenting adults,[6] in which one person assumes the dominant role of "Mommy" and the other plays the submissive role as the "Boy/Boi," the "Girl/Grrl," the "Little," the "Baby,"[7] or simply as the sub, or the bottom. A Mommy space was often described as being "loving and warm" (Velvet[8])—a safe, intimate, and smothering place steeped in nurturing, caring energy.

The majority of the Mommies I interviewed also strongly identified with a 1950s aesthetic, which was significant in itself. As Betty Freidan's *The Feminine Mystique* illustrates, the 1950s housewife cliché speaks of an era when the domestic realm, namely the kitchen, was portrayed as a woman's only stronghold—the one place where she was able to exercise any sense of independence and authority (15-19, 43-46, 238-42). Not only was the home marketed as the source of feminine power in the 1950s, but it was a space populated almost solely by women and children, with little interference by male authority. Ironically then, with men largely absent from the home and a bevy of disempowered housewives sitting bored in the kitchen, the 1950s, with its overbearing patriarchal potency, unwittingly creates the perfect backdrop for a lesbian Mommy play scene.

The 1950s domestic ideal, however, was largely aimed at white, middle-class women, as advertising omitted Black and working-class mothers, many of whom had no choice but to work outside the home. It is interesting, then, to draw parallels between the Mommies' fascination with the 1950s fetish and northern American BDSM culture in general, both of which draw on dominant white and Western hierarchies of power. As kink theorist Margot Weiss affirms, BDSM presents a microcosm of "broader social, political, and economic formations: the links (and tensions) between leisure and labor; consumerism and desire; race, class, and neoliberalism; and politics and privilege" (28). Unsurprisingly, in her studies of the San Francisco kink scene, Weiss found the perpetuation of normative values to be prevalent, and I found the queer leather Mommy community to be no exception—a point I find slightly amusing considering that in queer kink circles, the community is so dedicated and committed to subversion.

I spent eight months living in San Francisco studying the local queer leather Mommy community. A large portion of my methodology was participant observation. I was already personally involved in the queer kink community when I began my research, and midway through, I also began to engage in Mommy scenes myself. By attending gigs, sex parties, and lunches with people from the San Francisco queer BDSM community, where I interacted as both a participant (member of the community) and as an observer (researcher), I was able to familiarize myself with the community and to get to know some of the leather Mommies on a personal level. My research was not covert. Through word of mouth and because I discussed my work frequently and publicly, the Mommies soon became aware of both me and my research, and none of our informal interactions were directly referenced in my research notes or my findings.[9] Being a member of the community I was researching was useful not only in being accepted as a peer but also in the quality of information I was able to gather. I used my membership with the queer kink community as a method for connecting emotionally with my participants and creating a space where they felt comfortable enough to open up to me (Bolton; Hennen; Lunsing).

In addition to participant observation, I also conducted online ethnographic research in fetish chatrooms, and I interviewed seven self-identifying queer, San Francisco-based leather Mommies. The Mommies varied in age from their mid-twenties to late sixties. There were Brown, Black, and white women in the group, with and without disabilities, and from a mix of working- and middle-class backgrounds. It is impossible to portray a definitive picture of the leather Mommy, as desire is as multifaceted as the individuals who engage in it. Even when my interviewees diverted from the earlier generalized description of being nurturing and smothering they all still agreed that, just like a mother, the biggest allure of being Mommy was in occupying not just the centre of someone's universe but in being their whole universe: they got to be authoritative, omnipresent, and omnipotent.

The leather Mommy capitalizes on this position of maternal authority while fetishizing stereotypes of femininity and perverting conventional perceptions of phallo-centric power. She eroticizes maternal tropes, the power of the mother, and the vulnerability and helplessness of the child; she defies social taboos by revelling in the sexual maternal. The very things that oppress us as mothers—the policing of gender and the insistence on the interrelatedness of femininity, maternity, the home, domesticity, and childrearing—become erotic toys in the leather Mommy's hands.

The leather Mommy, therefore, appears to solve the problem of the uneasy relationship between the maternal and the sexual body by divorcing the maternal from any relationship to female instinct, biology, or acts of parenting; instead, she embraces the maternal as a purely hedonistic site of pleasure. Adrienne Rich describes the childless woman–mother dichotomy as the only two options available to women (250). The leather Mommy, in contrast, effectively straddles the middle ground between the two, creating a liminal space external to patriarchal conventions. Furthermore, because the leather Mommy is a self-defined identity, anyone can access it, regardless of their gender. The leather Mommy allows us to consider the possibilities of a maternal self that is not biologically determined or restricted, that can be performed and perverted, and that is accessible as an erotically pleasurable practice.

Troublesome Tits: Why the Leather Mommy Matters

"After having a baby, there was this way that I kept feeling, early on, that it was like falling in love because my pussy was sore, my tits were sore, and I was gazing into somebody's eyes in that way, that like, newly falling in love is.... My body kept telling me that it was, and I kept getting kind of confused and thinking it was sexual pleasure ... and it was, at times, breastfeeding.... I felt like I couldn't figure out who I was sexually, and so much of it had to do with nursing because I am completely identified around my tits, and those were utilitarian."

—Velvet

From a physiological perspective, the idea of separating the sexual and maternal bodies is completely ludicrous.[10] The severance of motherhood from sexuality filters down into the way children are educated about relationships and reproduction (Salsbury and Chapman, this volume): young children (mostly female) are instructed on how to look after a baby but are often not taught about how the baby was conceived or even about how the baby is born (Oakley 192-93). In terms of heterosexual unassisted reproduction, the vagina that (hopefully!)

orgasms during intercourse is the same vagina that can nine months later push out a baby; the nipples that were hard and erect during the moment of conception are the same nipples that are now breastfeeding that child (Hrdy 538; Rooks, Baida, this volume). Desire and utilitarianism cohabitate; it is impossible to separate the body.

A friend of mine who works with young, socially disadvantaged mothers once commented that most of her heterosexual clients had chosen not to breastfeed because it made their partners jealous. Young notes the same phenomenon: "The separation between motherhood and sexuality within a woman's own existence seems to ensure her dependence on the man for pleasure. If motherhood is sexual, the mother and child can be a circuit of pleasure for the mother, then the man may lose her allegiance and attachment" (87). It is incredible to imagine that because the male partner himself cannot differentiate the sexual and maternal body,[11] he is resentful of his own child seeking nourishment; however, the prevalence of negative reactions to public breastfeeding support this suspicion.

The tensions between sexual and nonsexual understandings of the maternal body are highlighted in the popular outcry that still occurs around public breastfeeding (Walks 136-37). Because the breast is first and foremost read as a sexual object, it is supposed to be kept away from public space, partly because breastfeeding introduces the breast into the public gaze but also because breastfeeding can be a pleasurable experience: "Breastfeeding entails prolonged stimulation of one of the most sensitive parts of the female body, which involves sensitive pleasure and causes the uterus to contract rhythmically.[12] In a culture which represses female sexuality, this is something to be avoided" (Oakley 195). Thus, although mothers are taught to ignore the pleasurable sensations of breastfeeding, the leather Mommy embraces them. For the majority of my participants, their sense of "Mommy" was deeply situated in the breasts, as they used the (nonlactating) nipple to soothe, calm, or smother their partners, and, of course, for the mutual pleasure of suckling.[13]

Young sees breastfeeding as both a site of empowerment and of rebellion. She provides an example of breastfeeding her daughter and describes her progression from the nursing chair to the bed:

> After some weeks, drowsy during the morning feeding, I went to
> bed with my baby. I felt that I had crossed a forbidden river as I

moved toward the bed, stretched her legs out alongside my reclining torso, me lying on my side like a cat or a mare while my baby suckled. This was pleasure, not work. I lay there as she made love to me, snuggling her legs up to my stomach, her hand stroking my breast, my chest. She lay between me and my lover, and she and I were a couple. From then on I looked forward with happy pleasure to our early-morning intercourse, she sucking at my hard fullness, relieving and warming me, while her father slept. (88-89)

Young is in no way advocating for the sexualization of children in this passage; rather, she is acknowledging that "love is partly selfish, and that a woman deserves her own irreducible pleasures" (90). The eroticism in this scene is unabashed; the pleasure she is taking in her maternal duties is palpable.

By embracing the sexual maternal, or more realistically, by admitting to the sexual pleasures of mothering, "we may find some means for challenging patriarchal divisions that seek to repress and silence those experiences" (Young 89). Young goes on to say the following: "Crashing the border means affirming that women, all women, can 'have it all.' It means creating and affirming a kind of love in which a woman does not have to choose between pursuing her own selfish, insatiable desire and giving pleasure and sustenance to another close to her, a nurturance that gives and also takes for itself" (90). In effect, Young argues for seeing the maternal as a site of pleasure and not one simply for service, which is specifically what the leather Mommy achieves. "Without the separation of motherhood and sexuality," Young says, "there can be no image of a love that is all give and no take" (87). The ideal of the selfless mother no longer carries any weight.

Of course, the leather Mommy is anything but selfless. She revels in the pleasures of mothering and blows apart the madonna myth by boldly declaring a decidedly nonvirginal relationship to the maternal. So does the leather Mommy have it all? As Young suggests, the leather Mommy is an embodied space that challenges patriarchal inscriptions on the maternal body by defiantly disrupting those divisions demanded of mothers. Yet the aversion to a sexual maternal is still played out in the way those who engage in Mommy play are received, even within the sex-positive, radical queer kink community, which, ironically, prides itself on breaking down and challenging norms and gender binaries. As

Momma Ruth explains, "It's been okay to be Daddy and to be Daddy's Girl, where it hasn't been okay for Momma to be sexual, because Momma[14] is the whore or the madonna, and being both is really, really hard." There was general agreement among the leather Mommies that members of the wider kink community often find the idea of a powerful and sexually active maternal figure to be disturbing or distressing. Similarly, this discomfort reveals that even among queer women, feminine sexuality is still perceived as a threat.

The Childless Maternal

Filling Mother's Shiny Boots—The Leather Mommy as a Substitute

"Motherhood ... well, I didn't like the term.... I mean that's been one of the main spaces that ... the feminine has been able to be glorified as motherhood. And oh, 'There's not a greater joy or privilege on this earth than to be a mother. Motherhood has given me an identity.' You know, well I say fuck that."

—Mistress Elizabeth

To see the leather Mommy as an expression of the sexual maternal, it must be understood how she can inhabit a maternal space despite being technically childless. Current readings of the maternal, which either define the mother through essentialist or child-centric terms, mean that the mother can only exist in the presence of a child, whereas the leather Mommy is an incongruous exception—she autonomously inhabits a maternal space in her own right. True, a Mommy scene will generally involve at least one person filling the role of a stand-in child; however, there was general agreement among my interview participants that Mommy is not defined by her Boy or Girl. Mommy is an independent and self-defined entity. Mommy would still be Mommy if she turned up to a play party alone, in ordinary clothes, did not engage in any scenes, and simply sat chatting to her friends all night by the chip bowl. She does not need anyone to make her a Mommy—if she calls herself "Mommy," that is enough.

A large portion of current maternal feminist discourse on the deessentialized maternal body focuses on a variety of expansive forms of mothering and the way they disrupt normative readings of the mother. Tuttle Hansen expands the definition of "mother" by arguing that the maternal is not dependent on the continued presence of a child who is given life, love, and protection; rather, the maternal is an act (433). She argues that a mother becomes a mother before the child is even born and stays a mother after the child dies, moves away, or in some other way leaves the mother's custody (445-46). The childless maternal body is defined by neither a child's presence nor its absence—that is, it is not necessary for a child to have ever existed. Perhaps, then, the best example of a childless maternal body is, therefore, the leather Mommy, in which the subject, the Mommy, exists[15] in her own right, independent of any object (child). The Mommy in this case comes into being not simply and exclusively because a child is born but because of her own self-determined and autonomous identification, as well as interaction, with the maternal.

Having said this, more often than not, the Mommies I interviewed did have a Boy or a Girl whom they actively mothered. Several of the Mommies felt that this mothering was equal to the care given to a child—using phrases such as "I raise her" or "I am responsible for him" to, in effect, describe their play as maternal labour—and some also spoke about the large sacrifices they had made in their lives for the sake of their subs, which is similar to the way Rich's ideal mother makes sacrifices for the sake of her children. Mistress Elizabeth always referred to her Boy as though he were her actual son (she even shared the same surname as her Boy—a chosen name, as opposed to legally recognized one). She describes her relationship with him as such: "I do feel like I've gone through motherhood with Scotty. I do feel as though I birthed him from my loins almost."

Mistress Elizabeth's relationship with Scotty raises a poignant question in the recurring debate over what makes someone a mother. If the leather Mommy provides care, love, financial support, guidance, and discipline, then how is her maternal labour so different from that of the parental mother? In answer, Andrea O'Reilly draws a differentiation between mothering (the chosen act) and motherhood (the institution): "The term motherhood refers to the patriarchal institution of motherhood which is male-defined and controlled and is deeply oppressive to women, while the word mothering refers to women's experiences of mothering which are female-defined and centred and potentially empowering to women" (35). She sees this differentiation as being integral to maternal activism. By removing mothering from the institution of motherhood and by challenging the constraints of the maternal (particularly those concerning maternal sexuality), mothering can be free to become not a site of oppression but one of "empowerment" and "social change" (35). Read in this light, then, Mommy play is a practice that occurs outside of the institution of motherhood, but it still involves mothering as an act and, consequently, provides us with an example of what I term the "empowered childless maternal."

Despite the pressure, as female-bodied people, to reproduce (or perhaps because of it in some cases), only one of the Mommies I interviewed expressed any (current) interest in birthing her own child. Most of the participants said they felt that being a leather Mommy satisfied their maternal urges and celebrated their maternal prowess without having to go through a drastic change in lifestyle and personal freedom and without having to engage in the long-term monetary, emotional, or even physical (pregnancy and childbirth) commitment of having an actual child. Jezebel explained it in the following way: "For me, it definitely does help fulfil a want to be maternal.... It's like I really like nurturing, I really like being maternal. I really don't want to have a child, so this is a way that I can be maternal ... without having to have a child." However, it is important to clarify that finding a substitute for motherhood was not a motivating force for any of these women. They all made it clear that they engaged in Mommy play primarily in the pursuit of erotic pleasure.

It may seem obvious at this point to state that despite their similarities, parenting and Mommy play are, of course, very different pursuits. Although many of the Mommies did talk about the huge amounts of work they put in to training and caring for their subs, Mommy play is at its core a fantasy—a (pleasurable) breach of a social taboo that through its reenactment of the maternal disassembles the power structures that establish motherhood as an act of labour. Miss Millie, who was one of the few Mommies who had never had a desire to have children and who also did not relate her Mommy interactions to a maternal identity, illustrates this distinction: "I don't want kids ever. They're expensive and sticky. So, the thing about adult children is ... first of all they're adults, and second of all, you can beat them, like really. You can put them in a closet for like thirty minutes. That's fine." Such a sentiment was echoed by all of the Mommies I met. Being a real-life mother would be nowhere near as fun, or at least not fun in the same ways, as Mommy play!

In a sense, the leather Mommy incorporates the fun parts of being a mother—lavishing love and affection, being adored and revered, and being the boss of everyone. She can forgo the dull bits: cleaning up vomit and shit, playing hide-and-seek for three hours straight, being woken up all through the night and again at 5:00 a.m. when they want breakfast, and rushing them off to school, cricket practice, doctor's appointments, and trombone lessons. The leather Mommy gets to be the fun mom, similar to the weekend dad,[16] who brings treats and takes the kids to MacDonald's and lets them stay up late. Furthermore, the leather Mommy can choose when to take the "Mommy" hat off, which is a luxury not afforded the parental mother.

Most of the Mommies acknowledged that perhaps they would not be so attracted to Mommy play if they had also reared their own children— after all, playing as Mommy is all about fantasy, and not reality. Mistress Elizabeth had this to say: "A lot of women do end up being moms and being a Mommy is not very sexual when you are really a mommy. So I think it would be very hard to eroticize that intense emotional closeness that we're talking about, and constant availability to your offspring." I only interviewed one Mommy who was also a parent. Velvet was the birth mother of a five-year-old, and since becoming a mother, she had ceased to engage in Mommy play. She said that this was partly because her current lover was not interested in that kind of play but also because her maternal urges were now being satisfied by her daughter: "I have been out of that world for long enough that it does seem really crazy to eroticize somebody being helpless, after I've had to like, really really take care of a tiny helpless being, and like, nurture her, into who she is now." Velvet said that her maternal side was now something reserved especially for her daughter and that she did not have the time, energy, or inclination to mother anyone else anymore.

Mommy play, like many sexual kinks, is a fantasy, and the fantasy often ceases to be a pleasure once it becomes a reality. A child loves to play with a toy vacuum, mimicking its mother, but the child does not want to actually vacuum the floor. The subversion, therefore, lies in taking pleasure where pleasure is ordinarily denied. As Velvet reiterated, being a mother was a lot of hard work, and although maternal labour is easily eroticized in fantasy play, the truth remains that it is not so hot in real life:

> Velvet: Let's pretend I have asked you ninety-nine times to pick up your toys and you don't do it.
>
> HZ: Could you eroticize that? No!
>
> Velvet (laughing): No! No.

However, as I anticipated, a large part of the reason Velvet no longer played as a Mommy also seemed to be due to her discomfort around mixing the maternal and the sexual and around being both a mother and a Mommy, which segues smoothly back to my first point—the sexual maternal is deeply feared and is a taboo that sometimes even the fiercest feminists are reluctant to breach.

Conclusion

Does breaking the sexual maternal taboo achieve anything new, or does it simply highlight the current constraints on femininity and the maternal? If nothing else, the leather Mommy shows us that it is possible to take pleasure in the maternal. She is an example of the sexual and the maternal being able to coexist, and she disrupts the expectation that a mother be selfless, self-sacrificing, and tied to the home and the child. She introduces the possibility that the maternal may be something more than just a birthright or a chore.

For the purposes of my argument, the most significant difference between raising a child and mothering in a BDSM context is also concerned with this erotic pleasure: the leather Mommy finds it a turn-on, whereas the parental mother is (supposed to be) turned off. The leather Mommy makes the maternal hot and kinky, and the parental mother takes much of her pleasure from the joy of selfless sacrifice. This conflict leads us to question whether it is possible to view motherhood as a mode of sexuality (as Rooks argues so eloquently earlier in this volume) instead of as a substitute for sexuality as it is traditionally upheld. It is this sensual pleasure that Young believes is the key to empowered mothering—by embracing as opposed to denying these corporeal eroticisms, mothers can reclaim the maternal for their own.

Mommy play also provides us with a model of the childless maternal, in which this pleasure can exist far removed from the materiality of reproduction. Leather Mommies are proof that the maternal cannot be contained by essentialist interpretations of the female body. The maternal is something available to everybody, regardless of gender, age, reproductive ability, or parental status. Yet the leather Mommy still does not transcend all issues related to gender and sexuality.

As Weiss concludes in her study of the San Francisco kink community, BDSM does not operate in its own bubble "outside of social relations and social norms" (6); all material for a BDSM scene is produced from the society in which we live, and, therefore, the players, too, enter the scene as bodies already inscribed by the pressures and pains of socialization and history. BDSM is not as transgressive as we think, since we cannot simply step outside of the power structures dominating our world. That said, the leather Mommy is somewhat unique, as motherhood is not generally considered to be particularly empowering. Therefore, the leather Mummy is not perpetuating a system of power that is already in existence; rather, she is inscribing power into a role that usually has none.

Weiss is not a romantic and does not cling to the queer idealism that BDSM is an emancipated space in which its players can build new worlds and identities that are free from the shackles of patriarchy. I am inclined to agree with Weiss's verdict. Simply performing the maternal is not a guarantee to have reclaimed and reinvented it, and drawing attention to the essentialism of motherhood does not mean that it is not simultaneously being reinforced. These ideas that we play with do not come out of thin air; rather, they emerge from beneath structures of race, class, gender, and sexuality, which are more often than not problematic. But if we can understand sexuality as fluid and the leather Mommy as the epitome of queer—containing within her all the contradictions and desires necessary for playing with the normative—then perhaps we can be content with simply knowing that through the queer leather Mommy, at least, the sexual maternal is able to flagrantly flourish in this space.

Endnotes

1. However this has not always been the case—pre-Christian images of fertility and the maternal figure differ greatly from this vision of the passive maternal. For example in *Larousse World Mythology* (47,

120-21, 223-24, 273, 346, 384, 472), it is claimed that pagan, Aztec, Egyptian, and Chinese maternal images and sculptures often presented the mother as strong, sometimes angry, often warlike, and generally indifferent to the child clinging to her breast or clambering on her knee.

2. All of the Mommies I interviewed used the female pronoun "she," and to varying degrees, all also identified as femme, although several were also either comfortable with gender-neutral or masculine pronouns, or they had butch and masculine-of-centre spaces they also liked to play in. I was briefly in contact with a trans man and also two butch-identifying women who identified as Mommy tops, but they were all unfortunately unavailable for interviewing.

3. The expectation that women are natural-born carers does not stop with children. Henrietta Moore points out that this expectation is also tied in to the assumption that women's jobs are more expendable than men's: "Women are at home in the community to care because they are mothers and do not work, or if they do work it is secondary to their maternal/caring role and they will therefore be happy to give it up" (Moore 98-99). The role of "carer" for the sick and the elderly also automatically falls to women: "No one in their right mind would suggest that a forty-year-old man should stay at home to look after a sick parent" (Moore 98).

4. Australia's discontinued Channel Ten talk show *Can of Worms* held a discussion in October 2012 about *Fifty Shades* asking whether portraying a female character in a sexually submissive role was demeaning to women. Interestingly, however, the discussion took an unexpected turn and instead ended up focusing on whether the term "mommy porn" was a condescending label, implying either that mothers are not sexual or that they require a watered-down version of sexuality.

5. Ironically, however, the taboo of the sexual maternal is also the source of plenty of mainstream pornography, including lactation porn (Giles, 303, 319-22), insemination fantasies (Fetlife.com), and MILF porn, which involves middle-aged women who are supposedly mothers). If the very point of kink is to be kinky, then on the surface this prevalence of MILF porn would appear to undermine my claim that the leather Mommy is subversive. However, the key

factor here is of autonomy: whereas the MILF is objectified, the leather Mommy is empowered. In the act of taking this power for herself, the leather Mommy exhibits her subversion.

6. It is possible that people who are unfamiliar with BDSM may incorrectly associate this kind of role play with pedophilia or child sexual abuse. It is, therefore, important to emphasize the phrase "consenting adults." Mommy play does not involve children and it is not an expression of pedophilic desires; it is a fantasy enacted by consenting adults who wish to embody either a dominant maternal or submissive childlike space themselves: "There is no indication that these individuals are searching for minors or re-enacting incestuous acts from their childhood" (Moser and Kleinplatz 43).

7. I have capitalized all of these titles in order to make it clear that I am referring to play identities as opposed to actual children.

8. All names used in this chapter are pseudonyms to protect the interviewees' identities.

9. Informed consent, minimal risk of harm to participants, including loss of privacy, and genuine knowledge of the aims of the research, are all key factors to consider when designing an ethical feminist methodology (Flick 46; Ferdinand et al. 519).

10. Sarah Blaffer Hrdy, a feminist anthropologist and primatologist, problematizes this grey area between the sexual and the maternal by questioning the way in which these two terms are defined and delineated: "To classify maternal sensations as 'sexual', and therefore in puritanical minds to condemn them, is to privilege sexuality in a very nonpuritanical way, implying that sexual sensations are more important than equally powerful sensations that reward women for caring for babies. We might just as logically describe various orgasmic contractions during lovemaking as 'maternal'" (537). Instead, Hrdy argues that long before humans related sucking breasts to a sexual act, women were experiencing pleasure while suckling children. She asks why the sexual is privileged over the maternal and maintains that "the feelings we identify as sexual were originally maternal" (537-38).

11. I believe that the repulsion directed at women breastfeeding older children originates from a similar space. Particularly in the case of male children, there seems to be an unspoken sentiment that once he has passed infancy and has begun his path to adulthood (and to a

sexual life in which breasts will potentially feature), the mother's breast is now too easily confused with a lover's and, therefore, becomes untouchable.

12. Breastfeeding actually produces sensations in both the mother and child that are akin to erotic pleasure—when a woman breastfeeds her womb contracts and her body releases oxytocin, which is the same hormone released during orgasm (Harel 5).

13. Incidentally, I could not help but notice that they all also seemed to have been blessed with splendidly voluptuous cleavages.

14. Momma Ruth's first use of the word "Momma" refers to mothering, whereas her second use refers to leather Mommies.

15. This idea of existence is borrowed from Judith Butler, who asserts that existence involves interacting with and interpreting gendered discourse within a social context (45), as opposed to simply being, which implies a state of passive inactivity.

16. This is a father who only has custody of his children on the weekends.

Works Cited

Bartlett, Alison. "Scandalous Practices and Political Performances: Breastfeeding in the City." *Motherhood: Power and Oppression*, edited by M. Porter, P. Short, and A. O'Reilly, Women's Press, 2005, pp. 57-76.

Bolton, Ralph. "Tricks, Friends, and Lovers: Erotic Encounters in the Field." *Taboo: Sex, Identity and Erotic Subjectivity in Anthropological Fieldwork*, edited by Don Kulick and Margaret Willson, Routledge, 1995, pp. 140-67.

Butler, Judith. "Sex and Gender in Simone De Beauvoir's Second Sex." *Yale French Studies*, vol. 72, 1986, pp. 35-49.

Colen, Shellee. "'Like a Mother to Them'": Stratified Reproduction and West Indian Childcare Workers and Employers in New York." *Conceiving the New World Order—The Global Politics of Reproduction*, edited by Faye D. Ginsberg and Rayna Rapp, University of California Press, 1995, pp. 78-102.

Beauvoir, Simone de. *The Second Sex*. Translated by Constance Borde and Sheila Malovany-Chevallier. Alfred A. Knopf, 2010.

Dodsworth, Jane. "Sex Worker and Mother: Managing Dual and Threatened Identities." *Child and Family Social Work*, vol. 19, no. 1, 2014, pp. 99-108.

Ferdinand, Jason, et al. "A Different Kind of Ethics." *Ethnography*, vol. 8, no. 4, 2007, pp. 519-43.

Flick, Uwe. *An Introduction to Qualitative Research*. 3rd ed. Sage, 2006.

Friedan, Betty. *The Feminine Mystique*. 2nd ed. Victor Gollancz Ltd., 1964.

Giles, Fiona. "The Well-Tempered Breast: Fostering Fluidity in Breastly Meaning and Function." *Women's Studies*, vol. 34, no. 4, 2005, pp. 310-26.

Grimal, Pierre, ed. *Larousse World Mythology*. Hamlyn, 1965.

Harel, Danielle. "Sexual Experiences of Women during Childbirth." 2007. The Institute for Advanced Study of Human Sexuality, dissertation.

Hawkins, Sophie B. "Damn I Wish I Was Your Lover." *Tongues and Tails*, Columbia, 1992.

Hennen, Peter. "Fae Spirits and Gender Trouble: Resistance and Compliance Among the Radical Faeries." *Journal of Contemporary Ethnography*, vol. 33, no. 5, 2004, pp. 499-533.

Hrdy, Sarah Blaffer. *Mother Nature—Maternal Instincts and How they Shape the Human Species*. Ballantine Books, 2000.

Longhurst, Robyn. *Maternities—Gender, Bodies and Space*. Routledge, 2008.

Lunsing, Wim. "Life on Mars: Love and Sex in Fieldwork on Sexuality and Gender in Urban Japan." *Sex, Sexuality, and the Anthropologist*, edited by Fran Markowitz and Michael Ashkenazi, University of Illinois Press, 1999, pp. 175-95.

Moore, Henrietta L. *A Passion for Difference—Essays in Anthropology and Gender*. Polity Press, 1994.

Moser, Charles, and Peggy J. Kleinplatz. "Themes of SM Expression." *Safe, Sane and Consensual: Contemporary Perspectives on Sadomasochism*, edited by Darren Langdridge and Meg Barker, Palgrave Macmillan, 2007, pp. 35-54.

"Mother and a Whore." *Because I'm a Whore.* 11 Sept. 2011, becauseima whore.wordpress.com/2011/09/11/mother-and-a-whore/. Accessed 5 Apr. 2020.

Nestle, Joan, and Barbara Cruishank. "I'll be the Girl: Generations of Fem." *Fem(me): Feminists, Lesbians, and Bad Girls,* edited by Laura Harris and Liz Crocker, Routledge, 1997, pp. 105-18.

Newby, Francesca. *Maternity—Real Stories of Motherhood.* Books Pty Ltd, 2006.

Oakley, Ann. *Housewife.* Penguin Books, 1976.

O'Reilly, Andrea. *Rocking the Cradle: Thoughts on Feminism, Motherhood and the Possibility of Empowered Mothering.* Demeter Press, 2006.

Rich, Adrienne. *Of Woman Born.* Norton, 1995.

Ruddick, Sara. *Maternal Thinking: Towards a Politics of Peace.* Ballantine Books, 1989.

Thompson, Julie. *Mommy Queerest: Contemporary Rhetorics of Lesbian Maternal Identity.* University of Massachusetts Press, 2002.

Tonkin, Lois. "Making Sense of Loss—The Disenfranchised Grief of Women Who Are 'Contingently Childless.'" *Journal of the Motherhood Initiative for Research and Community Involvement,* vol. 1, no. 2, 2010, pp. 177-87.

Tuttle Hansen, Elaine. "A Sketch in Progress: Introducing the Mother Without Child." *Maternal Theory,* edited by Andrea O'Reilly, Demeter Press, 2007, pp. 431-59.

Waifs, The. "Gillian." *The Waifs,* Self-Released, 1996.

Walks, Michelle. "Gender Identity and In/Fertility." 2013. University of British Columbia, dissertation.

Weiss, Margot. *Techniques of Pleasure: BDSM and the Circuits of Sexuality.* Duke University Press, 2011.

West, Carolyn M. "Mammy, Jezebel, and Sapphire: Developing an 'Oppositional Gaze' toward the Images of Black Women." *Lectures on the Psychology of Women,* edited by Joan C. Chrisler et al., McGraw-Hill, 2004, pp. 237-52.

Young, Iris Marion. "Breasted Experience: The Look and the Feeling." *On Female Body Experience: "Throwing Like a Girl" and Other Essays.* Oxford University Press, 2005, pp. 75-96.

Section III

Out of Line: Mothers Who Mess with the (Hetero) Maternal Model

Chapter Eight

Identity Shifts: Who Is the Postmodern Queer Mother?

Joani Mortenson

Thanks to your merciless expectations
    you may be surprised by what is not yet possible
We are here, and we are getting lost
    "Getting Lost" in the Latherian theoretical sense
Our identity is fluid, oceanic, multiple, layered, context informed,
thick, rhizomatic
    calling all the wildness out
    of the vestiges of our underground and horizontal Deluzian
roots

We are the new yawing chasm of birth
    we baste our turkeys with tiny tea cups and tablespoons

The Queer mother:
    Dykes with Tykes, from Twats to Tots
    We are here, queer, and used to you

You and your discursively articulated norms
    the formulaic cultural scripts of sedated suburbinites
We write our own scripts,
    one white ink at a time

We are the Laughing Medusa that you think is a nightmare,
> but truly, we are merely epistemologically and ontologically at odds
> slithering serpentine ball of confusion
> We, the chordata, vertebrata clarify, collude and qualify

We have been well trained in the organization of language
> We know we are the other othered mother,
> We are the comother, coparent, collaborative social mother
> That woman, yo' mama's girlfriend, the auntie, the whore who
stole mom from dad

Ripe, Round, Full, with child bearing hips chock full of stories
Our bodies,
> places and spaces without limits
designed, masterfully
> with well-hung words
> phallically challenged, we are the reckoning of vulvic moon-time
Our cunts are nebulas, our desire cosmic

We are semiotic, axiomatic, Socratic
> We have been and continue to be constructed, constituted,
recapitulated,
> Interpellated. Mother. Maiden. Crone.
I am your abject and my own symbolic architect

Our rapture ruptures the norms, frays the social fabric into too short
short-shorts
We wedge inside the official discourse of maternity
> And re-represent the site

If the world is worded by words, we are multisyllabic, formidable
homonyms,
> we are extravagant and palatial palindromes and acerbic syntax
We are the lesbian lexicon of sans-paternity postmodernist maternity

Chapter Nine

Love Bi the Book: A Chodorowian Examination of the Heterosexual Mother's Love for Nannies in Contemporary Culture

Katie B. Garner

Introduction

L iterature has the power to reflect our desires in ways that make us analyze them, and ourselves, more critically while shifting our understanding of human relationships, which is especially true of novels that centre on the mother-nanny relationship. The recent popular and critical success of Leïla Slimani's *The Perfect Nanny* highlights how complex and compelling this relationship can be and throws contemporary heterosexual relationships into sharp relief against a backdrop of financially procured emotional labour, the contractual conditions of which remain particularly questionable. A troubling recurrence in this genre is that English-language novels about mothers and nannies tend to depict a heterosexual mother in deteriorating or deteriorated relationships with her male partner, who is also often the father of the children, because the man has had an affair with the nanny. Frequently, this situation means the mother's trust has been broken by two people at once, both of whom she deeply values. In other novels, the marriage is damaged before the nanny enters the home. Outside of the childcare services she provides, the nanny invariably serves as a critical support person to the mother-employer herself—a role that is outside the formal purview of her job description. The nanny thus fulfills the role of caregiver not only to the children she has been hired to mind but also to the mother-employer. In both situations, the mother-employer appears to view her nanny as a replacement for both her own mother and her spouse, thereby encouraging the nanny to meet all of the needs these relationships typically fulfill. Although women in the carework field skew heavily towards financially insecure Brown and Black women, novels tend to shy away from this international consistency. A fair number of novels prefer to whitewash the class- and race-based power differences, as will be seen.

My literary analysis of five contemporary novels—*Sans Moi* by Marie Desplechin, *Lucy* by Jamaica Kincaid, *A Gate at the Stairs* by Lorrie Moore, *My Hollywood* by Mona Simpson, and *The Space between Us* by Thrity Umrigar—examines how the experience of enmeshment, as theorized by Nancy Chodorow and Hendrika Freud, is portrayed in novels about mothers and nannies. Only *Sans Moi* and *The Space between Us* take place outside the United States, with the former situated in Paris, France and the latter in Mumbai, India. I argue that the transfer of money in the employee-nanny labour relationship affects enmeshment primarily by offering the mother-employer the opportunity to be cared for as one would by one's own mother while still retaining the lion's share of power—a dynamic that is rarely encountered between a woman and either her husband or her mother. As a result the mother-nanny relationship becomes a terrain in which mother-employers relive past hurts, gain a false sense of empowerment, and exert control over another person.

Reproducing Theory

Nancy Chodorow and Hendrika Freud are two contemporary psycho-analytic psychologists who contend that women triangulate their relationships with their sexual partners to also include either their mothers or child(ren); women, in effect inhabiting both a parental and parented space concurrently. For Chodorow, a woman's desire to care for her children rests less in biology or culture and more in a child's identification and separation with, and from, her own mother. Women, she argues, seek to recreate the pleasant sense of enmeshment they experienced with their own mothers as newborns, which then plays out in adulthood as an attempt to include other women emotionally in their heterosexual relationships so as to replicate the relationships they experienced as infants.

Hendrika Freud, while less focused on the institution of motherhood than Chodorow, troubles the experience of enmeshment[1] and separation by claiming both mother and daughter remain ambivalent about this lifelong dance—a dance that Freud asserts remains more complex than what a mother and son experience because of their shared gender identification. According to Freud, as a girl matures, she "must free herself in part from the internal image of her mother" while establishing a way to accept her sexual feelings and sexual identity (83). Such an endeavour is challenging for women who ultimately identify as heterosexual because the "first love relationship and attachment" a girl experiences is "by definition, homosexual" (84). As a result of her constantly "renewed identification" and love, she remains "doubly linked to her mother" in a way that boys and men do not (84). Freud explains that a girl experiences ambivalence because she "would like to be independent and develop her own identity, [but] she yearns for reunification with her mother" (84). This desire for reunification is especially profound when she becomes a mother herself, according to Freud, because it is at this time, that the "young woman falls back on her own mother" and, as a result, "feels partly like a baby again because of this" (100). Following in this vein, Chodorow highlights that mothering an infant "involves a double identification for women, both as mother *and* as a child" (*Reproduction* 204).

Chodorow, similarly, suggests that female-female friendships become "harder to sustain" as heterosexual women mature and argues that these relationships are also "normatively expected to carry much less emotional weight and not to interfere with relationships to men" (Chodorow, "Mothering" 155). In this case, as in many others, a woman's psychological need for self-reflection, emotional companionship, and support as a mother remains out of sync with the contradictory cultural demands she experiences. It seems fair to suggest that male partners, regardless of data indicating an increase in hours of childcare and chores, still seldom satisfy their partner's needs.

The novels explored here present stories in which female-female relationships take centre stage and often trump the relationship the mother-employer has with her male spouse and/or the father of her children, as well as the relationship she has with her own mother, since older matriarchs seldom, if ever, appear as primary characters in these novels. This interests me for a few reasons. First, although the nanny is hired to care for the children in a family, she often provides some emotional or physical labour to the mother directly, even if this is only through her role as a sounding board for the mother's trials and triumphs. I argue that this role encourages the mother's emotional "regression," of which Chodorow and Freud speak. Second, she is paid help and not kin—a detail that changes the power dynamics of the relationship dramatically by awarding the mother-employer financial leverage she would not ordinarily have, even as an adult, in relation to her own mother, that she would not have as a child. Third, the men in all of these novels are largely absent, which invites readers to examine the ways in which Chodorow's and Freud's work on triangulation comes into play. Issues of enmeshment—the ways in which money and the inherent power struggles within labour relations affect mother-employers' relationships with their nannies as well as the ways in which heterosexual relationships are challenged by the presence of a nanny (who permits a mother-employer to relive the bond she had with her biological mother, albeit from a new place of privilege)—work together to allow readers to examine how nannies assume a unique role in a mother's life.

Enmeshment

In each of the examined novels, the mother-employer forms a bond with the nanny she hires that extends beyond the traditional mother-nanny relationship, which is already more intimate than most labour relationships. Additionally, in most of the novels, one or both of the women in the mother-nanny relationship are new to childcare. As Chodorow points out, new mothers often exist in a shared psychological space of both mother and infant, and as a result, it seems the nannies enter this dramatic tension acting as a proxy mother to both the children, who are her charges, as well as to the mother, who has employed her. This permits the employer to be mothered by a woman she often perceives as (or at least desires to be) wiser than she is about caregiving and mothering.

Mona Simpson, for instance, in her novel *My Hollywood*, illustrates how the triangulated relationship between the mother, child, and nanny can permit the mother to heal her own emotional wounds. Readers learn that Claire, a new mother, has recently hired a woman older than herself named Lola, who is a substitute for Claire's own mentally unstable mother. Claire believes that her "existence had caused too much pain," since "having a child wobbled and undid [her] mother," whereas Lola is strong, capable, and an experienced mother with her own successful, adult children back in the Philippines (Simpson 166). Not only is Claire unenthusiastic about the care she received from her mother, but she suggests she is mirroring her own mother's early anxiety. "Marriage hadn't changed me," Claire explains. "Having a child did. I was a dandelion blown" (24). She adores her son, William, but is apprehensive about the complexities of childcare that seem beyond her ability to master. As a mother of a new baby, Claire does not describe the self-gratifying enmeshment that Chodorow claims reenacts the pre-Oedipal pleasure of the mother-child bond, perhaps because she never experienced it herself as an infant. Instead, Claire identifies with Lola, specifically because, as she says, "I knew my deficiencies and so I selected a supplement. I hired a happy nanny" (12). She respects not only the fact that Lola has raised good, competent children but that she has done so, at least from Claire's perspective, without the ambivalence and guilt she feels so profoundly. Beyond looking for a mentor, Claire also seeks a proxy mother for herself. Lola is herself aware of this: "Americans enjoy to have done for them what a Filipina would do only for children small small" (Simpson 101). Lola claims she does not mind, and it seems she may derive some joy from feeling needed—a troubling narrative choice that reinforces ideas of motherly submission and altruism.

The spectrum of emotional and physical labour supplied by nannies to their employers is broad and diverse. In at least two novels herein, including *A Gate at the Stairs* by Lorrie Moore and *Sans Moi* by Marie Desplechin, readers encounter mother-employers who relish being gazed upon, like young children seeking their mothers' attention. In Moore's novel, a mother-employer named Sarah hires a nanny before she has completed the adoption of a child. The first several chapters consist of trips with Tassie, a young college student, to meetings Sarah has scheduled with prospective mothers, some of which are out of state. Tassie is paid, although Sarah invites her because, as Sarah tells her: "If we hire you, we would like you to be there with us for everything, from the very first day. We would like you to feel like part of our family, since of course you will be part of it" (24). Sarah's husband, however, rarely attends the adoption meetings. In light of Tassie's age, lack of experience, and unfamiliarity with Sarah, she cannot offer her employer much guidance regarding the choice to adopt, but Sarah craves a companion to witness the struggle she has undertaken. Tassie acts as someone for whom Sarah can perform her independence, within a dance of enmeshment and separation. Similarly, in *Sans Moi*, the unnamed narrator-mother describes this same intangible desire: "I was grateful for [our nanny Olivia] being there to witness my efforts. Thanks to her, what was just a sort of contemporary con trick took on the aspect of an epic. I was no longer just a divorced, spendthrift, disorganized woman, but the heroic captain of a ship in a storm" (Desplechin 71). These moments, which transgress boundaries between labour and friendship, are clearly important to the mother-employers but seem less so to the nannies. In *A Gate at the Stairs*, readers encounter Tassie's ambivalence when she asks rhetorically, "How long could this go on? And did it matter, as long as Sarah paid me?" (73). Whereas Sarah tells Tassie she wants her to be part of her family, Tassie feels emotionally removed from Sarah—the attachment is one-sided and unreciprocated.

Sans Moi's Olivia, a nanny who experiences a more symbiotic relationship with her employer, eventually disentangles herself from what she sees as an uncomfortably enmeshed relationship. In this novel, the mother-narrator becomes deeply involved in Olivia's troubled past, which included multiple rapes and drug addiction. Olivia takes the role of a child who needs tending, but she simultaneously leads the narrator into a dark, adult world in which the narrator must abandon her naiveté. The narrator explains, "I am growing in humanity. I don't know if I should thank Olivia for it, or curse her" (175). During this transformation, Olivia takes on a further maternal role by being instrumental in preventing the narrator's suicide. The mother-narrator describes the days during which Olivia watches over her while she is "between life and death" and is treated as a "sick child who's allowed to skip their homework" (191).

However, this dynamic is further complicated: although the mother-narrator frequently positions Olivia as a mother figure, she also mothers Olivia in return. The mother-narrator, who is about a decade older than

Olivia, claims that she is "responsible" for the younger woman, whom she helps by keeping drug-dealing acquaintances away from her (at Olivia's request). The mother-narrator tells Olivia: "You've no idea how much I believe you. I trust you to death" (133). When Olivia responds that that is nice of her, the narrator responds: "It's not nice at all. I haven't got a choice" (133). Her vulnerability and dependence shine through, mirroring a mother-child relationship, which indicates that the mother-nanny bond here transgresses traditional boundaries. The narrator does not indicate why she has no choice, but it seems that her emotional dependence and affection are factors. Although Olivia does not wholly return this feeling, in *Lucy* and *A Gate at the Stairs*, the young nannies almost view their employers as mother figures, or at least as mentors, even while the mother-employers place the young nannies in a similar position, ultimately triangulating their attachment between each other and the children in their care.

When Olivia leaves at the end of the novel, however, the narrator says that the nanny "doesn't look round, she's in a hurry, she's got things to do" (Desplechin 220). Olivia's departure stands in stark contrast to the narrator's now much narrower existence, living back in her childhood home with her parents as she recuperates from her suicide attempt. In the wake of her departure, it is clear that the mother-narrator views herself as the one who "encouraged" Olivia and "was looking forward to her being able to provide herself with a decent income, and a secure future," even though, she, the narrator, "didn't want to work at all" (205). This role reversal is not unlike that which typically happens between mothers and daughters; although the mother starts out as the teacher and protector, she becomes the one who often needs more help and care in later years. In *Sans Moi*, the narrator returns as an adult to her own mother to receive that care; she recognizes that she needs to be mothered herself, whereas Olivia walks away independently in good health.

Only *My Hollywood*'s Lola and *A Space between Us*'s Bhima, who are also the only middle-aged nannies in this corpus (and, for the most part, within the broader genre as well), seem to struggle with maintaining their emotional distance from the women who hired them. The three younger nannies do not. With Lola and Bhima being the only nannies who have their own children, it makes sense that they experience the mother-employer and nanny relationship differently than the younger, childless women do. However, the close, almost mother-child relation-ship the nannies have with the children is not limited to the older nannies—even Olivia tells the mother-narrator that she wants "visiting rights" when she leaves, alluding to the court-sanctioned time parents are permitted with their children after a divorce (213).

The blurred boundaries between being kin and paid help come to the fore in *The Space between Us*, when the housekeeper, Bhima, cares for her employer, Sera, after a particularly brutal beating from her husband. The verbiage is both maternal and sensual. As Bhima applies a salve to heal Sera's wounds, Sera feels "her whole body sigh" under "Bhima's thin but strong hands" as she experiences "life beginning to stir in her veins" (108). Comparing the sensation to the touch of her husband, Sera eloquently explains that "even at the sweetest moment of lovemaking with Feroz, it never felt as generous, as selfless, as this massage did" because "lovemaking always came with strings attached—the needs of the other had to be met" (108). Disregarding the strings she pulls via Bhima's salary, Sera decides that sex is "ultimately a selfish act, the expectations of one body intrinsically woven into the needs of the other," whereas "with Bhima, there was none of that" (108). Instead, "she could just listen to the sound of her body uncoiling" (108). In this scene, Umrigar successfully describes the ambivalence that Freud highlights in her own work. Sera is a passionate, sexual woman with her husband, but she delights in the sensual return to infancy under Bhima's confident and life-giving hands, which offer a physical manifestation of the platonic, albeit profound, love Sera has for Bhima, and which she craves to be reciprocated. Like a child, who tends to be blind to the labour that they require, Sera allows herself to believe that Bhima's work is done out of love.

Although the scene above echoes the maternal enmeshment Cho-dorow and Freud describe, it also summons a scene of profound sensu-ality. Sera, for instance, "almost groaned in frustration when Bhima stopped for a second," and as "Bhima was gently turning her on her stomach and undoing the back buttons of her dress," she could hear the woman murmur her name with pity and love (108-9). As her regression increases, Sera slips into an almost pre-Oedipal space: "Bhima kept talking to her in words and languages Sera barely understood" (109). Sera describes herself as "receding, moving backward in time" to when she was a "young bride sitting astride her new husband's lap as he rocked her back and forth in a sexual rhythm," and later, she moves all the way back to when "she was a small fish floating around in a warm world of darkness and fluids, a being as formless and translucent and liquidy as her bones felt right now" (109). Sera eventually fades, as she is "caught in the undertow of an ancient, primal memory, drowning in a pool of sensation and feeling, old hurts and fresh wounds being exorcised from her body, leaving her feeling as bright and new as the day she was born" (109). Here, along with Sera, Umrigar takes readers to their own infancy, to a point when a fetus is literally enmeshed and all needs are met. As she rests after the massage, Sera decides Bhima "had an eyeglass to her soul" and feels that she had "penetrated her body deeper than Feroz ever had" (110). The joyful enmeshment she experiences mirrors what Chodorow claims occurs between mothers and infant daughters and provides an explanation for why a male sexual partner cannot offer similar fulfillment, although few seem to try in these novels (Rooks, this volume). Whereas the above example is more dramatic than most, it is not surprising that nannies hired to care for children get positioned as mother proxies and also partner proxies to their employers, in arguably disconcerting ways.

Money and Power

I have argued that the relationship between mother-employers and nannies recreates the traditional mother-daughter dynamic described by Chodorow as permitting women an opportunity to (re)experience enmeshment. Yet there is a critical difference in the mother-nanny relationship—money. Caregivers are in a difficult position regarding the commodification of emotional labour. Nannies often report experiencing a genuine sense of affection for their charges, but at the end of the day, these caregivers are paid for their care and affection. The nanny is not paid to care for the mother, but it is often the mother who provides the pay (or at least the choice to pay), making it imperative that the nanny remain in her employer's good graces. Therefore, maintaining a serviceable relationship often involves meeting the spoken and unspoken needs of the mother-employer, not just the child(ren). Money and power are clearly at play in these relationships in ways that are extraneous to the child-mother dynamic, the salience of which appears in several of the novels.

It is not uncommon for mother-employers to experience a sense of benevolence when offering a paycheck for services rendered; they see the money almost as a gift to the nanny, who possesses fewer material and cultural means than the mother-employers. Viewing the situation this way permits mother-employers to overlook the fact that their relationship is commodified and is based on a traditional labour exchange. It also reasserts the mother-employer's power while down-playing her dependence. In *The Space between Us*, for example, Sera congratulates herself for the time and money she extends to secure an abortion for Bhima's granddaughter. And in *Lucy*, Mariah views her goodwill as a means of righting the historical injustice of colonization and makes many attempts to become friendly with her nanny, who is from the West Indies, because she is eager to be accepted by someone she sees as exotic. Like many mother-employers Sera and Mariah seem to believe that the women who work for them should be grateful for the "benevolent" working conditions they have provided. Still, these assumptions permit the women who work for them to gain a moral high ground and sense of power, particularly in Lucy's case. She does not permit Mariah to own the crown of saving a so-called backwards culture without forcing her to simultaneously adopt the roles of benefactor and colonizer by denying her the cultural acceptance she craves.

For another example, the generally modest narrator-mother in *Sans Moi* states the following: "I was incapable of putting a price on what I was offering: the upstairs maid's room ... which wasn't in a very good state.... I included life with us, a key to the flat, and the meals we had together, but how do you work out how much all that's worth?" (56). Olivia is working for free while she gets her life back in order, and the mother-employer tries to justify that what she gives Olivia in kind is sufficient. She recognizes, though, that Olivia's contributions easily outweigh the room and board she offers. Though a single mother, the narrator, who is a freelance writer, works from home, making her child-care needs for her school-age children somewhat manageable. As a result, she begins her relationship with Olivia feeling that she holds the monetary and emotional control; she, after all, is the one offering a young, troubled woman her surplus in exchange for unrequired help with her children.

In time, however, the undercurrent of power shifts: Olivia regains her footing, and the narrator slides into a state of severe depression. The mother-employer quickly grasps how necessary Olivia's companionship and support are, protesting that Olivia's additional help "wasn't fair" because it was not part of the original deal. She feels "indebted, grateful and embarrassed" (59). Although the mother-narrator had not overtly wielded her power previously, her transition from feeling that she is the one with the upper hand to feeling as though she is the one who needs Olivia—much more than Olivia needs her—strips her of her illusions of holding the power in their dyad.

It is interesting to consider the ways in which mothers and daughters may experience ambivalence about the ebb and flow of power between them. Indeed, independence may often be fought for even while a young woman (or an adult for that matter) is fearful of what it may truly require. With this in mind, I argue that the sense of benevolence some of the mother-employers experience when paying their nannies or offering extra financial assistance can morph into a means of acquiring power over the woman they view as a mother substitute. As sociologists Bridget Anderson, Cameron McDonald, and Judith Rollins all independently highlight, not only is benevolence a means of infantilizing the other person in the relationship, it can also serve as a reminder of who holds more material power. The guise of benevolence may mask the mother's insecurity, which is based on their simultaneous vulnerability and attachment, and mimics the dependence a child in a mother-daughter dyad experience. On the surface at least, money appears to invert this dynamic, but as literary critic Marianne Hirsch aptly points out, "a mother is simultaneously a daughter and a mother, a woman and a mother, in the house and in the world, powerful and powerless, nurturing and nurtured, dependent and depended upon" (196). Similarly, as Chodorow and Freud argue, the act of securing autonomy is just as fraught as the sense of enmeshment, and by exerting her power with money, the mother-employer may safely reexperience infancy's intrinsic and vast neediness with an added layer of power.

Simpson's *My Hollywood* provides the clearest example of this power play. In this novel, Claire is a semisuccessful composer and musician, who struggles to create music after her son, William, is born. Despite funding the family's move to California so her husband Paul can follow his dream of becoming a scriptwriter, Claire becomes painfully aware that her career is now technically funded by Paul, her salary being too low to cover the nanny's wages—a nanny who ironically is a requirement for Claire to be able to work. Initially, this insight, mixed with maternal insecurity and innate introversion, leads Claire to feel vulnerable and needy. Paul, who has only had passing contact with their nanny Lola, claims Claire is acquiescing too frequently to Lola's escalating demands and tells Claire she should refuse Lola's recent request for another raise. "There's got to be some point at which we say no," he tells her (172). Claire acquiesces and admits—only to herself—that "pushing Lola seemed more promising than pushing Paul" (170). The employee-employer labour contract is, thus, inherently different to the typically unspoken terms of a marriage-sex contract. At this point, Claire recognizes that although Paul's income covers Lola's salary, it, by extension, also permits Claire to control Lola and entice her to capitulate to Claire's own needs, which, in effect, rewrites her powerless relationship with her own mother.

Interestingly, though, *My Hollywood* is not a story of absolute power corrupting absolutely. Claire is reluctant to push Lola too hard, and although she is aware of the financial puppet strings she pulls, she also cares for her and values the close relationship between Lola and William. More importantly, she is cognizant of the benefits she herself reaps from Lola's companionship. Claire, who often had to mother her own mother due to a long history of mental illness, relishes being cared for herself. She feels important to Lola, even if that importance is tinged with the less romantic hue cast by a paycheck. (Lola, in turn, shows she cares deeply for William, and to a lesser extent Claire, when she turns down a better paying job to stay with them.) Moreover, as Claire's own mother failed to provide a suitable role model, Claire's choices suggest she has few options other than to pay for a mentor. Claire's relationship with Lola offers Claire the opportunity to mirror another woman and, in her opinion, allows her to be a better mother to her son. Consequently, Claire has few qualms about doing what she can do materially to secure Lola's allegiance, including offering her nanny a pair of diamond earrings that she herself covets.

When Claire tells Paul about the earrings, he points out that Lola would probably prefer cash, since she can send it home to her family in the Philippines. Claire, though, cannot comprehend this argument. Like a child offering a hurt parent their favourite toy, Claire can only imagine that Lola wants what she wants. Claire has difficulty deciphering the difference between Lola and herself, and I argue that this is, in part, because through Lola, she reexperiences the psychological enmeshment of infancy, which she did not experience with her mother. Through Lola, Claire has the opportunity to rewrite the dynamics that left her feeling isolated as a child, just as Chodorow suggests: "motherhood may be a (fantasied) attempt to make reparation to a mother's own mother for the injuries she did" (*Reproduction* 90). Claire's burgeoning identification with Lola encourages her to reenact the helplessness she felt as a child, in her relationship with her unstable mother. By helping Lola, she can now repair the memories of those times when her mother needed help and when she, particularly as a child, could not provide it. In other words, Claire wants to provide Lola with material items as a means of saving her substitute mother. It is only at the conclusion of the novel, after Claire separates from Paul and is raising William alone, that she returns to Lola to petition for a relationship based on parity, albeit one in which Lola would still be an employee. Claire seems to want to craft a new type of employer-employee relationship in which Lola has more power, and in which her emotional work and personal feelings are centered in addition to having her financial needs met. It is unclear if Claire's offer to share the work fifty-fifty comes from a place of need, maturity, or affection. Likely, it is all three.

Bisexual Love

Until now, I have largely focused on the mother-employer and her immediate relationship with her nanny, but what still undergirds this work is the question of why each of these female protagonists has such unsuccessful heterosexual relationships with their male partners and rather successful relationships with the nannies who care for their children, in some cases even after the nanny is no longer employed. In "The Cycle Completed: Mothers and Children," Chodorow argues that a (heterosexual) woman "cannot return to the mother in coitus as directly as can a man" (13). She further posits the following in *The Reproduction of Mothering*:

> While [women] are likely to become and remain erotically heterosexual, they are encouraged both by men's difficulties with love and by their own relational history with their mothers to look elsewhere for love and emotional gratification. One way that

women fulfill these needs is through the creation and maintenance of important personal relations with other women.
(200)

Although Chodorow clearly overlooks women who do not become
erotically heterosexual, the point remains that a nanny can rather
seamlessly supplant a heterosexual partner, particularly on an emotional
level. Interestingly, the male figures in these novels do not become
jealous of the nanny, even though the mother-employers develop
relationships that are more intense and possibly more toxic to the
marriage than an impetuous affair. Also, the novelists do not necessarily
suggest that the marriages fail because mother-employers develop such
deep relationships with the nannies they have hired; rather, they suggest
these relationships form because of the sense of lack these women feel
in their marriages and/or romantic partnerships— a lack that is evident
in all five of the novels despite their differing plots.

In *A Gate at the Stairs*, for instance, Sarah's husband Edward rarely
appears. He attends only one of a handful of adoption meetings, and at
the end of the novel he even asks Tassie on a date after her employment
has concluded.[2] Sarah, meanwhile, decides she wants a more involved
partner, and turns to a college student. This latter relationship permits
companionship while still allowing Sarah to see herself as a mentor. The
implicit differentials of control based on age, experience, education,
material wealth, and employment status all indicate that Sarah seeks
nonconfrontational endorsements of her choices rather than real
feedback from a coparent or partner. Similarly, the narrator in *Sans Moi*
is amiably divorced and has a handful of lovers, none of whom offer
substantial emotional connection. Although the narrator knows Olivia
has been doing drugs (even though she says that she quit), the narrator
claims that she did not want to end the relationship because of their
intense conversations (12). She explains: "I loved just being with her,
listening and talking to her," which contrasts with her lover of two
years, with whom she "didn't talk much" and who had not learned much
about her "family ... finances or ... past" (12, 17). Although the narrator
desires a closer relationship with one of the men she is seeing, he breaks
up with her, leaving Olivia to tend to the narrator's wounds. Interestingly,
the narrator, who finds her lover's emotional distance to be attractive,
is also drawn to Olivia because of the emotional intensity they share,
which, again, supports the notion that nannies fill the gaps of

heterosexual relationships in profound ways. Moreover, in part because this work is often the unpaid work of a mother-employer's own mother, nannies remain unremunerated as well.

A similar situation happens in *My Hollywood*. The opening chapter of the novel highlights Claire and Paul's first date, during which Claire describes her desire for a relationship based on equally shared responsibilities. Paul agrees, but his failure to adhere to their agreement leads to their divorce. At the end of the novel, Claire offers a similar (albeit platonic) proposition of shared labour to Lola, who accepts, leaves her children in the Philippines, divorces her own husband, and joins Claire and William in California. Money is no longer her primary motivator, which further complicates the traditional labour contract and more closely mirrors the emotional investment of kin. Lola calls William her true love, and Claire finds her emotional and practical needs are better met by Lola than Paul. Thus, these women willingly forge a relationship that is much closer to the fifty-fifty model Claire initially envisioned with Paul. Still, the financial aspects of the relationship do not permit the parity that is inferred by this fifty-fifty proposition. Simpson ultimately posits that the sexual contract, which Carole Pateman claims prevents women from being free due to their subjugation to men, remains in effect and suggests women may achieve better out-comes—personally, professionally, and as mothers—with one another rather than in heterosexual couplings. Simpson, however, does not show readers what this may look like, thus avoiding the significant problems of class, race, and employment status when it comes to achieving an equal partnership.

In *Lucy*, after Mariah discovers her husband has been having an affair with her best friend, their marriage dissolves, and he moves out. Mariah feels similarly betrayed after Lucy leaves her post before the agreed upon time. Arguably, the level of betrayal is different, but even as she breaks all contact with her husband, Mariah still reaches out to Lucy, hoping, it seems, to continue their relationship. Lucy, though, is less inclined to stay in touch; she seems eager to disengage from a relationship that had helped her confront the ambivalent feelings she had about her biological mother.

Similarly, in Umrigar's *The Space between Us*, Sera, who endured many physical beatings from her husband, grieves his death despite her relief of being free of his abuse. As she learns to live independent of his control, her relationship with her servant Bhima is a steadying force, and Bhima becomes a companion who helps her more than her adult children do. When Sera fires Bhima, based on an undiscovered lie from her son-in-law, it seems both women are bereft. Bhima drowns herself in despair and self-pity but ultimately retreats from the edge, emotionally scarred and alone but alive. Readers are not privy to Sera's grief, although it is evident that this separation will be more difficult than her husband's death. Like Simpson's *My Hollywood*, Umrigar's *The Space between Us* suggests that the relationship between the mother-employer and the nanny may be more rewarding and profoundly more emotional than the male-female relationship.

Both Chodorow and Freud argue that men experience separation from their mothers differently than women; men's separation occurs earlier and is more complete. Therefore, I argue that this difference may affect heterosexual relationships in adulthood and could be a contributing factor in women seeking female companionship outside of the marriage. One could surmise that a heterosexually partnered mother who hires a nanny may succeed in earning social approval for properly transferring her affection to a male partner while still fostering the sense of love and security provided by a mother. The relationship the mother-employer maintains with a nanny is socially sanctioned in the ways lesbian relationships sometimes are not (Pinterics, this volume), and, additionally, it does not undermine her status as a fully independent adult in the way continued dependence on one's mother may. Furthermore, she can reap the benefits of emotionally bonding with a woman whose role is designed to support her, even while maintaining control via the financial power she holds. Still, there seems to be a chicken-and-egg situation at play in the relationship between the mother, nanny, and husband, and it remains unclear whether the male partner becomes less engaged in the relationship as a result of the mother's incapacity to fully transfer her affection to him or whether she chooses the security of replicating the mother-infant relationship because her emotional needs are not met by her sexual partner. These novels do not highlight the early stages of these marital relationships enough to make a definitive assertion.

To be clear, none of the mother-employers in these novels develop a sexual relationship with the nannies they have hired, nor do any of the men, although in at least two of the novels this is not for a lack of trying. Interestingly, none of the husbands challenge their partners' emotional relationships with the nannies, and while it is possible that this is because they are disengaged from the marital relationship and, therefore, do not notice, it seems the male figures in these novels actually welcome the opportunity to have another person available in the domestic setting so that they do not have be fully engaged fathers and husbands. This speaks volumes about the division of parental labour being weighted heavily towards mothers and the subsequent absent father figure trope that prevails in contemporary society. Thus, the father's work and personal pursuits can remain his own in a way that would be impossible without paid help. Paul illustrates this most clearly in *My Hollywood*, when he gets called into work on Christmas day and tells Claire to contact Lola to fill in for him after she complains that she does not want to be alone. It should be noted that although Lola provides Claire companionship and lessens the physical demands of mothering a small child, this does not alter what Claire expects of Paul as a father or as a husband. Still, Lola acts as a placating presence and short-term salve for Claire. Additionally, Paul's later willingness to terminate Lola's employment demonstrates that he sees Lola as a placeholder, who permits him additional temporal and emotional freedom, rather than as an important person who has formed complex relationships with both his wife and child.

Despite these mother-nanny relationships not being sexual, they do, at times, mimic romantic relationships, particularly in the previously described scene from *The Space between Us* in which Bhima tends to the wounds inflicted by Sera's husband. Elsewhere in the book, Sera explains what she appreciates most about her relationship with Bhima: the "unspoken language, this intimacy that has developed between them over the years" (17). Sera describes the "silence that prevented her from reaching out to others, from sharing her darkest secret [that her husband beats her] with even her closest friends," but she notes that Bhima was the "only one who knew, the only one who felt the dampness of the pillowcase after long nights of shedding hot tears" (18). In this case, Sera describes the transparency and empathy that are absent in her relationship with her husband, which suggests that Bhima is privy to a more profound understanding of what occurs in the marital bed than Sera's own husband or her closest friends.

Sans Moi also features a mother-nanny relationship that goes beyond the platonic, as the mother-narrator describes a tension that would befit a romantic relationship: "Her voice affects me like the sound of a mountain spring. It wakes me up and enchants me. I stop working and get up from my desk, I follow her round the flat, everything she says interests me. In all the palpable substance of her body, in all the evanescent substance of her soul, I can't find a single thing that bores me" (128). Despite this emotional attachment, however, she keeps a physical distance from Olivia: "We never touched, it had become a rule between us. If we happened to brush against each other in the flat we apologized interminably. We never kissed each other hello or goodbye" (49). She later intensifies this stance: "The idea of inviting Olivia in [my bed] disgusts me. I'm very fond of her but I prefer everybody to keep their bodies to themselves" (101). This comes despite her somewhat frequent descriptions of enjoying the sensation of sleeping next to one of her handful of lovers, and, arguably, the very fact that she considered the idea suggests feelings that extend beyond friendship. Later, when the narrator attends a performance that Olivia is appearing in, she muses, "How alive my Olivia looks ... how effortlessly she distinguishes herself from the inert matter around her" (137). Although this observation could be interpreted as something akin to a mother's pride, others have attached a more sexual interpretation. Director Olivier Panchot's 2007 movie based on the book depicts a mother who is obsessed (sexually and emotionally) with the nanny—an interpretation that seems overreaching but alludes to the ambiguities of the novel.

Perhaps because the mother-employers all experience a push-and-pull pursuit of autonomy, an uneasy sense of dependency, and a tension between platonic and erotic feelings as they navigate these relationships, they also express chagrin at the lack of recognition that these relationships garner from family and friends. In *My Hollywood*, for instance, Claire mourns Lola's absence after her employment is terminated and compares it to her more recent separation from Paul: "When Lola left, no one had asked anything. The difference had been profound but private, like the end of an affair that turned out to be the love of your life" (329). Like Mariah, who desired a close relationship with Lucy after she left, Claire, too, rues Lola's departure. She misses their comradery but also realizes how much Lola did for her and Will only after she has left, and with this realization comes jealousy of Lola's talents. Later, however, Claire reframes Lola's strengths when she concludes that Lola's ability to be industrious yet not overtaxed was because "in the evening she had me"

Works Cited

Anderson, Bridget. *Doing the Dirty Work? The Global Politics of Domestic Labor.* Zed, 2000.

Chodorow, Nancy. "The Cycle Completed: Mothers and Children." *Feminism & Psychology*, vol. 12, no. 1, 2002, pp. 11-17.

Chodorow, Nancy. "Mothering, Object-Relations, and the Female Oedipal Configuration." *Feminist Studies*, vol. 4, no. 1, 1978, pp. 137-58.

Chodorow, Nancy. *The Reproduction of Mothering: Psychoanalysis and Sociology of Gender.* University of California Press. 1978.

Desplechin, Marie. *Sans Moi.* Translated by Will Hobson, Picador, 1998.

Edwards, Lee R. *Psyche as Hero: Female Heroism and Fictional Form.* Wesleyan University Press, 1984.

Freud, Hendrika C., *Electra vs Oedipus: The Drama of the Mother-Daughter Relationship.* Translated by Marjolijn de Jager, Routledge, 1997.

Hirsch, Marianne. *The Mother/Daughter Plot: Narrative, Psychoanalysis, Feminism.* Indiana University Press, 1989.

Kincaid, Jamaica. *Lucy.* Farrar, Straus and Giroux, 1990.

MacDonald, Cameron Lynne. *Shadow Mothers: Nannies, Au Pairs, and the Micropolitics of Mothering.* University of California Press, 2010.

Moore, Lorrie. *A Gate at the Stairs.* Vintage, 2009.

Nichols, Jennifer J. "'Poor Visitor': Mobility as/of Voice in Jamaica Kincaid's *Lucy*." *MELUS*, vol. 34, no. 4, 2009, pp. 187-207.

Pateman, Carole. *The Sexual Contract.* Stanford University Press, 1988.

Rollins, Judith. *Between Women: Domestics and Their Employers.* Temple University Press, 1985.

Sans Moi. Directed by Olivier Panchot, performances by Clémence Poésy, Yaël Abecassis, and Eric Ruf, Elzévir Films, 2007.

Simpson, Mona. *My Hollywood.* Knopf, 2010.

Umrigar, Thrity N. *The Space between Us.* William Morrow, 2005.

Chapter Ten

Excessive Maternal Embodiment: The Queer Danger of Desirous Mothers

Natasha Pinterics

Normative conceptions of bad mothers are frequently rendered in media and social discourses as, in some manner, lacking. These mothers are said to be missing something essential—skills, money, propriety, discipline, and so on. In her monograph *Maternities: Gender, Bodies and Space,* Robyn Longhurst elaborates on this idea:

> Lesbian mothers are thought to be lacking a man. Mothers on welfare are thought to be lacking financial resources. Drug dependent mothers are thought to be lacking willpower and the self-control to quit their drug habit. Mothers who do not live in nuclear families are thought to be lacking in "proper" families. Teenage mothers are thought to be lacking in maturity and mothering skills. (118)

The construction of poor mothering has been firmly attached to notions of maternal deficit, whether it be lack of proper skills, attributes, comportment, or values. In this chapter, I aim to both acknowledge and extend the trope of maternal lack towards the ways in which particular mothers are deemed unworthy, not because of lack but rather its opposite: excess. I maintain that cultural notions of maternal lack are intrinsically bound up with excess and that it is excess which, in fact, runs counter to our most closely held beliefs about acceptable bodies, desires, and mothering.

Excess in women has been assigned to particular kinds of female bodies—those marked "other" by fatness as well as by sexual desires and behaviours. In "Pathological Bodies," Samantha Murray argues, in line with many other fat and queer studies scholars, that the perception of excessive desire in women and "a refusal to regulate one's needs and impulses" (216) causes considerable moral panic. Women who (are perceived to) eat too much or who (are perceived to) fuck too much transgress the borders of moral and acceptable embodiment. The expectations around the regulation of desires are particularly stringent concerning the norms governing motherhood and maternal embodiment. These censures of excessive desire have rendered aberrant the bodies of queer mothers, mothers who are openly sexual, and fat mothers—they are failed maternal figures. In this manner, queer or overly sexual bodies are situated as unable (or unwilling) to adequately control who and how they fuck, and fat bodies are positioned as those who refuse to control what and how they eat. The act of sex and the act of eating become conflated through moralizing discourses that designate queerness, promiscuity, and fatness contaminated and excessive—capitulations to an overdrive of bodily desires.

Self-satisfaction through the drives of appetite for food or for sex—particularly sex outside of heteronuclear familial norms—is often referenced in terms of potential damage to children through tropes of figurative (or sometimes literal) contagion. Such contagion discourses mirror those of the North American AIDS panics of the 1980s (Esterik), which singled out particular (queer male) bodies as excessive in desire and, quite literally, contagious with HIV as a result of this excess. With this in mind, I want to begin a discussion of how locations of embodiment and excess may provide a particularly queer vantage point from which to examine the practice of mothering when performed by such objectionable, desirous bodies. In their 2011 monograph, *The Queer Art of Failure*, Jack Halberstam maintains that such failures are uniquely queer opportunities for shifting such discourses: "Failing, losing, forgetting, unmaking, undoing, unbecoming, not knowing may in fact offer more creative, more cooperative, more surprising ways of being in the world" (2-3). Analysis of these feared maternal bodies from a position of "queer failure" (Halberstam) provides forms of resistance or reframing to the cultural imperatives seeking to keep all mothering bodies contained, in control, and perpetually focused on the needs and desires of others.

"Reproductive citizenship" refers to the cultural imperative, under neoliberal social dictates, for total focus and strict self-government of the health and wellbeing of the pregnant and postpregnant maternal body (Salmon). As extensions of mothering bodies, reproductive citizenship requires that the health, nurturing, and wellbeing of children be stringently monitored and managed. In order to achieve the status of good motherhood, then, it is expected that "mothers are constantly engaged in caring for their children when young, that they meet their needs without fail ... to the detriment of their own, and that they are willing to take up expert advice in caring for their children" (Lupton 5). This model of reproductive citizenship works quite handily in conjunction with the dominant North American imperative of "intensive mothering," which advocates constant connection with, and attention to, one's offspring and their always arising needs and development (Lupton; McNaughton; Salmon). Some mothering scholars have argued that under the demands of intensive mothering, meeting the care and needs of children becomes tantamount to, or even more vital than, the care and needs of the self. Self-denial and self-control are central, though unspoken, elements of reproductive citizenship as well as the ensuing cultural projections of good motherhood. It is from this vantage point that examining expressions of, and reactions to, motherhood and excess becomes especially productive.

Too Much Mother: What's The Big Deal?

Jennifer Joyner writes in her memoir *Designated Fat Girl* that "A fat person might as well wear a sign with flashing neon lights: I CAN'T CONTROL MYSELF!" (23). Joyner points here to a central, prevailing idea about the relationship between fatness as the absence of self-control. This lack of self-control is linked to morality, overconsumption, and held up as proof of unruly, poorly managed desire (Boero; LeBesco; McNaughton; Murray; Saguy and Riley). Similarly, fat studies scholar Samantha Murray observes that "the 'fat' body is a site where numerous discourses intersect, including those concerning normative feminine beauty and sexuality, health and pathology, morality, anxieties about excess, and the centrality of the individual in the project of self-governance" (213). Each of these anxieties converges upon fat female bodies in Western culture, with significant ramifications for the fat mothering body. Mothers are expected to model appropriate self-management to their offspring. Failure on the part of fat mothers to manage themselves properly produces great anxieties about their capacity to instill both normative values and socially acceptable bodily comportment in their children. We need not look far to see connections between the treatment of queer bodies and fat bodies in white, Western neoliberal culture. The panicked antiqueer rhetorics of the AIDS epidemic are mirrored and repeated in the current rhetorical crisis of the supposed epidemic of obesity. Scientific inquiries, with poorly masked eugenic underpinnings, seek out gay genes and fat genes to rid future generations of both queerness and fat. Abigail Saguy and Kevin Riley significantly position the "epidemic of obesity [as representative of] concerns about the spread of immoral behavior" (913).

In order for fat mothers to appear fit (and the double meaning here is intended), they must affirm the notion that fat bodies cannot be inhabited by a good mothering subject. My own research has found that writing by fat mothers often involves narratives of weight loss that speak, in particular, to the goals of becoming better mothers and better citizens. As a blogger on the *Mamisphere* writes, "I want to set a good example for my children, especially for my two daughters. I want to have more energy to play with them all. And I really want to be able to fit my butt under the bed while playing hide and seek." This mother equates her ability to fit into size and body norms as central to her ability to provide a good example for her children. Similarly, Jacquie at *Fit Mommy Success Stories* says "For now, I just want to show my kids some self-control, what an active mom can look like." In order to access the embodied realm of the good mother, fat mothers must disassociate their fat bodies from the ability to provide adequate mothering and care, from personal wellbeing, and, crucially, from self-control. In other words, because adiposity is presented as deviant and unhealthy, fat mothers must denounce the fatness of their bodies as antithetical to responsible parenting in order to access the potential of good citizenship.

When Joni Edelman wrote her blog post "Why This Mom Is Happier When She's Fat," chronicling her former obsession with thinness and eventual transformation to being happy in and with her now fat body, she clearly struck a raw nerve among readers. The post went viral, garnering comments, tweets, blog re-postings, and countless shares on Facebook. Many of these responses were affirmative; they remarked on the bravery of Edelman's honesty and praised her journey to, and sharing of, fat positivity. Not surprisingly, given the heavy social weight of fat disapproval, her piece also spawned a vast array of negative responses and even rebuttal blog posts such as "Being Fat Didn't Make Me Happy But Being Thin Does." Many of these posts took Edelman to task for her embrace of a visibly "unhealthy body," and, significantly, many also challenged Edelman's ability to be a good mother and role model for her children. They clung to the misguided idea that fatness automatically invalidates the possibility of good health. Exemplary of these sentiments, one commentator says the following:

> I work out because I want to be able to see my kids grow old, I want to be able too [sic] see my grandkids grow up and I want to be able to travel, climb, hike, run around with my grandkids and do many many things are much harder to do when you are huffing and puffing…. I also want to set a good example for my kids and future grandkids in this age of "screen potatoes." It's easy to tell your kids to do the right things, but nothing is more powerful than leading by example.

Common social wisdom, though debunked by many fat studies researchers, maintains that fat people die earlier, and, thus, by virtue of being fat, one's children will be left motherless. Moreover, fat people are viewed as being inactive; therefore, they are unable to perform their role in keeping up with active children and are incapable of setting a good example of healthy living for their offspring. Another commenter on Edelman's blog post takes this everyday acumen a step further: "Stop trying to normalize obesity. It's bad for you, it's bad for your kids, it's bad for society." Such a response makes patently clear the links made between the fear of fatness and its contagions, and goes even further by connecting these contagions to the downfall of society itself. Fat mothers destroy their own bodies, damn the bodies of their present and future children to the same fate, and cause disruption to the individualized health norms and demands of advanced capitalist, neoliberal North American culture.

Too Much, Too Queer: Desiring Maternal Bodies

In *Mommy Queerest: Contemporary Rhetorics of Lesbian Maternal Identity,*
Julie Thomson explains that the cultural anxiety about queer mothering stems from the historical (and arguably ongoing) depictions of the
lesbian as sick, mentally ill, or criminally deviant. These ideologies
were medicalized in the fields of American sexology and psychoanalytic research, and from historical legal proscriptions dealing with non-
procreative sex, this historical baggage, Thomson notes, "anchors the
lesbian in an inherently illicit rhetorical space" (6). The "illicit rhetorical space" of queer motherhood is one that renders the term "lesbian"
or "queer mother" oxymoronic, as Thomson and other mothering
scholars (Mann; Epstein) have noted. If mothers are only to have or
desire sex for biological ends, then it stands to reason that by virtue of
queer women being (incorrectly assumed to be) unable to procreate,[1]
queerness and motherhood together create "a logical implausibility" at
the level of the symbolic (Thomson 6). According to Thomson, the
manner and means with which queer motherhood is deployed as oxymoronic in discourse is telling of "deeply rooted cultural anxieties"
about what motherhood and queerness mean and how they are performed (6), and of a deep-seated fear of the sexual maternal (Cass,
Rooks, and Zwalf, this volume). Part of this deeply rooted cultural
anxiety is the perceived sexual practices attached to the unavoidable
fact of queer and lesbian mother's sexuality, which is seemingly contradictory to maternal practice. Queer women and trans men sexualize
mothering simply by their queerness and cause cultural anxieties
borne of what Jacqui Gabb refers to as "a visible physicality that is
largely absent from traditional representation[s] of family life" (15).

It is not only the maternal that is discomfited by queerness. The
corollary is also true: there are fears within the queer community that
queerness as a category is also disrupted and sanitized by mothering and,
in particular, by the embodiment of homonormativity through
mothering. Queers who mother are often aware of the fears and cultural
prohibitions surrounding queer sexuality and the ability of queer bodies
to take part in what could be deemed appropriately chaste family life.
Perhaps as an attempt to distance themselves from these concept-
ualizations of queer embodiment, there is a tendency to depict lesbian
family life through the singular lens of desexualized maternal devotion,
using wholesome, smiling, and straight-passing images to represent

queer families. In this regard, Gabb comments that using such sanitized images in order to hold on to this claim to normalcy "may obscure our sexuality beneath the shroud of selfless maternal love [and that] images showing loving embraces, devoted smiles and wholesome values are great advertisements for the family [but] they deny our dangerous (queer) sexuality" (16). The problem with this denial, of course, is that queerness is construed as a problematic identity, and in order to properly embody the mother role, one's dangerous queer body, otherness, and sexuality must be fractured and disowned, hidden under a veil of straight-acting and staid-clothed heteronormativity. Given the longstanding history of heteronormativity as a pillar for the institution of the family, many in the queer community find such acquiescence untenable; it neither allows room for personal expression nor produces any lasting social change.

Laura Heston echoes this sentiment and acknowledges that although queers need not necessarily dequeer themselves to parent, those most commonly seen in the media and those who champion LGBT parenting have tended to thrive and be seen as nonthreatening because they perform and are read as normative sexual citizens. Thus, as white, able-bodied, gender-conforming, monogamously partnered, and middle-class gays have been deemed not excessive and, thus, not threatening to the heteronormative order, they reify the "exclusion of the poor, people of color, trans and genderqueer people, the polyamorous, the undocumented, and those practicing any form of sexual kink that might challenge the sanctity of marriage or its purpose as an institution bestowing rights and privileges to a particular relationship between adults (Heston 250-51). The dearth of sexually open, overtly queer mothers in the media and blogosphere speaks to the continuing invisibility of such excessive voices.[2]

Too Much Sex? Of Mothers and MILFS

Queer parents are not the only maternal bodies struggling against the strictures around sexual expression and activity. Heterosexual mothers who openly express their sexuality and desirousness are also subjects of social censure.[3] Take, for example, the viral Facebook image of Ashley Wright practicing pole dancing beside her toddler.[4] The response to this was swift and overwhelmingly vitriolic, accusing Wright of practicing sex work in front of her child and labelling her unfit to parent. Online comments ranged from hypercritical through to aggressively abusive:

> Come here baby and let me show you how I met your daddy and how I put food on the table and clothes on your back. She is teaching her daughter how to work for what she wants.

> How about teaching your daughter to read or count or spell, instill qualities in her that will make her bright and successful? Instead of instilling skills in her that will only benefit her if she needs to degrade herself for money.

> Well she should have some fucking clothes on her ass in front of her daughter... ur only teaching her it's okay to be half naked and dance around a pole and act like a slut yay a hand clap for u... she'll be knocked up by 14 very good mommy not [sic].

Evidently, for many, the act of dancing on a pole is innately sexual and, therefore, renders Wright an unfit mother. Wright has since posted another video, this time breastfeeding her child in a sling while pole dancing, which has similarly gone viral, and was even featured in *Cosmopolitan* online. The critical comments posted on both videos attest to the vitriol regarding the combining of maternal work with excessive sexuality. Responses to Wright, of course, cannot be discussed without also including a discussion of racism. Even without a pole, as a Black woman, Ashley Wright's body is already hypersexualized. Reading for raced and classed intersections with fatness and sexuality, women of colour and Indigenous women are viewed through colonial eyes as excessive and hypersexual by virtue of their race. Clearly, the dual positions of Black woman and pole dancer create a firestorm of reactions about the threat of the excessive, sexual maternal body.

Also relevant to this conversation is the recent memoir-turned-television-movie by white, affluent, Calgary writer Delaine Moore, *The Secret Sex Life of a Single Mom*, in which Moore delights in documenting her postdivorce journey to reclaiming sexual pleasure as a single mother. Although some reactions to Moore's work were positive, many of the critical responses attacked her suitability as a parent as well as questioned her morality, asking whether she was able to be both a sexual being and a decent and caring mother. Some comments have been overtly misogynist in nature: "LMAO! By looking at the photo, I'd say, 'I'd hit that,' but I think I may already have... ;-).'" Thetruthhurts999 writes: "I bet her kids are so proud of mom and can't wait to go to school tomorrow and face their school mates and teachers." Frank96 quips: "sorry kids, I'll be late tonight. Got tied up at the office," and Newtie says, "they are her kids to alienate ... visions of mom tied up in a sex club. Cool!" But it is Putinetrudeau who most plainly expresses the sentiment underlying these critiques: "Doting mothers don't write about sex clubs." Such reactions are patent in their judgments of Moore's sexual experiences and her decision to write about them publicly—and the criticism rests firmly on Moore as a failure in her role as an appropriate maternal figure. Of note here, and perhaps underlying the vehemence of the responses to both Wright and Moore, is a refusal on the part of these mothers to distance themselves from the excessive, a fracturing that is required from anyone seeking to be accepted as a good mother. These two women are overt in their presentation of excess, and this does not go unpunished.

On the surface, it seems puzzling how too much sexual expression on the part of mothers poses such a crisis of morality, especially at a time when it appears as though the sexualization of mothers seems to radiate from every available media outlet. Naked moms adorn the covers of magazines, and moms are working out at gyms on every corner to attain desirable mom bodies in order to be considered and/or feel sexy. Moreover, the ongoing expression of the MILF[5] phenomenon, and the relatively new but now skyrocketing industry of MILF[6] and pregnant and lactation[7] porn, all attest to the cultural acceptability of the sexualized maternal body (Cass, this volume). Yet the criticism directed at Ashley Wright's pole dancing and Delaine Moore's sexual adventures demonstrates that mothering and desire are not easily coupled, even though, at least in heterosexual culture, sex and childrearing are generally thought to be quite literally connected. Patricia DiQuinzio reminds us that "essential motherhood also represents women's sexuality in terms of mothering; it holds that the primary goal of women's sexual activity is motherhood and that women value sexual activity and pleasure primarily as a means to motherhood rather as ends in themselves" (DiQuinzio xiii). Essential motherhood depends on the notion that all women want to be mothers, which entails a valuing of heteronormativity, and of appropriate feminine comportment that is deemed unthreatening to these belief systems. One major point of departure, then, between our socially acceptable MILF and the sexually desiring and active mother seems to be that the figure of the MILF, as an icon in popular culture and pornography, is one to be conjured, gazed upon, fantasized about, and done to, by, and for the presumably straight male imaginary. The figure of the sexually desiring and sexually active mother, in contrast, is active rather than passive and is engaged and interested in fulfilling her own needs and desires (with or without the help of sexual partners).

As it is currently constructed, essential motherhood also demands that the work of mothering be all encompassing—a life's mission or a calling rather than just one part of a whole woman. In this way, mothering work entails the putting of one's own needs and desires on a near-permanent hiatus in order to meet the never ending and constantly shifting needs, desires, fulfillment, and education of one's offspring. To fail to do this adequately—to fail or refuse to engage in the project of containing one's own desires—is to put one's self at risk of being labelled a bad mother. And despite the seeming reclamation of bad motherhood in mothering memoirs of late,[8] those who have been labelled so on account of their maternal excesses experience material sociopolitical ramifications.

Gone Viral: The Contagion of Transgression

Adiposity, queerness, and promiscuity have each, in some way, been linked with concepts of disease and marked as contagious. Margrit Shildrick positions the idea of contagion as the spread of illness or bodily pollutants through touch or even propinquity. She maintains that this perception holds "that a contaminated object is one to be avoided or kept at a safe distance, lest we too become affected, our bodies opened up to the forces of disintegration" (154-55). When the idea of contagion via embodiment and embodied behaviours becomes attached to mothering subjects, the "forces of disintegration" threaten to carry over across generations, perpetuated through the children. Such contagions, those of perversity or fatness or other corporeal excess, are capable of endangering the very moral fibres of society—threatening an unravelling of bodily and social order across generations. In their outgrowing of the tightly bound social parameters of feminine and maternal behaviour, excessive mothers are considered morally suspect, at best, and unfit to undertake the practice of mothering, at worst. An area of paranoia concerning these sorts of unfit mothers is the perception that mothering bodies are conduits of cultural and physical contamination to their children or future children—"a reification of the myth of poor parenting and bodily failures ... reinscrib[ing] these failures on the bodies of the children described therein" (Friedman 15). Put differently, fat mothers, queer mothers, or mothers marked as inappropriately sexually active are contagious in their troubling excesses.

As Natalie Boero explains in *Killer Fat*, a broad range of embodied situations and experiences have been reread through a "postmodern epidemic" lens in order to be understood as medical problems and not as human experiences or differences. For Boero, a "postmodern epidemic" is created when the term "epidemic" is increasingly applied to diseases that are not contagious and for which "no discrete disease entity is required for a phenomena to be identified as epidemic" (4). She cites examples such as teenage pregnancy or school violence and bullying to demonstrate this form of nondisease application. Boero notes that health experts persist in using epidemic terminology for fatness, even though "there is currently no known biological cause of obesity" (4). The framing of adiposity as "epidemic" paves the way for medicalized interventions and the application of discourses of contagion.

The notion of obesity as a social contaminant—that the mere proximity of fat people can render a person at risk of becoming fat themselves—has gained traction in recent years. Tim Brown notes that "despite the lack of certainty about the aetiological pathways for obesity, 'contagion' and 'social contagion' appear increasingly to be the preferred terms used to connote the rapid spread of this particular 'medical(ised)' condition" (120). As Brown identifies here, recent theorizing in the area of obesity has labelled fatness as a disease category that can be physically, psychologically, and socially passed on to others. Fatness, then, has come to be understood as more than just one of many physical conditions of corporeality—it is a disease category that is transmissible to others socially as well as physically.

From this foundation, the notion of fat mothers passing on their unhealthy embodiment to their children is positioned as careless, toxic, and neglectful. The medicalization of fat and the individualistic nature of health prevention discourse in our culture frames such mothers as virtually indefensible and selfish: "Framing fat as an avoidable disease and a disease causing agent assists in characterizing fat women of childbearing age as irresponsible and dangerous to themselves, to their offspring, and to society. They are bad citizens and bad mothers" (McNaughton 185). Passing on fat to children is often seen as the result of teaching a lack of self-control and a propensity for overindulging in unhealthy foods. The notion of inherited obesity has also been blamed on mothers returning to the workplace and neglecting their proper role as caretakers (both nutritional and moral) of the family, relying instead on quick and easy convenience foods (Boero). Further studies, still, position the fat obesogenic mother as having a toxic womb that passes on obesity through unfortunate genes, poor fetal nutrition, or breastfeeding (Beerman; Saguy and Riley; McNaughton).[9]

This rhetoric is increasingly present in social and media depictions of fatness with respect to mothering capabilities, or lack thereof. Ruth J. Beerman, in her dissertation *Containing Fatness: Bodies, Motherhood, and Civic Identity in Contemporary Culture*, reminds us that "the good citizen requires a good body, and good mothers help mould children's bodies into good bodies. A mother failing to do so means a cultural failure of the institution of motherhood" (49). Such perceptions of maternal failure become obvious in repetitive alarmist headlines about the perils of childhood obesity and about fat mothers passing toxins through the womb to their unborn children. These discourses and actions are framed in a rhetoric of mistrust of fat women to make good choices, and they are frequently steeped in racist and classist assumptions about nutrition, bodies, and motherhood. In the words of fat theorist Amy Erdman Farrell, "fat denigration works in complicated ways to reinforce the existence of sexism, homophobia, and all other processes by which our culture categorizes and oppresses people through bodily hierarchies and stigmatization" (136). To compound this reality, the bodies of mothers (and their children's bodies) are differentially policed in terms of their race, class, sexual identities, and other identifiers. In her most recent article on fat stigma and mother-blame, Erdman Farrell maintains that the connection of fatness with racialized and classed identities compounds difficulties in fighting back against state and cultural sanctions, including child welfare seizures due to obesity.

Dangerous Sex

So-called improper sexual expression has long been considered menacing to the social fabric of moral, decent society, particularly that of women and queers who transgress sociosexual mores. David Plummer notes that "twentieth century political discourses on sexuality ... are founded on deep-seated fears of 'different' sexualities as transmissible and dangerous" (43). Determining parental fitness is principal to child custody decisions, and what defines the "fit parent" revolves around conventional notions of heterosexual dyads and of the good mother, which are synonymous with white, chaste, middle-class women (Schulenberg). Norrington explains that the "fear that homosexuality will 'spread' and cause a decrease in morals and procreation" (165) is persistent and demonstrates that fears of intergenerational transmission of queer deviance are still clearly functioning in the construction and maintenance of parenting norms.

Sex workers are also at risk of losing custody of their children by virtue of falling into the excessive sexual activity category and by the perceived irresponsibility of those who would undertake such work. As sex work activist, writer, and mother Annie Temple explains, "social wisdom would have us believe that sex industry workers are terrible parents who routinely jeopardize their children's safety by bringing 'perverts' around, leaving them to raise themselves, and setting an example of depravity." The fear of the viral mother is enacted in both figurative and literal senses when sexual excess is concerned, as sex workers, as well as others who are seen as highly sexual, including (nonhomonormative) queers, are thought to partake in riskier sexual behaviours and, thus, are more susceptible to sexually transmitted infections which can, in turn, be passed along to children in pregnancy. Hausman notes the following:

> The image of the viral mother focuses attention on her body as the conduit for disease, drug addiction, or contamination that ends up in the body of her innocent—and pure—infant.... The viral mother is so because she conceivably could have avoided the infection or contamination of her infant but, having engaged in risky, immoral, or illegal behaviors, she endangers the infant anyway. Choice is thus an aspect contributing to her deviance. (148)

The threat of contagion for excessive mothers, as I argue, is both literal (as with the cases of fatness and sexually transmissible infections) and social (as with fatness, queerness, and other sexual behaviours deemed unmotherly). Key, here, are the ideas that mothers can, and should, choose different and more mainstream normative paths for the good of their children and for the good of moral society.

M/others Gone Wild: Maternal Failures

Samantha Murray has been direct in her criticism of the politics of recuperation in the fat pride movement: a strategic insistence on the autonomous, unambiguous, and self-authoring subject leaves no room for the complexities and negativity that arises from living in fat bodies. In the same vein, Rachel Epstein urges those undertaking queer maternal work to resist the urge to oversimplify this labour and, in particular, to refuse collusion with the disavowal of sexuality from our maternal identities. She explains that it is paramount to be critical "about how we maintain and build on the radical history we have inherited as sex and gender outsiders, as lesbians, as gay men, as bisexuals, as transsexual and transgender people, as queer people ... and as parents" (9) and to consider how to work against the projection of queer families as sanitized replications of the traditional heterosexualized nuclear family ideal. Further to these entreaties, Judith Butler has argued that "discourse becomes oppressive when it requires that the speaking subject, in order to speak, participate in the very terms of that oppression—that is, take for granted the speaking subject's own impossibility or intelligibility" (157). When good, safe lesbian moms eschew what is taboo about queer sexuality and good fat moms espouse weight loss as a necessity of adequate parenting, their repudiation of excess in order to grasp at mainstream good mothering does exactly what Butler warns against: "they participate in the very terms of their oppression" (157).

These discourses reference the mother's literal children but also address the metaphorical futuristic child, the "innocent" that speaks of responsible moral citizenship, a concept Lee Edelman has famously coined "reproductive futurism" (Sperring and Stardust, this volume). The connection of small children to the idea of larger identificatory processes is not without cause. The rallying cries of "but what about the children?" speak to protecting literal children, certainly, but also to the preservation of the culture at large as well as our collective futures through avoidance of the social contagions of maternal excess. In the name of reproductive futurism, both fatness and the hypersexuality of queerness are rendered a threat to the moral fabric and reproduction of good society. Edelman contends:

> The disciplinary image of the "innocent" Child perform[s] its mandatory cultural labor of social reproduction. We encounter this image on every side as the lives, the speech, and the freedom of adults face constant threat of legal curtailment out of deference to imaginary Children whose futures ... are construed as endangered by the social disease as which queer sexualities register. (19)

Similarly, the frequently employed trope of the "obesity timebomb" in mainstream media is used to invoke an apocalyptic future in which healthcare and welfare systems are destroyed and society is doomed to general misery.

It is here that Halberstam's monograph *The Queer Art of Failure* can be of use when looking for an ontological home for mothers who refuse to fit the containment of the dominant mother mould. Halberstam notes the power of such refusals and argues that to become antisocial queer figures "we must be willing to turn away from the comfort zone of polite exchange in order ... to fail, to make a mess, to fuck shit up, to be loud, to bash back, to speak up and out, to disrupt, assassinate, shock, and annihilate" (110). I would argue that despite the obvious literal futurity of reproduction, the fat mother, the queer mother, and the promiscuous mother all loudly answer this call. Mothers who insist on complicating their queerness and fatness as maternal subjects refuse the terms of maternal intelligibility and social acceptability. To be critical and oppositional about motherhood and mothering clearly run counter to normative projections of motherhood. Therefore, despite her seemingly unshakeable link to social discourses of reproductive futurism, the fat mother is also able, as Halberstam puts it, to "fuck shit up" by queering the maternal body. I echo Halberstam in citing the need to

> craft a queer agenda that works cooperatively with the many other heads of the monstrous entity that opposes global capitalism,

and to define queerness as a mode of crafting alternatives with others, alternatives which are not naively oriented to a liberal notion of progressive entitlement but a queer politics which is also not tied to a nihilism which always lines up against women, domesticity and reproduction. (15)

Part of this agenda must be to strive to realize a queer maternal embodiment that neither fractures from the queer nor the maternal but that instead seeks to widen the parameters of both.

How might we use our failed maternal identities and excessive maternal bodies to mark a refusal to play nicely with others? Can we inhabit the "now" of queerly excessive mothering bodies in ways that change future bodies and practices of motherhood? How can we negotiate a place for excess and desire and for the excessiveness of desire? Bringing queer antisocial theory into the maternal consciousness provides us with a way to promote excessive queer and fat activisms that do not make use of defensive strategies that appeal to the good mother, which instead push back, embrace the impolite, and wholly reject the terms of the debate upon which good motherhood and mothering embodiment are based. If we use Halberstam's failure as a strategy, we can imagine what it is we are failing for and to what ends. If we can manage to conjure what our futures might look like, perhaps we can begin to stumble towards them through a critical maternity in our failed and failing excessive bodies, rejecting the social safety with which our mothering roles are supposedly imbued.

Acknowledgment

Natasha Pinterics gratefully acknowledges the support of the Social Sciences and Humanities Research Council (SSHRC). Special thanks also go to Holly Zwalf for her editorial insights.

Endnotes

1. Of course, this assumption erases bisexual women or women with trans or nonbinary partners who have sperm.·

2. Two notable exceptions to this are *Feminist Pigs: Welcome to the Queer Feminist Homestead* (by Jane Ward)—a blog that discusses the politics

of queer life, queer sexuality, and queer parenting, and also *Queer Brown Girl Trying to be a Parent* (by Deb Singh)—a blog at *Shameless Magazine*, which has chronicled both postpregnancy queer sexual expression and parenting in polyamorous partnerships.

3. I note here that relative to the few depictions of excessive lesbian motherhood and sexual activity available, there are significantly higher numbers of heterosexual women advocating their right to be both mothers and sexual beings.

4. https://www.facebook.com/MsWrightsWay

5. The acronym MILF refers to "Mother/Mom I'd Like To Fuck." The term itself was first documented in Internet newsgroups during the 1990s, the earliest known online reference being in a 1995 *Usenet* post about a *Playboy* pictorial of attractive mothers. The term "MILF" was popularized by the 1999 film *American Pie*, and pop group Fountains of Wayne's song "Stacy's Mom" (2003) also took up the MILF phenomenon; their video famously starred Rachel Hunter as the love interest of her teenage daughter's boyfriend.

6. MILF porn is a genre of pornography in which the actresses are usually women in the forty to fifty age group, although many actresses who play MILFs are actually much younger. Central to the typical MILF narrative is an age-play dynamic of older women and younger lovers, both male and female (Friedman).

7. Pregnant porn features women at varying stages of pregnancy. In lactation porn, lactating breasts are eroticized, and, in particular, focus is placed on the spray of milk itself. Some scholars have likened the role of squirting breastmilk to a type of female ejaculation or "money shot" (Musial).

8. The "bad mommy" memoir boom took on a life of its own after the sweeping success of Ayelet Waldman's compelling tell-all *Bad Mother: A Chronicle of Maternal Crimes, Minor Calamities, and Occasional Moments of Grace*. Numerous books and blogs followed in a similar vein, for example, *Confessions of a Scary Mommy; Reasons Mommy Drinks;* and *Toddlers Are A**holes: It's Not Your Fault*. All of these works likewise embrace the label of the trash-talking, no-holds-barred, bad mother, in the face of the ever-mounting pressures of modern motherhood. Significantly, the authors of such works are overwhelmingly white, upper-middle-class, heterosexual,

married, and cis gendered women, with the attendant sociocultural privilege such positionality entails.

9. See www.mommyish.com/2015/09/17/breastfeeding-nutrition-junk-food-ad-campaign-photos/ for a description of a recent ad campaign from the Pediatric Society of Rio Grande positioning breastfeeding mothers as viral conduits for poor fetal nutrition.

Works Cited

Beerman, Ruth J. *Containing Fatness: Bodies, Motherhood, and Civic Identity in Contemporary Culture.* 2015. University of Wisconsin-Milwaukee, dissertation.

"Being Fat Didn't Make Me Happy But Being Thin Does." *Wildly Charmed,* 2015, wildlycharmed.com/2015/02/being-fat-didnt-make-me-happy-but-being-thin-does.html. Accessed Apr. 7 2020.

Boero, Natalie. *Killer Fat: Medicine, Media, and Morals in the American "Obesity Epidemic."* Rutgers University, 2012.

Brown, Tim. "Differences by Degree: Fatness, Contagion and Pre-emption." *Health,* vol. 18, no. 2, 2014, pp. 117-29.

Butler, Judith. *Gender Trouble: Feminism and the Subversion of Identity.* Routledge, 1990.

DiQuinzio, Patrice. *The Impossibility of Motherhood: Feminism, Individualism, and the Problem of Mothering.* Routledge, 1999.

Edelman, Joni. "Why This Mom Is Happier When She's Fat." *Baby Center,* blogs.babycenter.com/mom_stories/2232014-why-this-mom-is-happier-when-shes-fat/#disqus_thread. Accessed Apr.7 2020.

Edelman, Lee. *No Future: Queer Theory and the Death Drive.* Duke University Press, 2004.

Epstein, Rachel. "Queer Parenting in the New Millenium: Resisting Normal." *Canadian Women Studies/Les Cahiers de la Femme,* vol. 24, no. 2-3, 2005, pp. 7-14.

Erdman Farrell, Amy. *Fat Shame: Stigma and the Body in American Culture.* New York University Press, 2011.

Esterik, Penny van. "Contemporary Trends in Infant Feeding Research." *Annual Review of Anthropology,* vol. 31, 2002, pp. 257-78.

Friedman, May. "Mother Blame, Fat Shame, and Moral Panic: "Obesity and Child Welfare." *Fat Studies*, vol. 4, 2015, pp. 14-27.

Gabb, Jacqui. "Imag(in)ing the Queer Lesbian Family." *Journal of the Association for Research on Mothering*, vol. 1, no. 2, 2006, pp. 9-20.

Halberstam, Jack. *The Queer Art of Failure*. Duke University Press, 2011.

Hausman, Bernice. "Contamination and Contagion: Environmental Toxins, HIV/AIDS, and the Problem of the Maternal Body." *Hypatia*, vol. 21, no. 1, 2006, pp. 137-56.

Heston, Laura. "Utopian Kinship?: The Possibilities of Queer Parenting." *A Critical Inquiry into Queer Utopias*, edited by Angela Jones, Palgrave MacMillan, 2013, pp. 245-267.

Joyner, Jennifer. *Designated Fat Girl*. Rowman and Littlefield Publishers, 2010.

Laditan, Bunmi. *Toddlers Are A**holes: It's Not Your Fault*. Workman Publishing Company, 2015.

LeBesco, Kathleen. "Neoliberalism, Public Health, and the Moral Perils of Fatness." *Critical Public Health*, vol. 21, no. 2, 2011, pp. 153-64.

LeBesco, Kathleen. "Quest for a Cause: The Fat Gene, the Gay Gene, and the New Eugenics." *The Fat Studies Reader*, edited by Esther Rothblum and Sandra Solovay, New York University Press, 2009, pp. 65-74.

LeBesco, Kathleen. *Revolting Bodies? The Struggle to Redefine Fat Identity*. University of Massachusetts Press, 2004.

Longhurst, Robyn. *Maternities: Gender, Bodies and Space*.Routledge, 2008.

Licata, Elizabeth. "Awful New Campaign Shames Mothers for Eating Junk Food While Breastfeeding Because Nothing You Do Will Ever Be Good Enough." Mommyish, Sept. 17, 2015, www.mommyish.com/breastfeeding-nutrition-junk-food-ad-campaign-photos/. Accessed Apr. 7 2020.

Lupton, Deborah. *Medicine as Culture: Illness, Disease and the Body*, 3rd ed. Sage, 2012.

Mann, Bonnie. "The Lesbian June Cleaver: Heterosexism and Lesbian Mothering." *Hypatia*, vol. 22, no. 1, 2007, pp. 149-65.

Martin-Evans, Lyranda, and Fiona Stevenson. *Reasons Mommy Drinks.* Three Rivers Press, 2013.

McNaughton, Darlene. "From the Womb to the Tomb: Obesity and Maternal Responsibility." *Critical Public Health*, vol. 21, no. 2, 2011, pp. 179-90.

Moore, Delaine. *The Secret Sex Life of a Single Mom.* Seal Press, 2012.

Murray, Samantha "Normative Imperatives vs Pathological Bodies: Constructing the 'Fat' Woman." *Australian Feminist Studies*, vol. 23, no. 56, 2008, pp. 213-24.

Musial, Jennifer. "From 'Madonna' to 'Whore': Sexuality, Pregnancy, and Popular Culture." *Sexualities*, vol. 17, no. 4, June 2014, pp. 394-411.

Norrington, Janette. "Does Parental Sexual Behavior Influence 'Parental Fitness' and Child Custody Determinations?" *The University of Maryland McNair Scholars Undergraduate Research Journal*, vol. 3, 2011, pp. 161-69.

Plummer, David. "Girls' Germs: Sexuality, Gender, Health and Metaphors of Contagion." *Health Sociology Review*, vol. 16, no. 1, 2007, pp. 43-52.

Saguy, Abigail, and Kevin Riley. "Weighing Both Sides: Morality, Mortality, and Framing Contests over Obesity." *Journal of Health Politics, Policy and Law* 30, no. 5, 2005, pp. 869-923.

Salmon, Amy. "Aboriginal Mothering, FASD Prevention and the Contestations of Neoliberal Citizenship." *Alcohol, Tobacco and Obesity: Morality, Mortality and the New Public Health*, edited by Kirsten Bell et al., Routledge, 2011, pp. 212-25.

Schulenberg, Jennifer. "Same-Sex Rights for Lesbian Mothers: Child Custody and Adoption." *Canadian Woman Studies/Les Cahiers de la Femme*, vol. 19, no. 45, 1999, pp. 45-51.

Shildrick, Margrit. *Embodying the Monster: Encounters with the Vulnerable Self.* Sage, 2002.

Smokler, Jill. *Confessions of a Scary Mommy: An Honest and Irreverent Book About Motherhood: The Good, the Bad, and the Scary.* Simon & Schuster, Inc., 2012.

Temple, Annie. "10 Reasons Sex Workers Are Great Mothers." *The Naked Truth*. Apr. 24, 2015, www.nakedtruth.ca/2015/04/ten-reasons-sex-workers-are-great.html. Accessed Apr. 7 2020.

Thomson, Julie. *Mommy Queerest: Contemporary Rhetorics of Lesbian Maternal Identity.* University of Massachusetts Press, 2002.

Waldman, Ayelet. *Bad Mother: A Chronicle of Maternal Crimes, Minor Calamities, and Occasional Moments of Grace.* Anchor Press, 2009.

Chapter Eleven

Engorged: Fucking (with) the Maternal–An Analysis of Antinormativity, Cultural Legitimacy, and Queer Authenticity

Sam Sperring and Zahra Stardust

"I sat in that fertility clinic waiting room, on my own, surrounded by heterosexual couples, while taking thesis notes in my 'erotic maternal and kink' text books and fielding off questions from the receptionist and from the other patients about when my husband was going to arrive."

—Holly Zwalf, *Engorged: Fucking (with) the Maternal*

It was cozy inside The Red Rattler Theatre, a popular queer activist hub in Sydney's Inner West, where we settled in for a one-off event called *Engorged: Fucking (with) the Maternal*. Holly Zwalf, the organizer and MC, was approaching eight months pregnant on the night of the event. Holly is a queer woman, a kinkster, a smutty spoken word artist, and a solo parent by choice with a PhD on leather Mummies; on this night, her stomach was swollen, and her curves stretched tight under a leopard print dress.

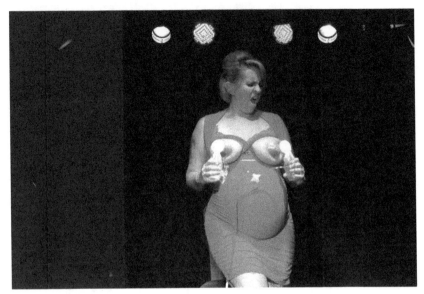

Figure 1: Holly Zwalf, Photo by Grace Kingston

We both had a personal and professional relationship with the *Red Rattler,* a volunteer, artist-run warehouse and one of the few licenced premises in Sydney for experimental performance art and live music that professed queer, feminist, and antiracist politics. We were both writing PhDs that explored queer activism and world-building projects—Sam studying the relationship between queer theory and queer activist practice and Zahra examining queer and feminist pornographies. At the time of *Engorged*, Sam was on the Red Rattler's board of directors, having spent a significant part of her twenties in that space. Zahra had performed at many Rattler events since its establishment in 2009, including film festivals, fundraisers, community panels, and workshops. Concerning the *Engorged* performance, we were excited to hear local stories about queer experiences of parenthood but also to witness how narratives (and critiques) around breeders, world making, and futurity came into tension with one another.

The evening commenced with an acknowledgement of the traditional owners of the land on which we met, the Gadigal people of the Eora Nation. This was not a fleeting reference—we were there to talk about family, both biological and chosen, and to remember the thousands of Aboriginal parents whose children were stolen by the Australian government in the name of protection. We were there to remember that it is not over—as the Northern Territory Emergency Response continues with welfare restrictions and income quarantine for remote Aboriginal communities (Stringer), and the postcolonizing relationship of dispossession and displacement of Aboriginal people remains ongoing (Moreton-Robinson), Aboriginal children continue to be removed from their families and remain overrepresented in out-of-home care at ten times the rate of non-Aboriginal children and rising (Evershed and Allen 2018). Grandmothers Against Removals, who received the profits from the event, continue to fight against forced adoption.

This was the backdrop against which queers—queer parents, trans parents, femme parents, butch parents, foster parents, adoptive parents, solo parents by chance, solo parents by choice, sex worker parents, fat (activist) parents, differently abled parents, prospective parents, leather families, kink families, chosen families, and people who have decided not to have families—had been invited to come together and imagine (and fuck with) the maternal. The callout for performers invited anyone, from spoken-word artists through to dancers and singers, to help put on "a night of entertainment that explores the queering of/fucking with the maternal in all its wonderful, perverse, transgressive, subversive beauty."

The callout for *Engorged* spoke to the ways in which queers have reimagined family in ways that constitute and consolidate nonhetero-sexual identities. The kinds of relationships that queers have forged with motherhood and parenting have emerged directly because of our different relationships, by both desire and necessity, to reproduction and the state. Sex workers, for example, in facing criminalization and the threat of social services removing their children, have worked collectively to share resources and have "created communities of mutual aid, sharing income and childcare" (Smith and Mac 6). Among African American women—"who often feel accountable to all the Black community's children" (Collins 130)—Patricia Hill Collins argues that the experience of nonbiological mothers ("othermothers"), who share mothering responsibilities with biological parents ("bloodmothers"), constitute nurturing family networks that contribute to "building a different type of community" based on an "ethic of caring and personal accountability" (130). Intergenerational kinship networks are also foundational to Aboriginal Australian systems of care, and they govern the individual's roles, responsibilities, and relationships to culture, land, ceremony, and others. The work of vogue "house mothers" in ballroom communities in Western Sydney, such as Bhenji Ra, who are overwhelmingly trans women of colour, involves taking responsibility for the community's children (younger members of the community) and looking after one another in a world that will not look out for you. In these contexts, nonnuclear, nonbiological, nonheteronormative forms of mothering become crucial to surviving and thriving.

Engorged was both a playful and sombre affair: queers arrived with stories about their interactions with the "straight state" (Canaday) and with what Lauren Berlant and Michael Warner have referred to as "a constellation of practices that everywhere disperses heterosexual privilege as a tacit but central organizing index of social membership" (555). Various acts at *Engorged* described barriers in a system in which heterosexuality is assumed and inscribed at multiple levels: paternalistic attitudes towards single parents in the welfare system, lack of visual representation of multiple family configurations in popular culture, and repetitive conversations about male role models at fertility clinic counselling sessions. In reaction to these barriers, queers have reimagined nuclear family forms in ways that constitute and consolidate nonheterosexual identities, such as through the cultivation of nonbiological or chosen families (Weston), gender-norm-resistant parenting, and Mummy or Daddy kink play (Weiss), to name a few. The pervasive inscription of hetero norms onto nonheterosexual kinship and family systems, alongside increasing queer resistance to heteronormative domesticity, raises a contradiction made evident through *Engorged* that this chapter will, in part pursue—that queer parents are simultaneously positioned as insufficiently heterosexual by straight state institutions (Pinterics, this volume) and not queer enough (and, subsequently, "unfuckable") within certain queer social networks.

Engorged told stories of heartache: experiences of abuse, of miscarriage, and of navigating mental health. There were reflections about being a mother, losing a mother, being wounded by a mother, and becoming estranged from a mother. And these stories were overlaid with saucy tales of finding pleasures in bodies, fluids, and transgressions, and of reclaiming reproduction from the realm of medicine or even from the human. From bare-breasted breastfeeding poetry to tales of pregnant cruising on hook-up apps, conception role-play, and play parties, sex was ever present in the room.

The use of the word "fucking" in the title of the show also spoke to a queering of motherhood, which we saw represented quite literally through the gender identities of the parents and prospective parents involved in the event. "Motherhood" was not positioned as inherently connected to gender: the DJ for the event, b(racket), was a masculine-identified birthing parent, who proudly navigated chest feeding his baby for eighteen months. When the MC introduced him, she related the story to the audience that his toddler had eloquently said, in the week leading up to the show, "him's my mummy." Bastian Le Gîte, a queer nonbinary person and sex worker activist—whose work was read by kink performer and trans rights advocate Danny Xanadu—relayed the emotional impacts of existing outside a procreative, heteronormative system and the sheer exhaustion of trying to fit that system:

> But no, no amount of queer drunk toilet fucking can take away the fact that now you are trying to fit "into" the system, just enough to be able to carry out a function that most every other straight XX bodied person has fucking done (from the looks of it anyway), and that you don't fit into the system. Not only do you not have a partner, not female and XX, let alone a cis-dude, you don't have a stable job, you don't fit into the gender binary (but you are sure as hell trying). You don't fit all these criteria you need to get help here. Hell, it's not even "help" cos you are paying for it on top of all this, as the government does not sponsor "people like you" to reproduce. So you'd better be rich. You'd better fit into this gender stereotype. Maybe even it would be beneficial to start selling your arse again. Maybe that would increase access to this ever-evading sperm pool, plus help with funds. So yep, you femme it up. But then realize that it's not easy.

Figure 2: Danny Xanadu, Reading a Piece by Bastian le Gîte,
Photo by Grace Kingston

Bastian's reflection that the government "does not sponsor 'people like
you' to reproduce" speaks to the biopolitical organization of populations—a focus taken up by queer theorist Paul B. Preciado writing on
state heterosexualism. Although in Australia queers can access assisted
reproduction services at fertility clinics, a diagnosis of infertility and a
doctor's referral are required in order to access the Medicare rebate for
subsidized treatments. Many queers will not be medically infertile,
meaning they cannot presumptively access the rebate. Instead, they
are considered, on paper, "socially infertile": as a couple or as a solo
person, they may be incapable of producing sperm or having a uterus.
Social infertility does not attract subsidies from the state. In practice,
many fertility donors are willing to declare a queer woman infertile if
she has had two to three failed IUIs. However, heterosexual couples do
not face the same burden. This is not because heterosexual reproduction is natural; rather, as Preciado writes, heterosexual reproduction is
merely politically assisted procreation. Preciado reminds us that "Mol-
ecules do not care about the conventions of social gender, marriage, or
heterosexuality, yet all human procreation is politically assisted,
requiring a collectivization of a body's genetic material through a more
or less regulated social practice" (405). Doctors continue to act as

gatekeepers of assisted reproductive technologies, making quotidian determinations about who is eligible and who can access parenthood.

One art installation at *Engorged* explored the potential erotics of assisted reproduction technologies in order to disrupt the medical gaze. Viewers were invited to peer inside a box with the words "Live Sex Peepshow" emblazoned on a banner above the peephole, at photos of porn performer Zahra Stardust undergoing an intrauterine insemination (IUI) procedure. The artist statement asked, "Is this sex?" In another photo, a nurse is seen injecting donor sperm into Stardust's cervix with a syringe. The erotic experience of looking in through a peephole, down a speculum, and into a dark cavity was intended to blur the boundaries between clinical procedure, procreative penetration, medical fetish, and sexual voyeurism.

Figure 3: Zahra Stardust, Installation, Live Sex Peepshow. Photo by Grace Kingston

The narratives of *Engorged* are replete not only with reminders of social, cultural, economic, and infrastructural barriers to reproduction but also with examples of reconnaissance and resistance, such as forging new relationships to make pregnancy, parenting, and family (in multiple manifestations) possible. Reinscribing and re-working the popular narrative of procreation, Zwalf recounts: "I'm going to tell you a little story about where babies really come from. When a person with some sperm loves a person with a uterus very much, as friends, the person with the sperm hangs out in my apartment with a jar and his boyfriend and spoofs into the jar while I pretend to hang the washing out."

Although finding humour in uncomfortable moments was a reoccurring theme of the performances, *Engorged* was also bursting with tales of sexual pleasure told with candour and pride. Performers revelled in exploring and enjoying their pregnant and postpartum bodies and functions in the face of social scripts that render them undesirable or unnatural. Smash E'Claire, sitting on stage in a domestic setting while folding clothes, squirted her own breastmilk into a glass of gin and devoured it. Such uses of breastmilk are not isolated. In her book *Fresh Milk: The Secret Life of Breasts*, Fiona Giles documents the multiple ways in which people share and enjoy breastmilk, from grandmothers breastfeeding grandchildren through to strippers squirting breastmilk at clients (Giles xi-xvi). In honour of her breasts, Meredith Dreha performed this poem at *Engorged* while another woman stood beside her with her breasts exposed, wearing a tight leather skirt and standing proudly in an erotic pose:

> ode to thyne breasts
> oh my breasts, my breasts, sweet sagging breasts
> rippled with stretch marks across my chest
> the right (shhh don't tell) and larger left, were put to the test
> prodded, scanned, squished, biopsied, no less
> my two friends have passed these arduous tests
> SIMPLY LABELLED LUMPY
> a fountain of feasts had my son from these breasts
> survived another day to nurture, rest, and play
> no longer a weak man's toy
> forever mine to pierce and enjoy.

Not only are breasts here removed from a positioning through the male gaze, but Dreha is also reclaiming her body and sexuality away from ownership by others; she is restating her own capacity to make decisions about risk, safety, and pleasure, and is reinscribing the maternal while nurturing the breast with an autonomous sexuality (Baida, this volume).

Alice, who passed her eight-week-old baby to a friend before climbing onstage, described with much delight her experience of being fisted at a crowded play party while heavily pregnant ("Be shocked, or incredulous, or horrified, or even judgy: Yes, I was pregnant, and one day, I knowingly walked into a smoke-filled room filled with filthy perverts"). Her piece detailed her experience of grazing her urethra whilst having sex because her copious ejaculate had washed away the lube. Of her subsequent experience in the emergency department, she recalled the following with a sense of pride:

> The clinicians were kind but incredulous. They could not stop asking me what I was doing to sustain gashes like that. The only other time they can recall having to put a few stitches in someone *before* they gave birth was this one time a woman "overdid" the perineal massage.

The confusion of the medical staff here echoes recurring narratives in queer literature concerning the medical profession's distrust in individuals' knowledge and understandings of their bodies, an experience that is common for trans and gender diverse people. Dean Spade, for example, writes of the acute "gulf between trans community understandings of our bodies, our experiences, and our liberation, and the medical interpretations of our lives" (24). For lesbian, bisexual, and queer women, interactions with clinicians often illustrate a lack of knowledge about the sexual health needs of these populations and position their sexual practices as risky, dangerous, and irresponsible. The apparent surprise over the appearance of a heavily pregnant woman in emergency due to injuries sustained from adventurous sexual activity speaks to the medical expectation that mothers will be asexual or sexually conservative (Cass, this volume).

By contrast, practices of fisting can actually be useful in the preparation for childbirth. Queer literature on fisting describes the practice as one that—like childbirth—requires cooperation between the body and mind. Dinesh Wadiwel writes the following in his piece "Sex and the Lubricative Ethic":

> The practice is by nature gentle and ... requires care and skill on the part of its practitioners... fisting also involves an elaborate web of communication strategies, as well as the often painstaking process of "coaxing" the body into a position of comfort where this practice may become possible ... a connection and synergy between body organs. (495-96)

Preparation for childbirth—through breath, perennial massage, and muscle relaxation—is not dissimilar.

In another example of the disjuncture between medical and individual understandings of queer bodies, Zwalf tells of being heavily pregnant and visiting a chemist for thrush cream with her Tinder date, where despite her reassurances, she received a long schooling from the pharmacist, presumably concerned about her duty of care and about how she should not use the cream applicator because she might accidently break her own waters:

> She obviously can't tell that I'm a slutty single mum. In the last three days, I have had two different sets of fingers and tongues on and in my cunt. I've had two different fists inside me. I've been fucked with a speculum. I've had two cocks, at the same time. And now Tinder woman is grinning because she happens to know that I've even had a whole string of fairy lights inside me in the last twenty-four hours. And the pharmacist turns to me and says, "I'm just going to take the applicator out of the packet to make sure you don't use it." How fucking patronizing.

Throughout the event, Zwalf tells multiple stories about her pregnant dating adventures on Tinder. These stories are told in defiance of expectations that mothers are bad mothers if they have casual sex, multiple lovers, or work in the sex industry ("Mother and a Whore"; Dodsworth 100). But Zwalf's stories also reveal contradictory responses within queer communities about the place of pregnancy in queer sexual practices:

> There was the woman who was all up for it right until the moment I said, "So meet me tomorrow night? And just so there's no

surprises, I'm five months pregnant." Silence. "Don't worry, I'm not looking for a co-parent, just a shag! Lol!" More silence. Luckily I had a backup swipe waiting in the wings. Backup woman barely bat an eyelid. "Yeah cool, so what hotel are you at, and what toys do you want me to bring?" Score.

In some cases, the Tinder tales provide examples of strangers learning to navigate desires, risks, and pleasures without assumptions about people's bodies, kinks, traumas and needs—approaches that queer sexual cultures aspire to. Zwalf tells of 'kinky poly spunks who have researched how to do Shibari safely on a pregnant body" and gives examples of navigating potentially awkward encounters using clear boundaries, consent, and communication:

I can't lie on my stomach.
I should only really lie on my left side.
I find it hard to come unless I'm on my back, but I should only be on my back for about five minutes.
If I lie flat I feel sick, so I need to be propped up a bit.
Can we move out of the kitchen? Because the food is making me feel a bit queasy.
Sorry, pregnancy makes me fart sometimes.

In these examples, pregnancy becomes an ordinary part of queer life that can be navigated frankly, openly, and unashamedly during intimate encounters rather than a state of being that exists outside of, or acts as a barrier to, sexual subcultures or pleasures.

In a further step towards complicating the pregnant and sexual bodies, at one point in the evening Calmbirth—a childbirth education program aiming to inspire "couples to experience birth with knowledge and confidence [that] prepares couples mentally, emotionally and physically"—is compared to being "just like conscious kink." This comparison offers an example of approaching childbirth queerly; *Engorged* performers can transfer the skills they have learned in the BDSM scene about transforming pain to pleasure and apply them to childbirth. Scholarship has documented the ways BDSM and kink players manage and reorient experiences of pain, with a focus on negotiation, skills, and safety (Wiseman; Weal; Easton and Hardy; Thorne). Queer poet and author Maggie Nelson reaffirms the relationship of BDSM and kink to childbirth with regard to her own pregnancy. She writes that concerns over "shit and labour" or accommodating a baby's head "did not strike me as exceedingly distinct from what happens during sex, or at least some sex, or at least some of the sex I had heretofore taken to be good" (84). Immersion in queer cultures and practices then has the ability to shape our orientations towards desire, pregnancy, and labour.

This blurring between sex and childbirth shares common ground with the movement for orgasmic birthing, which rejects the medicalization and alienation of the birth process and seeks pleasurable, "empowering, [and] memorable births" (Davis and Pascali-Bonaro). The use of BDSM skills in pain management, pleasure maximization, and communication for the purposes of birthing also shares similarities with the movement for active birthing (Balaskas), which advocates for people to have more control and decision making over their birthing experience in order to become active participants rather than passive observers. Lived experiences of bodily pleasure during birth, breastfeeding, and mothering complicate normative scripts about mothering as simply a turn off that is mutually exclusive to eroticism; they reinforce Zwalf's conceptualization of motherhood (this volume) as a model of sexuality rather than as a substitute for it.

Figure 4: Smash E'Claire, Photo by Grace Kingston

The stories were not all celebratory. Facing each other onstage and sharing letters about how they coped (or did not) when they came out as queer and bisexual, a mother and daughter shared with each other their personal stories of the effects of mental illness, queerness, as well as mothering and daughtering upon their relationship over time. Another performer delivered a heavy spoken word piece titled "The Living Daylights," which was written "for all the other survivors" and was steeped in the weight of memories of her abusive mother. Remembering in flashes the heat and terror, threats and beatings, she towered over the audience in high-heeled leather boots, covered her scars and asked "Is this why I am kinky? What we do with this intergenerational trauma, and how do we recover?"

Figure 5: Stella Delight and Her Daughter, Missy, Photo by Grace Kingston

Later in the night, some *Engorged* performers delved into their experiences as sex-working parents. They shared experiences in which their sexual labour had been read by others as inconsistent with parenting and used as grounds for mandatory reporting to demonstrate their unfitness in child custody cases or used as a tool for blackmail by former partners. One of the *Engorged* performers compared her reception as a pregnant woman from sex work clients in contrast to prospective queer dates. Recalling Tinder stories in which queers had expressed discomfort or unease around engaging sexually with a pregnant body, recounting what she perceived as queers' conservative attitude towards breeding, she contrasted this with the enthusiasm over her pregnancy in sex work spaces: "I've charged an astronomical amount to straight men who desperately want to have sex with a pregnant woman." In this account, despite general queer celebration of nonnormative sexual practices, she found more openness from heterosexual men than from the queer (non–sex working) community to finding pleasure in the erotic maternal.

Queer sex workers are in a unique position because despite engaging directly in sex for work, there remain barriers to conception. As Bastian le Gîte said in their spoken word piece, despite an oversaturation of semen in the workplace, access to sperm for the purposes of reproduction can be particularly fraught:

> dominating rich American businessmen on a daily basis, and all those nights (and days) of queer riot lovin' ... regardless of all these years of naked business dudes, their money, their fantasies, hell, even their jizz, when it comes down to it, even after all these years, when you really need some sperm, some good quality fucking jizz, it's really hard to find it!

This conundrum of being surrounded by sperm but having difficulty finding a sperm donor is also shared in one performer's story about managing to inject her in vitro fertilization (IVF) drugs in secret during an overnight escorting booking with a regular client, who has woken up ready for sex. She joked about the irony of having sex with a condom on to make money to pay for her IVF treatment. In this sense, queer temporality disrupts the normative linear narrative between sex and conception, as conception for queers (as well as for some heterosexuals) is often necessarily removed from the sexual act. "Queer time" follows a different temporal logic that does not engender heteronormative benchmarks of success. Queer theorist Jack Halberstam argues that "queer uses of time and space develop ... in opposition to the institutions of family, heterosexuality, and reproduction" (1). Queerness itself is "an outcome of strange temporalities, imaginative life schedules, and eccentric economic practices" (Halberstam 1). In this context, queer pregnancy, sex work, and the paradoxical obstacle to obtaining "some good quality fucking jizz" become a queer "time-warping" experience.

Although they aimed to deessentialize the maternal body, most creative pieces showcased at *Engorged* still focused on biological aspects of reproduction. However, reproduction has also been theorized more broadly: invisible, feminized, and sexual labour, for example, have been conceptualized as forms of social reproduction, providing emotional regeneration of workforces on a daily or intergenerational level (Federici). Sensate Film's piece *Fertile*, also shown at *Engorged*, places reproduction outside the human body and positions it as something more omnipresent than a mere function of biology. Offered as a piece of "ecosexual smut," *Fertile* features erotic imaginist and pleasure activist Gala Vanting alongside ephemeral images of bones, leaves, dirt, and organisms to explore imaginings of reproduction, generation, and life cycles with an "erotic charge":

And so i sprout seeds and i spill blood and i dig into myself with a desire to test the viability of my own earth, so that things and people and ideas and loves may find roots within me, may grow themselves in this vessel, the container i make of myself, may ripen themselves within me in so sympathetic a fashion that i too experience that bursting sensation, that roundness, that swelling, that fullness that unfolds itself out and spills sweetly over all that is. fruitful. fecund. fertile.

In the film, Vanting explores her relationship to her own fertility— not only her embodied, procreative fertility but her capacity as a maker of things, a holder of space, and a container for growth. Reproduction and generation are all around us, not only in the natural environment but also in the cycles we nurture, the energies we radiate, and the relationships we forge.

Figure 6: Gala Vanting in Fertile, Photo by Sensate Films

The stories told at *Engorged* also reveal tensions within queer studies, particularly concerning what constitutes queer and what function it should have. Within queer studies, the various interpretations of queer as a form of self-shattering and antisociality are often played against scholarship that focuses on queer world making and futurity. Tensions within activist networks in Sydney, Australia, parallel this tendency, in which "*queerness* names the side of those *not* 'fighting for the children'" (Edelman 3), rendering engagements with ostensibly heteronormative ways of life—such as childrearing—decidedly unqueer. It is this reading that Zwalf took up in *Engorged*, alongside others who have written about the generative possibilities of creating and building radical families for the future.

Originating in the work of Leo Bersani, the antisocial turn in queer studies is an antiutopian move away from idealism and humanistic notions of community. It emerged in response to liberal gay rights agendas of the 1980s and 1990s, which "either advanced a humanist demand for equal rights by downplaying sex and emphasizing identity, or promoted the value of sex and sexual subcultures through notions of diversity, pluralism, social wellbeing, community and connectedness" (Breckon 515). Refusing to indulge gay intimacies or identitarian concerns as a means to community formation, Bersani claims that homosexuality is intrinsically antirelational; its opposition to community—and by extension, the social—is what makes homosexuality "politically indispens-

able." The psychic rupture induced by gay sex is a momentarily self-shattering force in that it "disrupts the ego's coherence and dissolves its
boundaries," ultimately driving its subjects apart (Bersani 101).

Following Bersani, Lee Edelman's widely debated polemic *No Future*
outlines a radically uncompromising queer antisociality based on a
fundamental rejection of the symbolic figure of the Child, and,
subsequently, what he calls reproductive futurism—the stubborn and
unwavering investment in child protection discourse that "invariably
shapes the logic within which the political itself must be thought ...
preserving in the process the absolute privilege of heteronormativity by
rendering unthinkable ... the possibility of a queer resistance to this
organizing principle of communal relations" (2).

"Won't somebody please think of the children?," "Children are the
future," or "Fight for the children"—such refrains are the self-evident
and "unquestioned, because so obviously unquestionable" slogans of a
capitalist heteropatriarchal politics geared towards the ideological
necessity of the nuclear family under the all-encompassing guise of the
Child (Edelman 2). Although Edelman's is not a material critique—he
is not referring to a physical child, children, or to actual queer lives per
se—materiality matters. And to this extent, his critique is attractive to
a privileged (gay, white, and middle-class male) minority, as illustrated
by the innumerable backlashes from queer utopian scholars who
variously unpack the immense privilege required to refuse a future. As
Hilary Malatino points out, "Minoritarian queers—trans folk, folks of
color, economically disenfranchised, gender non-conforming queers—
have never had the privilege of refusing the social contract of reproductive
futurism, of *deciding* to embrace an alternative lifestyle modeled on what
are quite obviously gay-male-specific sexual practices and asocial hook-
ups" (209). Indeed, the privilege to refuse a future requires having a
foreseeable future to begin with.

Robert Teixeira echoes this sentiment but goes further to problematize
the relationship between theory and activist praxis: "Works of 'high
theory' are always difficult to translate into the kinds of critical, cognitive
and emotional resources suitable for contemporary activists who are
interested in anti-capitalist resistance and the development of autonomous
spaces" (154). Without attempting to answer larger questions concerning
the responsibility of theoretical work to individual and collective
capacities to act, through examining the stories told at *Engorged*, we can

explore how the anarchic allure of no future is expressed on a practical and corporeal level within the queer activist communities and how some queers—particularly those with families and investments in a collective and different future—have responded.

Resistance against motherhood as an institution is found in both feminist and queer theories. As Zwalf's chapter in this volume details, motherhood—and the associated expectations of selflessness, domesticity, and emotional labour—has been conceptualized as a component of women's oppression (Beauvoir; Rich). From haughty mumblings of the repurposed slur "breeders" to the lack of child-friendly queer spaces—or events that even entertain the provision of childcare—to the increasing emphasis on nonprocreative (e.g., families of choice and non-biological) families as the queer epitome du jour, it is as though to be queer and a parent renders one socially and politically infertile, so to speak.

Pregnancy, Zwalf argued in her performances at *Engorged*, can prompt various forms of invisibility and estrangement, particularly within the queer community. Holly is hard to miss, yet she has insisted that erasure happens twofold when you are a queer, pregnant, and femme-presenting woman. Smash E'Claire, reflecting on her divorce from queer community postpregnancy, described this erasure as "The Great Disappearing Act." During her performance, she discussed how she is read as heterosexual or unfuckable, or is fetishized within and outside her community due to the double whammy of being simultaneously maternal and gender conforming:

As a femme, I know what it's like to disappear

As a femme mother my problems are magnified

Every time someone sees me alone with my child I am read as straight

Even by queers

If I look like a mother, my queerness disappears; my dresses and makeup become oppressive tools of the patriarchy, not subversive acts of radical femmeness

If I look like a mother, my queer capital disappears—I am no longer the subject of queer desire. I am an enemy

Engorged is Zwalf's attempt to prompt questions surrounding her already signified (that is, signifying futurity) pregnant body, to educate others about "different family models," and to show how "incredibly queer parenting can be" in an attempt to combat claims of homonormativity and to challenge the divorcing of the sexual from the maternal that she has encountered in queer communities. Here, she imagines queer as the ability to subvert, to make strange, and to reinscribe.

Zwalf's blog *The Cabbage Patch Fib*, which aims to debunk pregnancy myths and "start a much-needed discussion about queer fertility and solo parenting," reiterates this desire. She writes the following: "Having a baby does not make you straight or heteronormative, or even a sell-out breeder. I am no less queer for having a baby. In fact, in one sense I have become even more queer than I was before, because now I am big time queering, or fucking with, traditional notions of family and motherhood." Zwalf's use of "queer" and "queering" here as verbs signifies a challenge to heteronormativity and, consequently, situates queer as inherently antinormative (as so much of queer theorizing and queer activist practice does). Interestingly, Zwalf then reaffirms the stabilizing dangers of this kind of guarantee—this certainty that antinormativity (or the antisocial) is the defining politic of queer studies and praxis—in her following paragraph:

> I deeply resent the idea that to be queer you need to remain static—still dancing to the same shit worn-out dance music at 6am thirty years later, and still covered in glitter. Don't get me wrong—most of my friends are almost as excited as me that I'm pregnant. But step outside my inner circle and you often hear a different story.... I've wondered whether it has something to do with queers feeling that their identity is threatened by my choice to procreate. And by identity I mean carefree single drug-taking party-animals.

This queer identity based on sexual availability, drug experimentation, and partying is illustrative of Edelman's call for queers to take up the "culture of death" that is always-already ascribed to them in the face of reproductive futurism (39). That being, to embrace a "will-to-enjoyment perversely obedient to the superego's insatiable and masochistic demands" despite the threat of futurity signified by queers like Zwalf (Edelman 46). Queers like Zwalf, queers who do not sufficiently embrace their figural association with the death drive,[1] can't sit with Edelman. As Smash É Claire illustrated in her spoken-word piece on motherhood, "I got told by a queer person that there is no way I could be queer if I become a mother, because queers must pursue a nihilistic death drive, and motherhood is repulsive."

During a phone interview with Zwalf post-*Engorged*, she discussed the stigmatization of breeders to the "good old radical feminist debates of the 70s where to have children was viewed as buying into patriarchy by sacrificing your body as a baby machine." "Contemporary attitudes towards childrearing within the queer community are not dissimilar," she further said. "It's another iteration of that. People who decide to have children are looked down on; the more non-normative, the more queer you are." The narratives Zwalf references are longstanding—and in some cases, still relevant—critiques of assimilation into heteronormativity, patriarchy, and middle-class conformism. Her complaint is how they have been used to create new regimes of queer hierarchy and stigma.

This shortsighted conceptualization of procreativity sustains the relationship between queer and antinormativity, which is a largely unquestioned allegiance within queer studies and queer community politics. Because antinormativity functions as the driving force behind queer thinking, which is always interventional, those who invoke the term and those who critique normativities in general are led to believe their work is by extension necessarily progressive. The routine refusal implied by the claim that queerness is, or should be, by definition oppositional (and yet simultaneously opposed to the logic of opposition) is not only at odds with the field's mobile and fluid origins but guarantees a return to identity categories—and categorisations of all kinds—newly fashioned. The conviction that queerness is inherently antinormative gains traction precisely because it is recurrently pitched against heteronormativity, a tendency that James Penney claims is "drawn upon to attribute by specious opposition a minoritorian or vanguard edge to the queer" (Penney 184).

Figure 7: Liz Stokes as Sister Muscle Mary, Photo by Grace Kingston

In a 2015 issue of *Differences* journal, aiming to decentralise anti-normativity in order to rethink queer theory, Robyn Weigman and Elizabeth Wilson argue that we must reconsider what is hetero about heteronormativity and reproductive futurism other than "their insistence of the rule of two (man and woman; normal and abnormal) ... their barely containable, ever-mobile hetero-geneity" (17). Ultimately, Weigman and Wilson show that norms are far more politically dynamic than queer critique has previously allowed them credit for. When I asked Zwalf her opinion on the status of norms, she laughed:

We're [queers are] quite superficial with what we see as outside the norm ... If you don't look a certain way, if you don't wear the queer uniform, if you don't do relationships in a certain way, polyamorous, kinky—only certain kinds of kink—then you're not conforming to the idea of queer, you're outside of it. I kind of end up concluding that you can't get outside of norms; whether you're adhering to them or fucking with them, norms are still the base that we start with.

Here, critical belonging to queer community and to the field of queer studies is, as Weigman states, "implicitly organized along epistemological lines, as critical authority is dispensed (or withheld) on the basis of *always* knowing the difference between normativity and the value of being queerly set against it" (55). However, if, as Zwalf points out, we are never outside of norms as they are the basis of society, then we cannot logically ever be in opposition to them, which begs the question of what actually constitutes the political and how to distinguish between norms that are productive and those that are pernicious.

Without posing a unified stance on what queer theory and praxis without normativity could mean, approaching politics from a position of complicity over oppositionality where antinormativity does not become a stand in or benchmark for all that is queer allows for a practice that is "contestatory, highly mobile, and decentered ... one dedicated less to resolution than to serious engagement with the content and consequences of its own political and critical commitments" (Weigman 3). We argue then that queer attachments to antinormativity— exemplified in arguments such as Edelman's reproductive futurism and reiterated locally on a practical and corporeal level—have ultimately served to betray queer studies' anti-identitarian and ethical origins. The fixing of some queer authenticity to antisocial or antinormative praxis has effectively hierarchized expressions of queerness and queer legitimacy within activist communities, rendering some more socially valuable and culturally legitimate than others. Again, Smash E 'Claire, reiterated this tendency in relation to her disappearance as a femme mother embedded in queer community—a magical act of presumed conformity, of homonormativity, and, hence, of invisibility:

I go out when I can, but people don't see me
They see mother

They see only the iterations of motherhood that have been fed to us all
They see a woman (I don't even identify as a woman) who has given
    in and given up
They see their own mother and all the pain they have been
    subjected to
They never see the MILF [mother I'd like to fuck]
I'm never the MILF
Maybe because I'm a good mother
Maybe because pregnancy has transformed my body from being
    a pleasantly plump hourglass to a misshapen, stretched, saggy
    sack of fat flesh—my curves no longer full with the blush of
    youth, the hourglass pushed out by muscles no longer connected
Maybe because I'm exhausted
So they see a mother who has let herself go

People don't see me
Only one trick, and I never even meant to learn it
Only one trick, but it works so well
The greatest magician on earth
The amazing disappearing mother

The self-fashioning of identity signifiers—here the conflation of "femme," "mother," and "unfuckability" as always-already antithetical to 'queer' (insofar as these categories are taken to be assimilatory and hence at odds with anti-normativity)—ultimately contradicts the anti-identitarian and ethical origins of queer studies. Smash E'Claire's words are indicative of how the choice to have children refigures one's relation to and within queer community along "the tired binary that places femininity, reproduction, and normativity on the one side and masculinity, sexuality and queer resistance on the other" (Fraiman qtd. in Nelson 75). The implication is that in order to perform an intelligible queer selfhood and to participate in, or belong to, a queer community, one faces considerable pressure to adapt their sense of identity. The antinormative sensibility structuring "queer" (theorizing, politics, and activism), therefore, has the practical effect of excluding and rendering invisible some of its key constituents—in this case, queer mothers. This prompts ethical questions over the capacity to fulfil queer antinorms alongside who is and who is not represented within queer scholarship and communities.

In her own statement about the (un)fuckability of mothers and to challenge the notion that pregnancy renders the body less queer, Zwalf came out for the final act of the evening and performed an erotic striptease to The Supremes' "Baby Love." She performed classic stripper choreography in a hospital gown, featuring twirls and chair work, interspersed with moments to stretch out her hips, rub her lower back, roll her sore neck, take off her heels, and read a book (*Motherlove*). As the music changed to Kelis's "Milkshake," with the unforgettable lyrics "my milkshake brings all the boys to the yard," Zwalf hoisted up her red dress, pulled out her breasts, unclipped her maternity bra, and began to shimmy for the audience. As the audience laughed, she revealed a breast pump and began exaggerated pumping to the beat of the song. In the final track, Flume's "Holding On" to the lyrics "Oh hip-shaking mama, I love you," Zwalf made a deliberately ungraceful transition to the floor, performed a classic striptease "trucker pose," and then concluded by penetrating herself with an inflatable dilator, designed to help pregnant people stretch their vaginas in preparation for childbirth. In this moment, and against a backdrop of desexualisation and hierarchies of queer authenticity, Zwalf presented the queer pregnant body as a site of resistance, medical equipment as ripe for reworking, pregnancy as at once sexy and laborious, and the maternal body as both desiring and desirable. As she pulled out her sizeable dilator, she was both fucking, and fucking with, the maternal.

Figure 8: Holly Zwalf, Photo by Grace Kingston

Endnotes

1. "The death drive names what the queer, in the order of the social, is called forth to figure: the negativity opposed to every form of social viability" (Edelman 9).

Works Cited

Balaskas, Janet. *Active Birth-Revised Edition: The New Approach to Giving Birth Naturally.* Harvard Common Press, 1992.

Beauvoir, Simone de. *The Second Sex.* Translated by Constance Borde and Sheila Malovany-Chevallier, Alfred A. Knopf, 2010.

Berlant, Lauren, and Michael Warner. "Sex in Public." *Critical Inquiry,* vol. 24, no. 2, 1998, pp. 547-66.

Bersani, Leo. "Is the Rectum a Grave?" *Cultural Analysis/Cultural Activism,* vol. 43, 1987, pp. 197-222.

Breckon, Anna. "The Erotic Politics of Disgust: Pink Flamingos as Queer Political Cinema." *Screen,* vol. 54, no. 4, 2013, pp. 514-33.

Canaday, Margot. *The Straight State: Sexuality and Citizenship in Twentieth-Century America.* Princeton University Press, 2009.

Davis, Elizabeth, and Debra Pascali-Bonaro. *Orgasmic Birth: Your Guide to a Safe, Satisfying, and Pleasurable Birth experience.* Rodale, 2010.

Dodsworth, Jane. "Sex Worker and Mother: Managing Dual and Threatened Identities." *Child and Family Social Work,* vol. 19, no. 1, 2014, pp. 99-108.

Easton, Dossie, and Janet Hardy. *The New Topping Book.* Greenery Press, 2003.

Edelman, Lee. *No Future: Queer Theory and the Death Drive.* Duke University Press, 2004.

Evershed, Nick, Lorena and Allam, Lorena. "Indigenous Children's Removal On the Rise 21 Years after Bringing Them Home." *The Guardian.* 25 May 2018. www.theguardian.com/australia-news/ 2018/may/25/australia-fails-to-curb-childrens-removal-from- indigenous-families-figures-show. Accessed Apr. 8 2020.

Federici, Silvia. *Revolution at Point Zero: Housework, Reproduction, and Feminist Struggle.* PM Press, 2012.

Giles, Fiona. *Fresh Milk: The Secret Life of Breasts*. Allen and Unwin, 2003.

Halberstam, Jack. *In a Queer Time and Place*. New York University Press, 2005.

Hill Collins, Patricia. "Black Women and Motherhood." *Justice and Care: Essential Readings in Feminist Ethics*, edited by Virginia Held, Westview Press, 1995, pp. 117-138.

Malatino, Hilary. "Utopian Pragmatics: Bash Back! and the Temporality of Radical Queer Action." *A Critical Inquiry into Queer Utopias*, edited by Angela Jones, Palgrave MacMillan, 2013, pp. 205-227.

Moreton-Robinson, Aileen M. "I Still Call Australia Home: Indigenous Belonging and Place in a White Postcolonising Society." Uprootings/Regroundings: Questions of Home and Migration, edited by Sara Ahmed et al., Berg Publishing, 2003, pp. 23-40.

"Mother and a Whore." *Because I'm a Whore*. 11 Sept. 2011, because imawhore.wordpress.com/2011/09/11/mother-and-a-whore/. Accessed Apr. 8 2020.

Nelson, Maggie. *The Argonauts*. Graywolf Press, 2015.

Penney, James. *After Queer Theory*. Pluto Press, 2014.

Preciado, Paul B. "Politically Assisted Procreation and State Heterosexualism." South Atlantic Quarterly, vol. 115, no. 2, 2016, pp. 405-10.

Rich, Adrienne. *Of Woman Born*. Norton, 1995.

Smith, Molly, and Juno Mac. *Revolting Prostitutes: The Fight for Sex Workers' Rights*. Verso Trade, 2018.

Spade, Dean. "Resisting Medicine, Re/modeling Gender." *Berkeley Women's LJ*, vol. 18, 2003, pp. 15-39.

Stringer, Rebecca. "A Nightmare of the Neocolonial Kind: Politics of Suffering in Howard's Northern Territory Intervention." *Borderlands*, vol. 6, no. 2, 2007, go.gale.com/ps/anonymous? id=GALE%7CA553004470&sid=google Scholar&v= 2.1&it=r&linkaccess= abs&issn=14470810&p=AONE&sw=w. Accessed Apr. 8 2020.

Teixeira, Robert. "Lee Edelman (2004) No Future: Queer Theory and the Death Drive." *Graduate Journal of Social Science*, vol. 6, no. 1, 2009, pp. 149-61.

Thorne, Clarisse. *The SM Feminist*. Amazon Digital Services, 2012.

Vanting, G., Frey, A. *Fertile*, Sensate Films, 2013.

Wadiwel, Dinesh. "Sex and Lubricative Ethic." *The Ashgate Research Companion to Queer Theory*, edited by Noreen Giffney and Michael O'Rourke, Routledge, 2009, pp. 491-506.

Weal, John D. *The Leatherman's Protocol Handbook*. Nazca Plains, 2010.

Weigman, Robyn. "Eve's Triangles, or Queer Studies beside Itself." *Differences*, vol. 26, no. 1, 2015, pp. 48-731.

Weigman, Robyn, and Elizabeth A. Wilson. "Introduction: Antinormativity's Queer Conventions." *Differences*, vol. 26, no. 1, 2015, pp. 1-25.

Weiss, Margot D. "Working at Play: BDSM Sexuality in the San Francisco Bay Area."*Anthropologica*, vol. 48, no. 2, 2006, pp. 229-45.

Weston, Kath. *Families We Choose: Lesbians, Gays, Kinship.*: Columbia University Press, 1991.

Wiseman, Jay. *SM 101: A Realistic Introduction*. Greenery Press, 1996.

Zwalf, Holly. *The Cabbage Patch Fib*, 2015, thecabbagepatchfib.wordpress.com/. Accessed Apr. 8 2020.

Notes on Contributors

Christa Baiada is an associate professor of English at Borough of Manhattan Community College of the City University of New York. She holds a PhD from the CUNY Graduate Center. Her area of specialization is American literature. She has published literary analysis and pedagogy essays in various journals, including *Asian American Literature: Discourses and Pedagogy*; *Journal of Men's Studies*; and *Teaching English in the Two Year College*. Her current research focuses on literary representations of embodied motherhood, particularly pregnancy, childbirth, and breastfeeding, in twentieth- and twenty-first-century American fiction.

Vivienne Cass (PhD) is a clinical psychologist and specialist in human sexuality. She has held positions at several universities in Western Australia and ran a private practice for over thirty years. She continues to teach in sexual therapy, supervise and mentor, give conference presentations and media interviews, and write in her field. She is the author of the *Cass Theory of Lesbian and Gay Identity Formation* and has published book chapters and papers on the topic of sexual orientation, including chapters in the *Encyclopaedia of Reproduction*, *Textbook on Homosexuality and Mental Health*, and the Kinsey Institute publication *Homosexuality-Heterosexuality*. Dr. Cass has also published two books— *The Elusive Orgasm: A Woman's Guide to Why She Can't and How She Can Orgasm* (2004), now in seven languages, and *There's More To Sex Than AIDS: The A To Z Guide To Safe Sex* (1988)—and also a set of clitoral anatomy posters titled *The Illustrated Clitoris*. In 2011, following the introduction of apps, she created and developed a sex education app for the iPhone and iPad, titled *Explore Women's Sex*.

Erin Chapman is a sexuality educator and assistant associate professor of child, family, and consumer studies at the University of Idaho. She has taught three cohorts of the Our Whole Lives (OWL) program in the local community. Working in collaboration with the Women's

Center, LGBTQA Office, Student Health peer educators, and Violence Prevention Programs, Erin is passionate about campus efforts to educate about and raise awareness around sexual health and healthy relationships. Her research interests include the study of inclusive and positive sexuality education, healthy relationships across the lifespan, and adolescent and emerging adult development, all within a feminist framework. In addition to collaborating on research around OWL, Erin is the cocreator of Got Sex?—a sexuality education forum for college students at the University of Idaho.

Katie B. Garner's research focuses on the culture of motherhood in the United States, labour equality, childcare, class and race in the mother-nanny relationship, and feminism. Dr. Garner wants to encourage conversations on these topics in order to increase progressive political will and ultimately change American policy. She is currently working on a book tentatively titled *The Catch-22 of Childcare*, which combines her research with interviews conducted with nearly one hundred mothers around the United States. She has taught at colleges in the Chicago area and has led feminist workshops for mothers and teens. More information can be found at *www. drkatiebgarner.com.*

Grace Kingston is a multidisciplinary artist; she conducts research in the fields of social media, digital culture, networks, environments, and spatial-contextual awareness. Raised in Sydney, Australia, Kingston's formal study was undertaken at the University of New South Wales Faculty of Art and Design. She is currently a lecturer at SAE Creative Media Institute and a current board member of *Runway Experimental Art Journal*. After receiving a first class honours award in 2009, Kingston was awarded an Australian Postgraduate Award scholarship to continue her practice in the University of New South Wales masters of fine art program. Supervised by Professor Paul Thomas, she completed her MFA in 2012, and her thesis findings were published in the peer-reviewed journal *Scandal in European and American Culture, Vol. 1.*

Joani Mortenson, MSW, RSW, E-RYT, is a queer mama and grandmother who lives in White Rock, British Columbia. Having led many lives and worn many hats, including a long stint in academia as a multidisciplinary grad student, researcher and sessional professor, she now has a private movement therapy practice where she focuses her work in early childhood development. She refers to herself as a "social working yogi." Joani values diversity, health, community, and her proximity to the ocean.

Natasha Pinterics lives in Edmonton, Alberta with her partner, and a wild, wonderful blended family of four kids, two dogs, two cats, two birds, and numerous fish. Natasha teaches English, Critical Thinking and Gender Studies at NorQuest College, and dreams of the spare time to plant more flowers, do more crafts, and make the world change faster.

Amanda Kane Rooks is an academic in the School of Access Education, CQUniversity. She is currently finalising her PhD in Literary and Cultural Studies with a focus on motherhood and female sexuality in fictional representation. Her work has been published in a number of peer reviewed journals, including Women's Studies: *An Interdisciplinary Journal, CLCWeb: Comparative Literature and Culture, Literature/Film Quarterly, Film Criticism, Antipodes,* and *LiNQ.*

Lysa Salsbury is the director of the University of Idaho Women's Center. Both of her teenage children have participated in the Our Whole Lives (OWL) program. Lysa leads campus outreach, education, and engagement efforts around women's and gender issues, and serves on a number of institutional and local committees that focus on pro-moting inclusion and diversity at the university and in the surrounding community. Her research interests include respectful communication, feminist mothering, and inclusive sexuality education. In addition to collaborating on research around OWL, she is the cocreator of Got Sex?—a sexuality education forum for college students at the University of Idaho.

Sam Sperring is a PhD candidate at the Translational Health Research Institute at the University of Western Sydney, writing her dissertation on the cancer experiences of gender and sexuality diverse women. She is a sessional academic in the Faculty of Arts and Social Sciences at the University of Technology, Sydney, and her research here has concerned the empirical exploration of the relationship between queer theory and the material practices of local queer activist communities. She has spoken on these areas in various forums, and has related works published in the journal *Assuming Gender, The SAGE Encyclopedia of Trans Studies,* and *Voiceworks.*

Zahra Stardust completed her PhD at the University of New South Wales on the regulation of pornography in Australia, specializing in queer and feminist approaches to production. Her research is concerned with intersections between criminal law, sexuality, and justice. She has published chapters in *New Feminist Literary Studies* (Cambridge University Press, 2019), *Orienting Feminisms* (Palgrave, 2018), and *Queer Sex Work* (Routledge, 2015) and has published articles in *Porn Studies*, the *Journal of Sexual Health*, and the *World Journal of AIDS*. She has worked as the policy advisor at the AIDS council of NSW and Scarlet Alliance (Australian Sex Workers Association), as a teaching fellow in criminology at University of New South Wales, on the board of the Gay and Lesbian Rights Lobby, as a member of the Australian Lawyers for Human Rights LGBTI Sub-Committee, and as a mentor for the Women's Justice Network supporting women recently released from prison. Her research interests include queer theories, feminisms, peer methodologies, and critical legal studies.

Francisca Vanderwoude is an emerging multidisciplinary visual artist and researcher based in Brisbane, Australia. Drawing from her experiences as a mother and sex worker and working predominantly with video, performance, soft sculpture, and installation, Francisca is currently completing a master of arts (visual arts) at Griffith University through an arts-based research project. With a focus on maternal practice in relation to intersections of class, gender and sexuality, her work explores themes such as autonomy, agency, bodily pleasure, relationality, and intersubjectivity.

Michelle Walks is a feminist medical anthropologist who balances quality time with her family and her precarious labour at institutions around British Columbia and the Yukon. She teaches anthropology, sociology, gender and sexuality, and women's studies, and depending on the semester, she will acknowledge that each discipline is her favourite to teach. Until her feet required fashionable orthotic footwear, she would roam the classrooms barefoot, being grounded in her teaching. Her research has focused on queer and trans reproduction; she is now looking to develop and teach sexual health education through a local NGO that does transnational work. Dr. Walks previously coedited *An Anthropology of Mothering*, with Dr. Naomi McPherson.

Angelina Weenie is a Plains Cree woman from Sweetgrass First Nation, Saskatchewan, Canada. She is a faculty member of Indigenous education at the First Nations University of Canada. She completed her PhD at the University of Regina, and her research was on Indigenous teaching and learning.

Zairunisha is a PhD scholar in the Centre for Philosophy, School of Social Sciences at Jawaharlal Nehru University, Delhi, India. She is presently working on a thesis about motherhood, reproductive technology, and feminist bioethics. She has published articles and chapters on motherhood in many national and international journals and books. As an assistant professor, she has taught courses in philosophy at University of Delhi, Delhi, India.

Holly Zwalf has a PhD from the University of New South Wales on queer kink and the erotic maternal. She has presented on various topics relating to mothers and sex at the American Anthropological Association, the Australian Motherhood Initiative for Research and Community Involvement conference, and at the Lilith Feminist History Symposium. Holly is a queer solo parent by choice and lives in the Australian bush with her wild little toddler. She is a film maker, and a smutty spoken word performer. She writes professionally on the topics of feminism, sex, and relationships and has a blog about queer solo conception: *thecabbagepatchfib.wordpress.com.*